THE UNITED EMPIRE LOYALISTS

AMS PRESS
NEW YORK

SIR GUY CARLETON (LORD DORCHESTER)
From a drawing after an old engraving by MARIAN E. G. BRADLEY

THE UNITED EMPIRE LOYALISTS

Founders of British Canada

BY

A. G. BRADLEY

THORNTON BUTTERWORTH LIMITED
15 BEDFORD STREET, LONDON, W.C.2

This edition reprinted from an original copy contained in the collection of the University of Michigan Library, Ann Arbor.

Reprinted from the edition of 1932: London

First AMS edition published in 1971

Manufactured in the United States of America

International Standard Book Number: 0-404-00927-1

Library of Congress Catalog Card Number: 75-136413

AMS PRESS INC.
NEW YORK, N.Y. 10003

CONTENTS

LIST OF ILLUSTRATIONS

PREFACE

I HAVE sometimes ventured to wonder in what form those English historians, distinguished or otherwise, who have dealt with American history, visualise the American of the eighteenth century. Visits to the cultured circles of latter-day Boston or New York, even if achieved, would be useless for such a purpose. Almost inevitably, and quite obviously, they picture the Colonists of the Revolutionary period merely as Englishmen living beyond the Atlantic. As a matter of fact, they were nothing of the kind. Their type and the atmosphere in which they lived, developed through generations of isolation from the Mother Country, were things quite remote from anything within the experience or even the conception of the English man of letters. It is unfortunate, too, that most English accounts of the War of Independence have been written with a strong Whig bias. Americans frankly admitted that Sir George Trevelyan, the most notable English authority on the period, held a strong brief for them. Nearly as much may be said of Lecky. The lesser fry, in dealing with the war, as an incident in English history, are obviously influenced by American writers, who have naturally dealt most voluminously with the period.

The late Dr. Belcher is the only recent English historian who, in a fairly copious work on the War of Independence, has declared boldly for the Loyalist side of the question. It is a most painstaking book, and many of his conclusions the Whig writers would find it difficult to confute. Moreover, Dr. Belcher took the trouble to pay many private visits of inspection and research to America, and it is even possible that in some backwaters of American life he found social material that helped him to realise the rank and file of the Revolutionary period with greater accuracy than more famous writers, who had made no attempts at such personal investigation.

In regard to pre-Revolutionary Colonial America, the late Mr. J. A. Doyle is the only English historian who has dealt seriously with this most interesting subject. I had the privilege of knowing that versatile genius. A South Wales squire, master of hounds, breeder and expert judge of racehorses, county councillor, Fellow of All Souls, scholar and historian, his wide interests and knowledge of men well fitted him to write his two volumes on the *English in America*; and he paid one visit, I well remember, to the Southern States. But even Mr. Doyle was too much inclined to regard the eighteenth-century Americans outside New England as just oversea Englishmen. For myself, though I grudge the space and regret the egotistical note inevitable to the process, I feel I must in some sort justify this measure of criticism and my interest in these matters.

In truth, I derived this interest from the soil itself. For from the year 1874 onward to the mid-eighties, I owned land in Virginia and mostly lived on it—with interludes spent elsewhere, on both sides of the Atlantic—I had occasion to go about the State a great deal and sometimes into the adjoining States. Naturally, I came to know these sociable people and their country pretty intimately, and they were well worth knowing. They were just out of the disastrous Civil War. The slaves were still working on the land as paid labourers. Most of the landowners, large, middling and small, were in their old homes. They were all in their degree, with trifling exceptions, amazingly old-fashioned. The late Civil War had been one of defence, fought largely on portions of their own soil or in kindred Southern territory, and they were quite untravelled. The essentials of life had remained practically unaltered for a century. My neighbours were the grandsons of the men who had followed Washington and applauded Patrick Henry, or sometimes sat on the fence, and I am quite sure that they represented the same type. Superficially, and in outlook, they were quite unlike Englishmen. But owing possibly to fundamental causes, and to their inherited attachment to country life, they assimilated better than any other Americans with settlers or visitors from the mother country.

Things had not moved much with these folk for generations. Railroads were then few, and people still travelled mainly on horseback with saddlebags. When necessary, carriages were dragged over the rough, red roads or through the winter mud by struggling horses. A centenarian negro tenant of my own remembered the local festivities at the peace of 1783. Another near by had been servant boy to Patrick Henry. The leading miller of the district had marched, in youth, with Harrison's Kentucky Militia to the invasion of Canada in 1812. Many sons of Revolutionary soldiers were still living and known to me as hale old men. The country was beautiful. The social atmosphere, though far from ornate, was undeniably picturesque and indeed a hundred years behind the times in many ways. The people were fluent and often entertaining talkers, very much on the reminiscent note. I contributed papers on the country and neighbouring states from time to time, to *Blackwood*, *Macmillan's Magazine* and the *Pall Mall Gazette*, and, more frequently, to the *Field*. This, together with a sort of subconsciousness that some day I might be glad of such experiences, stimulated me to far wider wanderings than would have been otherwise the case, not merely in the South but occasionally in the Northern States, with visits to the chief cities. For this subconsciousness, this instinct, for it was nothing more, I have had infinite cause to be thankful. In Boston particularly, that feeling for the past inspired by the outdoor Virginia atmosphere and the indoor talk of Virginia veterans, too old to have had their past blotted out for the moment by service in the recent Civil War, received a decided impetus.

For by the accident of an old family friendship, I used to find myself there lodged in the very heart of things Bostonian, where the Olympians of that great era—Longfellow, Emerson, Wendell Holmes, Ticknor and others—could be met informally face to face. But it was Francis Parkman who mattered most to me. For that famous historian and delightful writer was at the moment especially interested in Virginia, which, like most Bostonians in those days, he knew, if at all, merely as a battlefield. This interest of his led to talks which easily bridged the years between us, talks that I have never forgotten. What is more, it introduced me to his works, which in later years inspired my own modest ventures into North American and Canadian history. It was then, too, in middle life, that I felt thankful for the background with which I had so fortunately and without definite design provided myself. For I had spent most of 1873 in Canada, part of it in camping and canoeing on the lakes and rivers that thread what was then the virgin forest hinterland of Ontario, now everywhere exploited by American and Canadian tourists and sportsmen; the remainder in various parts of the settled portion of the country. It was an utterly different Canada from that of to-day, or even of thirty years later. There was practically no North-West. Toronto was hardly more than a big country town with plank side-walks. The traditions of the U.E. Loyalists, the Family Compact, and the war of 1812, of which there were many survivors, were still in the air, though Federation had just been achieved, and were blended with the influence of the large British garrisons, only just withdrawn. There was no wealth to speak of, things moved slowly, and the social atmosphere was still undemocratic.

My first host in Toronto had come there before 1812 as a child, with his family and their household gods, by *bateau* up Lake Ontario. His well-appointed house and grounds stood upon the spot where his father had cut down the woods and erected his first dwelling, near the embryo town. By that time it stood in the suburbs. To-day it is enclosed in the city. Like everybody else of seventy and over, my host well remembered the war of 1812, and there were many older men still about who had fought in it. During that year in Canada I formed ties which took me back there from time to time till thirty years later, when the Dominion had grown out of all former knowledge in wealth and population, and the outlook had vastly altered. By that time, I had a fair working knowledge of the country from the Atlantic to the Pacific, and incidentally a good deal of use for that knowledge.

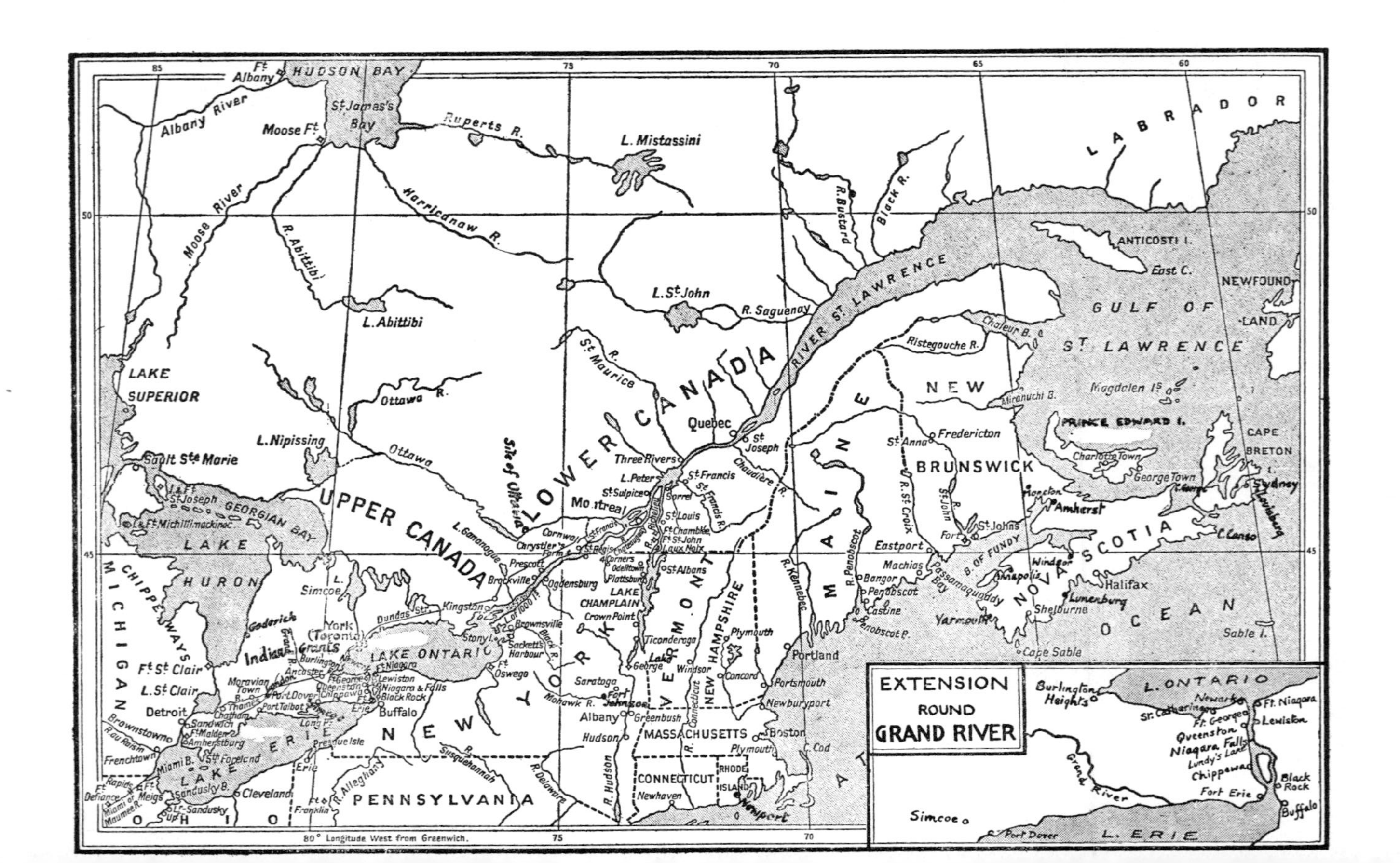
HUDSON BAY
St. James's Bay
Albany River
Moose Fᵗ
Moose River
Ruperts R.
Harricanaw R.
R. Abittibi
L. Abittibi
L. Mistassini
L. Sᵗ John
R. Saguenay
R. Bustard
Black R.
LABRADOR
ANTICOSTI I.
East C.
NEWFOUNDLAND
GULF OF ST LAWRENCE
RIVER Sᵗ LAWRENCE
Magdalen Iˢ
PRINCE EDWARD I.
Charlotte Town
George Town
CAPE BRETON I.
Sydney
C. Canso
NOVA SCOTIA
Halifax
Shelburne
Cape Sable
Sable I.
OCEAN
NEW BRUNSWICK
Fredericton
Sᵗ Anna
Ristegouche R.
Chaleur B.
Miranuchi B.
R. Sᵗ Croix
Sᵗ Johns
B. OF FUNDY
Passamaquoddy Bay
Eastport
Machias
Bangor
Penobscot
Castine
Penobscot B.
R. Penobscot
Amherst
Windsor
Annapolis
Lunenburg
Yarmouth
MAINE
R. Kennebec
Portland
Portsmouth
Newburyport
Boston
Plymouth
C. Cod
MASSACHUSETTS
CONNECTICUT
RHODE ISLAND
Newport
Newhaven
NEW HAMPSHIRE
Concord
Connecticut R.
Windsor
VERMONT
Ticonderoga
Lake George
LAKE CHAMPLAIN
Crown Point
Plattsburg
Odelltown
Sᵗ Albans
NEW YORK
Saratoga
Fort Johnson
Mohawk R.
Albany
Greenbush
Hudson
R. Hudson
R. Delaware
PENNSYLVANIA
R. Susquehannah
R. Allegheny
Fᵗ Franklin
Erie
Presque Isle
OHIO
Cleveland
Sandusky B.
LAKE ERIE
LOWER CANADA
Quebec
Sᵗ Joseph
Chaudière R.
Three Rivers
L. Peter
Sᵗ Francis
Sᵗ Francis R.
Sorrel
Sᵗ Sulpice
Sᵗ Maurice R.
Montreal
Sᵗ Louis
Fᵗ Chamblee
Fᵗ Sᵗ John
Isle aux Noix
Four Corners
Sᵗ Regis
Cornwall
Chrystler's Farm
Ogdensburg
Prescott
Brockville
L. Gananoque
Site of Ottawa
Ottawa
Ottawa R.
L. Nipissing
UPPER CANADA
Kingston
L. of 1000 Iˢ
Brownsville
Sackett's Harbour
Black R.
Oswego
LAKE ONTARIO
Fᵗ Niagara
Lewiston
Niagara & Falls
Black Rock
Buffalo
Dundas Stᵗ
York (Toronto)
L. Simcoe
Burlington
Ancaster
Indian Grants
Goderich
Grand R.
Moravian Town
Thames R.
Port Dover
Port Talbot
Long Pᵗ
Chatham
Sandwich
Fᵗ Malden
Amherstburg
Detroit
L. Sᵗ Clair
Fᵗ Sᵗ Clair
Brownstown
Frenchtown
Rau Raisin
Miami B.
Sᵗ Foreland
Fᵗ Meigs
Fᵗ Defiance
Maumee R.
Lr. Sandusky
LAKE SUPERIOR
Sault Sᵗᵉ Marie
Sᵗ Joseph
Michillimackinac
GEORGIAN BAY
LAKE HURON
CHIPPEWAYS
MICHIGAN
80° Longitude West from Greenwich.
EXTENSION ROUND GRAND RIVER
L. ONTARIO
Burlington Heights
Sᵗ Catherines
Newark
Fᵗ George
Fᵗ Niagara
Lewiston
Queenston
Niagara Falls
Lundy's Lane
Chippewa
Black Rock
Fort Erie
Buffalo
Grand River
Simcoe
Port Dover
L. ERIE

CHAPTER I

INTRODUCTORY

BEFORE proceeding to the main subject of this book —those Colonial Americans who favoured or fought for the Revolution and those who adhered actively or passively to the side of the Crown—it will be well, I think, to take a brief glance at the ingredients of which the thirteen colonies were respectively composed. The reader may be reminded too that, taking their average of life, these last had been in organized and orderly existence for about a century and a half, and in all the main essentials under English laws and customs locally administered. Furthermore, their term of life till 1776, it is interesting to note, was approximately identical with that which to-day divides us from the date of their independence. To begin with, the American Colonies fall at once into three main groups: the four New England colonies of Massachusetts, Connecticut, Rhode Island, and Vermont, with the still unincorporated territories of New Hampshire and Maine; the three middle colonies, New York, New Jersey, and Pennsylvania; and the six southern provinces, Virginia, Maryland, Delaware, North and South Carolina and Georgia. The cleavage between the groups was not merely geographical, though climate had much to do with it. Race, again, had very little to say in the matter, for British blood was in those days everywhere overwhelmingly predominant. In the New England group sectarianism had been, of course, their very foundation, and though by this time much softened and ameliorated, Puritanism was still the distinguishing characteristic. Of these colonies it made a comparatively close and homogeneous group. In a broad view they may be treated as one, though even so they did not love each other too ardently and had frequent inter-colonial disputes.

The middle colonies of New York, New Jersey and Pennsylvania hated one another only less than they all disliked the New Englanders. This last antipathy we may fairly call temperamental, and it was pretty general. Moreover, the Puritan Colonies had never been what in this connection is called loyal. They had left the Mother Country with soreness against her in their hearts, and the tradition had long outlasted the cause. They had come to regard themselves almost as Independent Republics, though when their interests had been at one with the Mother Country, as in the then recent French Wars, they had been active enough. More than one official in the early 18th Century had reported to the Home Government that the New Englanders had practically ceased to recognize any tie with Great Britain. Their Constitutions were on the usual Colonial and English model—a Governor representing the Crown (though two of their Provinces elected their own), a nominated Council forming the Upper House, with an elected Assembly representing the various towns and districts, while the Governor in Council had a veto on the measures of the popular House. The typical New Englander farmed his own land, generally one or two hundred acres of rather poor quality, with the labour of himself and family, sometimes aided by an indentured servant or a negro slave. A large number, however, were engaged in ocean trade, shipping and shipbuilding, in which pursuits they greatly excelled. Besides Boston, there were many important little towns. New Englanders as a whole were far the most advanced of all the Colonists in education, though in religion the most intolerant. Their Calvinism, however, had been greatly modified since the days when they had burned witches and compelled every incomer to conform and contribute to their churches and subscribe to their form of worship. Other sects were now tolerated, and even the Church of England, as will be seen, had made considerable way among the higher class. A few Scotsmen and a small stream of the Ulster Protestant emigration, of which a word later, had settled in New England; but Presbyterianism, as represented by both these types, was even more antipathetic to New England theologians than Episcopacy with its terrible suggestions of bishops and the Scarlet Woman. Lastly, a fondness for the dollar and keenness in bargains, though by no means confined to the colonists of New England, was a distinguishing trait dwelt upon by every traveller. Though eminently democratic in habit, they no longer exemplified the democracy of a pioneering country. Grades of society had inevitably developed. Wealth and education can never be discounted, in any civilized form of society. There were no recognized territorial magnates, conditions forbidding such a possibility; but the bigger shipowners and merchants, the lawyers, ministers and professors, formed a modified aristocracy in the towns that despite a popular franchise, and a politically sensitive proletariat, actually controlled these New England Provinces, as in a more open manner other colonies were controlled by their big landowners and merchants.

New York, again, was quite different. Settled originally by the Dutch and annexed by England under James II,[1] it retained a strong substratum of the pioneer race, which amalgamated reasonably well with the English newcomers. These Dutchmen included Patroons with large estates and a numerous tenantry on a quasi-Feudal system. There were also small freeholders, fur-traders, merchants and shipowners. By the time of the Revolution, there had been added to these, large landowners of English blood with a somewhat similar tenantry of British, German, or Dutch nationality, and a vast number of freehold farmers both those of the family-farm type and others who worked larger farms with slave or white labour. There was no uniform or distinguishing trait in the Province. Its note was tolerant and easy-going. The Church of England was automatically the recognized and established creed, and its support officially maintained where possible. But toleration of all creeds gradually evolved. The big landowners, Dutch and English, may have had trouble with their tenantry, probably they did in such a country,

[1] As an alien wedge driven into the heart of the English colonies, it made the regulation of the Navigation laws and the prevention of smuggling impossible.

but they judiciously increased their holdings by interest at Headquarters, for there was a great deal of such land-jobbing everywhere. The gentleman-farmer, if the term may be used, with one or two thousand acres, and employing half a dozen negro slaves, was also a feature of this colony, and there were, besides, innumerable small freeholders of the usual New England and normal American settler type. Slavery was legal in all the colonies till the Revolution, though sparingly utilised in these Northern Provinces. There was a lot of good land in the colony. The Hudson River, too, was a great artery of commerce and transport, and was to make of the colony and its capital in later days the greatest State and the greatest city in America. At this time, New York City with 30,000 population was slightly inferior in numbers as well as in attractiveness to Philadelphia and Boston, though already forging ahead in commercial importance.

New Jersey, adjoining New York to the southward, may be briefly described as a rather pale replica of its greater neighbour, and in intimate contact with it. For, containing on its edge a large slice of Greater New York City, it runs southward, a broad strip along the sea coast, with the Delaware forming the inner boundary, and Philadelphia at the south-west set upon that river's farther bank. Industrious farmers, British, German, Dutch and Swedes, cultivated its mostly smooth-lying surface, which became the scene of much fighting in the war.

Pennsylvania, on the other hand, was a large wide-spreading province, and had a character of its own. For it was founded much later than the others, namely in 1686, by the Penn family[1] to whom it was granted, absorbing at the same time some small groups of Dutch and Swedes already settled within its boundaries. As everyone knows, the Quakers, elsewhere persecuted, were here made welcome and well repaid the privilege by their substantial contribution to the rapid success of the colony. Philadelphia grew with a rapidity unprecedented in colonial enterprise; the fair and fertile country round it kept pace with the growth of the city, which by

[1] Penn hoped to produce crops there that could not be grown in England. This hope was only fulfilled in the case of Indian corn.

the Revolution was not only larger than Boston and New York, but exceeded both in those things which make for solid comfort both in appearance and in reality. If the Quakers were a leading factor in the prosperity of the City, Palatine Germans and British of all denominations attracted by the tolerant and democratic atmosphere of the colony were a strong support. Under the Penn dispensation, the surrounding country was settled equitably on the " family farm " system, and a freeholding yeomanry, both British and German, spread rapidly towards the Alleghany Mountains in the rear, which from hence southward begin to influence so greatly the situation and condition of the colonies. This, the youngest and most hospitable to immigrants, received also a large supply of Ulster Protestants. It is the only part of North America too, to which the Welsh as agricultural settlers have ever made a recognized group contribution. The Province was thoroughly democratic outside Philadelphia, which naturally fell into the inevitable social cleavages. In regard to these Ulstermen, it was early in the 18th century that there arose that movement from North-Eastern Ireland, which made such an impress on American history, and to a certain extent on the War of Independence. The " Six Counties," largely cleared of their native population and planted with Anglo-Scottish Protestants a century earlier, together with the two northerly counties of Antrim and Down, already more or less Scottish,[1] had begun to get restless. The Anglican Establishment, which excluded the Presbyterians from full civil rights, though their creed was the established religion of their Scottish Fatherland, was one most justifiable grievance. Another arose later on with the termination of many of the long leases, covering two or three generations, on certain great estates. For the opportunity to raise these unduly tempted the landlords to what was, in a long view, an act of insensate folly. These hardy colonists, who had practically made the country, and had a shrewd knowledge of its rental values, were now confronted with demands that they felt they could not meet, and were in consequence displaced by the native Irish who in days gone by had themselves been

[1] See "The Government Survey of Ulster, by Capt. Pynner, 1616."

dispossessed of the country in its more elementary condition. To get back these, more sanguine and less practical people offered higher rents without much thought of an audit day, a very old story in Ireland.

To these two causes are justly attributed the great exodus which set in from Ulster and continued through the century, till over a hundred thousand of these sturdy people, who incidentally had staunchly supported the English rule in Ireland, had left her shores. A mad policy, and it provoked the exodus, though alone it would hardly have maintained it. The further fact is not generally recognized by historians that the success of the earlier settlers duly transmitted to those left behind created a very natural desire to follow in their steps. And yet more, the captains and owners of ships sailing from Derry, Belfast and elsewhere advertised the country and their cheap fares with all the zeal of modern steamship agencies and with even less discretion. Most of these emigrants landed in Philadelphia. They were all intending farmers. Some of them with a little money secured farms in the home districts, but most of them, either at once or after a short pause in the Settlement, made straight for the Alleghanies beyond the fringe of civilization. There, as backwoodsmen, half-farmers, half-hunters, they established a belt of rude civilization extending itself southward along the foot of the mountains through Maryland, Virginia and the Carolinas. Here, confronting the Indian within and beyond the mountains, they awoke by their very industrial aggression his slumbering hostility. To their skill with axe and rifle they were compelled to add that of Indian warfare, and in time they formed automatically a long wedge of fighting men thrust in between the settled Colonies and their Indian-haunted hinterland. Technically, they were Pennsylvanians, Virginians and so forth, but actually they governed themselves so far as government was necessary, and in their isolation recognized no control from Colonial Legislatures. They were Presbyterians mostly, and a few of their ministers followed them. They attracted and absorbed a few other types, German and Dutch Calvinists, besides mere adventurers from the old settlements. But as Scotch-Irish Presbyterians they were not liked by the Philadelphians, who attributed, and with justice, all Indian disturbances to their attitude. The Quakers had prided themselves, and in the retrospect still pride themselves, on their peaceful relations with the Indians, but then the neighbouring colonies, by pushing back the savages, had made things much easier for Penn's settlement. These others, however, were restless pioneers and held the frontier. In later days, they crossed the mountains and became the chief founders of the States beyond, Ohio, Tennessee and Kentucky. A virile race, not gregarious haunters of cities and incidentally traffickers in votes like the Catholic Irish of the 19th century immigrations, but genuine lovers and tillers of the soil and jealous of their rights—rough, pugnacious democrats, with a strain of Calvinism and its attendant cruelty, particularly where the heathen were concerned. For according to the familiar shibboleth of their creed, an Indian had no saving merits except when he was dead! Lesser streams of this immigration from Northern Ireland arrived from time to time at Charleston, and thence making for the mountains of South Carolina crept up their base, till in course of time the link was completed with their friends pressing down from the north. Such was the stock that held and pushed back the frontier through most of the 18th century, the "mountainy men" of the then current speech; a people apart from the civilization of the lower planting and farming districts, the security of which from all chance of recrudescent Indian attacks they incidentally guaranteed—though after Braddock's defeat in 1775 they were rolled back by hundreds on the terrified settlements with fire and slaughter. Reared in danger, hardship and industry, when these people of the third and fourth generation emerged into a normal civilization, they proved the best and thriftiest of farmers, the most vigorous men of affairs. To none of the stocks engaged in the making of the United States does that country owe more than to the Scotch-Irish, the "second time" colonists from Ulster, and no well-informed American would hesitate to admit it. In 18th century documents they are nearly always alluded to simply as "Irish," since the other breed, the Southern and Catholic

Irish, were as yet, for sufficient reasons, almost non-extant in America.[1]

With Maryland we come to the first of the colonies committed largely to negro slavery and to a single crop, in this case, tobacco. This does not mean that tobacco was their only crop, far from it, but it was the chief article of export and revenue. Most other products were mainly for home consumption, though they covered many times the area occupied by tobacco, which is a rather intensive crop. It requires much labour with hand and hoe, and is proportionally more productive per acre than maize, wheat, oats and grass, which were grown mainly for local consumption of men and stock. This applies to all the tobacco colonies. Devotion to a single 'cash crop' is apt to involve slovenliness in the mere maintenance crops and the deterioration of land. Such were the characteristics of all the slave States in varying degrees, till the abolition of slavery in 1861-5, left a trail disfigured by patches of practically irrecoverable waste. Maryland, however, suffered less in this respect than the others. The colony had been founded in 1632 by George Calvert, Lord Baltimore. He had already sunk a fortune and incidentally ruined his health by a similar enterprise in Newfoundland, which failed through the severity of the climate and its attendant drawbacks, not previously realised. Undismayed by these mishaps, Baltimore got a further grant from Charles I of this more congenial territory and named it Maryland, after Henrietta Maria. Virginia, which claimed prior ownership, had objected vigorously, but vainly, this being the first of many disputes, sometimes ending in blows between the Provinces, which then hated one another heartily. The Calverts were Catholics, and Maryland was intended, as it proved to be, a refuge for immigrants of that faith who were excluded elsewhere. Complete

[1] A few years ago during a debate in Congress on some matter touching the Revolutionary war, an Irish-American politician of the modern type out of the fulness of his historical knowledge informed an edified House that fifty per cent. of the patriot armies were composed of Irishmen, whereupon a gentleman named Field arose and stated that he had made an exhaustive study of the racial ingredients of the patriot armies which revealed the fact that six per cent. were Irishmen but all Ulster-Scotch-Irishmen. Of the late speaker's compatriots, he said, there were practically none fighting, save in the ranks of the British army, where there were some thousands.

toleration for all, however, was Baltimore's most liberal policy. Maryland was a proprietary Province, like Pennsylvania. Either personally, or through appointed governors, under the usual quasi-popular machinery, the Calverts governed it wisely till the Revolution, at which moment, curiously enough, their Governor, Eden, was immensely popular. Speaking broadly, a minority of Catholic gentry with liberal land grants and an inflow of other settlers of various creeds, developed the Province. Before the Revolution, however, the Anglican Church had come to predominate and rather ungratefully aspired to Establishment, though nothing serious came of it.

At the close of the 17th century, Maryland, like Virginia, imported negro slaves in great numbers, and a sort of Planter aristocracy arose along the tidal districts, with a prosperous working-farmer community developing the hinterland towards the mountains and the growing Scotch-Irish belt along their base. When the war broke out, Maryland contained 150,000 people, of which only fifteen per cent. were Catholics and a third negro slaves. Life here seems to have been singularly happy, for the whites at any rate, save among that fraction of them who were indentured servants, persons whose lot here as elsewhere was often very hard. That of the negro slave, though easier in these higher Southern States than farther south and in the West Indies, had not yet softened into the generally benignant attitude towards him of these States in the 19th century. Interior Maryland, however, was neither then, nor at any time, much of a slave-owning country. It was chiefly opened and worked by white labour, in most cases that of the freeholder and his family. Annapolis, its little capital, had already, before the Revolution, been outstripped in importance by Baltimore, at the head of the Chesapeake Bay.

And now we come to Virginia, about which a good deal more must be said. For she was much the most populous and important of the Southern Colonies, Massachusetts alone in the North aspiring to rivalry. All things considered, Virginia, in 1775, was the most prominent of the Colonies, with a population of 600,000, of which more than a third were negro slaves. There is probably not a soul in England with the faintest knowledge of the colonial or social history of Virginia. Yet everyone, as the saying goes, has a vague notion that Virginia is distinguished for its "old families," with a further impression that these owe that distinction to aristocratic English origin. The first is a half-truth, the second is pure fiction. Again, Virginia, occasionally coupled with her neighbours, is quite commonly styled, even in England following American picturesque historians and fiction writers, the "Cavalier State." Critical American historians have been recently endeavouring to kill this amazing superstition with gentle ridicule. But they won't do it. It is too good copy for magazine and fiction writers, and the modern Americans, as no discerning visitor or reader of their lighter literature could fail to realise, have a flair for genealogy, not necessarily personal. That there was a considerable movement out of England after the Civil War of men of all classes and occupations, who had lost property or employment through espousing the King's side is true enough. But Virginia by that time, say 1650, was a going concern. Some of the better-class refugees most naturally went to Virginia, as its people were not schismatics, but ordinary Englishmen, and the country was attractive. But a great many more of this class went to the West Indies where they could buy slaves and work plantations. There was no labour to speak of, either white or black, in Virginia in 1650. Nearly everyone did his own work, much modified by the long, open season and the abundance of game and fish. The original settlers in Virginia were socially as varied as those in all the colonies—middling and lower-class folk with the sprinkling of country squires' sons that has distinguished every single colonial movement from that day to this, and never so much as in, say, the last eighty years. Australia, New Zealand, Africa, Canada, the West Indies, Ceylon, have always been full of them as a matter of course. It may be remembered that the abounding younger sons of the Squirearchy in the 17th and early 18th century followed occupations that their successors would have thought derogatory. A common alternative to emigration was apprenticeship to a wholesale or retail tradesman in London or the country.

Virginia had accepted Cromwell without demur. The sight of a battleship had settled the matter at once. A few offices changed hands, but nothing else was altered save in connection with Cromwell's freer trade policy, which was, of course, very popular. Maryland accepted the Parliament much less placidly, while in Barbados, civil war raged between the Royalist and Cromwellian factions. When peace returned in England, fugitive loyalists with some means crossed the Atlantic especially to the West Indies, where both land and slaves to work were procurable. In Virginia, there was plenty of free or cheap land, but the Virginia settlers, as already stated and contrary to a baseless legend, had generally to do their own clearing and cultivating. For it was all primeval forest. Undoubtedly, many ex-soldiers or sympathisers with the Royalist cause came to Virginia as to other provinces. Some of these immigrants were well connected and their names are preserved. Most who could afford it returned at the Restoration. The country was not ready for the spacious planter aristocracy, using the term in the limited colonial sense, that sprang up when the negroes came.

Whatever the supposed devotion of Virginia to the Stuarts, she rose in rebellion against Charles II in 1676, exactly a century before the Great Revolution, drove out the old "Cavalier" Governor, burned the little capitol of Jamestown, and created a chaos of several months. A young English gentleman, Bacon, was the leader, and his death caused the ultimate collapse of the rising. A battalion of the Guards was sent out and many gibbets erected, and decorated by the restored and vengeful Governor, Sir William Berkeley, with the swinging bodies of insubordinate planters. The King's laconic remark on his too faithful zeal was characteristic: "That old fool has hung more men in that naked country than I have punished for the murder of my father." This was the greatest political event in Colonial America prior to the final Revolution. But scarcely anyone on this side of the Atlantic, and by no means everyone on the other, has so much as heard of it.

English laws and customs were as closely adhered to in Virginia from the first as circumstances allowed. County and vestry administration, churches with parishes of huge extent, a handful of State salaried clergy, and rigid suppression of dissent were the order of that day. But religion in practice was utterly slack till in the 18th century a wave of dissenting fervour, stimulated mostly among the rougher classes by the preaching of Whitefield, virtually defied the establishment and its church dues, then paid in tobacco. The Church of England clergy, though upheld by the upper class, were admittedly a very poor lot. The more fervent of the laity were quite conscious of this, and a deputation of two or three Virginians in the 18th century waited on the Minister of the day, Walpole, I think, requesting, quite reasonably, the appointment of a bishop to America. The Minister was so short with his visitors that they were provoked to ask him if he did not think that Virginians, like Englishmen, had souls to be saved. "Damn your souls," was the ungracious retort of the great man, "go home and grow tobacco!" This at any rate was the time-honoured story told in Virginia. Education was casual and voluntary. The better sort had tutors, such as they were, and occasionally sent sons home to England. Eton has altogether six colonial Virginians on her register. The bulk of the people had no education at all, though little private schools sprang up and a college was founded at Williamsburg.

And now for the truth about these old Virginia families of which most of the English-speaking world has vaguely heard—though mainly through the decorative pictures drawn by uncritical American novelists. Through the 17th century, the first century, speaking broadly, of Virginian history, a small group of successful families acquired prominence as was inevitably the case in almost every British colony. For one thing, there were always several Government posts paid by the Crown, which in themselves gave consequence and led in an unscrupulous age to further opportunities of personal aggrandisement—as in land for instance. One need not labour the other causes—energy, shrewdness, or ability—that brought power and wealth to the more fortunate colonists. But this group seems to have remained a small one through the 17th century, at the close of which there were only

2,000 negro slaves to about 50,000 whites in the colony, figures which in themselves are a negation to the existence of a large slave-owning planter aristocracy. It is true, there were at least as many convicts and indentured servants —voluntary or kidnapped. But these unfortunates were widely distributed. In short, Virginia was in the main developed with white labour on " family farms " in freehold grants or purchases usually of 500 acres, more or less—much as the other colonies. The contemporary accounts of Bacon's Rebellion, when several thousand mounted men turned out on one side or the other, suggest rather a yeomanry of substantial freeholders—" House-keepers," as the contemporary account calls them. Beyond a doubt, even then, there were a few large estates cultivated by slaves. But they were not the leading characteristic of the country. Land too was always cheap and abundant in Virginia.

But land, beyond a mere " family farm," was no good without workers. About 1700, there came a rush of slave labour at prices which the Virginians could afford to pay. Slavery had already brought wealth to the West Indies, and it now came within reach of the Virginia tobacco growers, both from the West Indian surplus supplies and direct from Africa. It was now that the large planters and slave owners arose in appreciable numbers, and as such became a power in the land for seventy or eighty years. By the Revolution there were 250,000 slaves in Virginia to 350,000 whites. But then great numbers of the ordinary farmers owned a few slaves. One of the many delusions concerning the Slavery States is that the ownership of negroes was of itself a sort of social distinction. This was only true upon a low social plane. Thousands of common farmers, who would not pass under the most liberal construction as anything else, acquired slaves. A few prominent families were already to the fore, but most of the " Old Virginia families " rose into gentility with this 18th century. Many made the leap, if the phrase may be used, where the boundary line was not very sharply defined, as late as the 19th century. Slaves were more evenly distributed in Virginia and Maryland than is generally supposed.[1]

[1] " Moll Flanders " (Defoe).

By the Revolution, however, there had arisen a quite numerous planter aristocracy. There is no evidence that it paid any regard to its respective origins, which were undoubtedly various. Washington, admittedly the "first gentleman in Virginia," obviously neither knew nor cared anything about his English descent. His pedigree had to be puzzled out quite recently by moderns, though he was socially rather proud and stand-offish. It is certain that he never thought of Virginia as the "Cavalier State." None of his distinguished contemporaries, or immediate predecessors, betray in their writings any interest whatever in their ancestors. They were fairly tenacious, however, of the substantial position they had inherited or acquired. Nominally, a democracy with a freehold franchise, they had plenty of opposition. The larger estates were then mostly in the Tidewater district, that tier of counties lying on or near the sea, threaded by tidal rivers. On these navigable waters they had their own wharves, from which English vessels took their tobacco direct to England, returning with the manufactured articles necessary to their lives.

In the higher country behind Tidewater, and stretching towards the Alleghanies, which chain of mountains rose like a faint blue wall along the whole Western frontier of the Colony, lay many counties of later settlement. Here there were pioneers in different stages of development, either from Europe or the superfluous sons of the Tidewater planters. These people, with few or no slaves, cutting out farms with their own labour, represented another class, who in time came to resent the domination of the big Eastern magnates, and returned by degrees an actual majority to the Legislature, in opposition to the party of the *Nabobs* and *Bashaws*, as they styled them. Ill-educated, of course, as a class, their majority of about six to five did not carry them very far, but it was a protest against privilege in the monopoly of Crown offices, the irregular patenting of Crown lands, a general assumption of superiority, and so forth.

In time these pleasant-lying upland counties themselves became thickly sprinkled with slaves, and many an upland farmer rose into the class above. But prior to the

Revolution there was a sufficiently strong opposition jealous of the Tidewater aristocracy to influence greatly the course of that vital movement, as will be shown later. These Virginia democrats thought that a movement proclaiming such high-sounding notions of equality as those emphasized by Patrick Henry and Jefferson, both demagogues, though of the planter class, entailed a more equal division of power and such good things as belonged to it in their own State. So at the Revolution they supported the Eastern Oligarchy who, contrary to the general outside expectation, became the leaders in the popular cause. This may be confidently set down to the fact that the Virginia aristocracy was essentially a home-made one and owed nothing to English associations. There had been no immigration that seriously counted since the preceding century. The Virginians, though in some ways very English and attached to the Mother Country, had for three generations maintained little personal touch with it. They were neither travellers nor sea-goers. Few had ever been out of the Province. In all the gossip and personal memoirs of the 17th and 18th centuries, there is no mention of a Virginian appearing in London Society, whereas many Americans from other colonies come on the scene, while, as everyone knows, West Indian heiresses were notable items on the marriage market.

But at home the Virginia aristocracy ruled the roost. This very isolation and class predominance made, no doubt, for a more sensitive attitude towards interference from outside. Most of them went into rebellion. But their idea of the future was merely the removal of the Royal Governor and of English rule. Everything else was to be as before. The Provincial democracy had quite other ideas, as when the stress of war was over, the oligarchy found out. For at least a generation the latter had to swallow a good deal that was distasteful. Primogeniture and entail were swept away. So too was their Church Establishment, while fifty or more of its actual buildings were wantonly destroyed and their sacred vessels and vestments profanely ravaged by "patriot" dissenters and Presbyterians. To these Yahoos they represented the Tory faith; though the gentry themselves were on the popular side they were powerless in the matter. Their churchmanship, to be sure, was political and social rather than religious. A recent Virginia historian of their Church describes them as "polite pagans." The slovenliness of Georgian England was intensified a hundred-fold in these far scattered barn-like brick or wooden buildings served by a clergy who, by all accounts, could often have given points in unclerical conduct to their Hogarthian contemporaries in the Mother Country, whence they mostly came. Still they were not the provocative cause of the ruffianism that burned the churches and robbed them of their plate and vestments. It is an admittedly black page in the story of Revolutionary Virginia, and a reproach to the class that failed to prevent it.

In due course, however, after the war, the Virginia aristocracy made a pretty good recovery, and, reinforced by a number of new families, resulting from the upset of the Revolution with its subdivision and confiscation of loyalist estates, got back into the saddle again[1]. Many superficial concessions in phraseology became necessary. Greetings in the market place ignored the class distinction. The "common people" as even Madison and Jefferson called them, became the "plain people," a phrase, it will be remembered, beloved by the late President Wilson, himself a Southerner of that origin. The gentry were no longer classified under that title, but found other phrases to distinguish themselves, much helped by the negroes, who were keenly alive to such distinctions. "But Democracy everywhere, even in America, felt the setback given to it by the overthrow of Napoleon in Europe. In Virginia, other reasons contributed to the checking of Liberalism. The development of the South and West drew from the old Dominion its best young manhood and brought on a disastrous economic competition. Virginia lost rank as the greatest of American States and rapidly sank to a secondary position. It was no longer a land of energetic and forward-looking men, but of memories, a place of social amenities and soft dreaming. Under the influence of Sir Walter Scott's novels glorifying the feudal

[1] "Sketches from Old Virginia" (A.G.B.).

age, the new generation constructed in imagination a colonial past of splendour which had small part in reality. The old aristocratic spirit revived and existed alongside the democratic theories of government which Jefferson had introduced. But the fact remains, that in Virginia the swing back from democracy was steadily increasing in momentum from the fall of Napoleon to the Civil War." [1]

Thus the author of *The Revolution in Virginia*, the latest and best Virginia authority, puts the matter in a nutshell, and it will equally apply to the slave-owning half of Maryland, and to the smaller aristocracy of North Carolina. The amazing influence of Scott's novels on an educated but isolated rural community, not well supplied with current literature, and personally unfamiliar with contemporary Europe, is now recognized by critical investigators of this period. By sheer imagination they transformed their forebears into a sort of Feudal magnates, oblivious to the absurdity of comparing tobacco-planting by negro labour with Feudalism, and the background of a new country to the historic soil of Feudal England. It was then the "Cavalier ancestor" crept into existence. That familiar expression, "Southern Chivalry," was adopted by them long before the Civil War, which would have given it some point. It was quite meaningless as applied to a peaceful home-staying community, chiefly concerned with agriculture and section politics. Moderate country houses of ten or a dozen rooms with a pillared wooden portico, became stately mansions and even "Baronial halls." The whole phraseology of the South took an unintentionally whimsical turn. The men at a country dance became in local print the "Chivalry" of the district. The ladies were attended by "cavaliers" and became themselves "demoiselles," although French was almost an unknown tongue. Southerners never played outdoor games, but sometimes held tournaments, tilting at the ring and crowning "Queens of Beauty" and "Maids of Honour." There was a queer fancy, too, quite common among middle-aged or elderly men, to be thought "proud and dignified," detrimental to the good manners that were general, and an obituary notice was hardly satisfactory that failed to credit

[1] Ekenrode.

the deceased with the latter quality at any rate. All this, now, no doubt long extinct, is only interesting as so out of its period and place and so curiously exotic.

In the half-century between the world peace of 1815 and the Civil War, Virginia as a whole and in a material sense, went steadily downhill, her lands, in great part either worn out or naturally poor, under the deplorable system of farming engendered by slavery. Olmstead, the Arthur Young of America, a New York gentleman farmer, who toured the South on horseback in the eighteen-forties, described Virginia as drifting hopelessly and carelessly towards a general insolvency. The old Tidewater country of colonial days, mainly of a light sandy soil, had been in part deserted for the middle and western belts towards the mountains; and they in turn, had been, and were still being, treated to the same merciless cropping. A naturally beautiful country was thus sadly disfigured. Its storm-gullied, red hillsides, its briary, sedgy wastes of "turned-out" old-field, and big patches of scrub pine where oak forests had once waved, were cruel eyesores and were even reckoned as such. But to the vast majority, who had known no other country—for the Civil War was fought in the South—such conditions, naturally enough, seemed almost normal. There were exceptional districts, however, and even whole counties, showing a different face, and a fair proportion of individuals, who benefited by the better farming of their forebears. But there were far more, who in the eighteen-seventies, deplored the condition to which their lands had been reduced, and with means crippled by the Civil War, struggled valiantly to restore their fertility.

But the crisis Olmstead writes of was for the moment averted. The importation of slaves from Africa had been suppressed. The rice and indigo plantations of South Carolina wore out their negroes rapidly. The cotton industry of the great South-west was just beginning and calling aloud for labour. For all this demand the surplus stock of Virginia, and in a less degree of her neighbours, were the sole source of supply. The price of negroes rose greatly, and carried Virginia on till the Civil War put an end to the whole business. Though living before that war in elementary and unexacting comfort, her landowners were still poor in money judged by outside standards, and rather widely in debt. Slaves had become the chief financial security, for the ill-treated lands were cheap and not always saleable. When these were freed, their owners seemed in a bad way, though if the lands had been as reasonably treated in the past as those of Pennsylvania and New York, with this new, cheap and quite good labour of the freed slaves, all would have gone well —better indeed than before. For slavery was an expense and incubus on inferior land. It took so much of it to "bread" the slaves with the current bad farming, and three-fourths of the soil of Virginia was either naturally poor or exhausted and steadily running down.

American novelists and even many local historians, with a quite curious addiction to overcolouring the amenities of bygone days and careless of hard facts in Virginia especially, write airily of "princely mansions" and "hordes of slaves." The best houses in the State, generally late eighteenth century, were no larger than the smaller squires' houses in England, or indeed than many spacious rectories and even farmhouses I could name myself. And as they are mostly still standing, this obvious fact can be readily verified. As regards slaves, there were far too many in the State for its good. But of these, the Government Statistics of 1861 tell us 22,000 families owned but four or less apiece, while only 117 owned 100 and over. Now, 100 negroes meant roughly about 15 families of both sexes and all ages housed in log cabins—in other words, the white labour strength and cottage accommodation of a fair-sized Lincolnshire or Norfolk tenant farmer of the same period. Compared, for instance, with the West Indies, where 5,000 slaves were sometimes owned by a single family, the American figures were insignificant, just as the incomes of the chief landowners in Virginia, Maryland and North Carolina rarely approached the revenues of the larger Barbados and Jamaica planters.

Maryland, indeed, had so compromised with slavery by 1861, that almost half the state was virtually as its neighbours, Pennsylvania or New Jersey, and was thus fortunate. The Scotch-Irish who at the Revolution had been still borderers and incidentally Indian fighters at the back of Virginia, had already developed the fertile valley between the Blue Ridge, that noble outwork of the Alleghanies and the main chain, now roughly defined as the Shenandoah Valley. Their descendants mainly occupy it to-day, and still form a sharp contrast to their fellow Virginians of English stock east of the Blue Ridge. Thrifty farmers even to nearness on these good limestone lands, slavery had never appealed to them. Their country at "abolition" wore a different aspect and showed another face to that of their slave-ridden Anglo-Virginian neighbours.

South Carolina at the Revolution differed from the other Slave States. She too had developed an aristocracy which mostly owned and cultivated rice and indigo plantations near the coast. It was a smaller and even then individually richer body than the others and owned more slaves, approximating more nearly to the West Indian colonies, though these conditions became more marked later on. The rice plantations being of necessity damp and unhealthy, much time was spent at the capital, Charleston, where the larger planters had residences and were often directly concerned with the shipping trade. This province was more in touch, too, with England than the other Southern Colonies, while in the matter of social and educational amenities Charleston was noted as being almost the rival of Boston and Philadelphia, with characteristics of its own superadded. In the country, as elsewhere, there was a large population of yeoman farmers, English, Scotch, Germans, Dutch, Swiss and French Huguenots. North and South Carolina had been colonised later in the 17th century than their neighbours and had been originally one Province. They had been settled by all kinds of people, both British and Continental in origin, not generally schismatics, though little groups of sectaries were among them. When North and South Carolina fell apart, the former, as already noted, developed into a paler and inferior reflex of Virginia. The jest, still current in the old Dominion, "Yes, Sir, I come from North Carolina, but right close to the Virginia line," aptly expresses the situation. But South Carolina became ultimately the antithesis of its former partner. The name came to stand especially for a small and wealthy aristocracy of rice and indigo planters and slave owners on a larger scale than elsewhere. Virginians and Marylanders had more than once suggested the abolition of slavery, as an undesirable and uneconomical institution, but were baffled, partly by the British interests in the slave trade and partly by the difficulties consequent on manumission. The South Carolinians, as slave-owners, operating mostly in semi-tropical and often unhealthy lowlands, steadily supported the "Institution." It was South Carolina, as we know, that led secession, provoked the Civil War, and dragged into it the Slave States to the north of her. Yet even before the Revolution there were thousands of small farmers in the back-lying uplands of the Colony. But the large planters on Tidewater ruled the Province, howsoever divided in opinions as to the Mother Country when the crucial hour arrived. Charles II had divided the Province among several English proprietors as a reward for their fidelity to his father's cause. Only one went to reside there[1], though all drew some sort of revenue from their grant till the Revolution. After that, the South Carolina aristocracy though not a large one, grew into the wealthiest body of the kind in the American Union. They had more slaves, worked them out more quickly, and had less personal regard for them than the States to the northward, for which climate and their larger scale of operations were chiefly responsible. They were the wealthiest, the most travelled, and least provincial of the Southern slave-owners. As regards origin, the "Cavalier" legend had penetrated even the Carolinas. Professor Morrison, of Harvard, in his recent *History of the United States*, draws a humorous picture of a rough little up-country South Carolina farmer, without refinement or education, in possession of a dozen negroes, alluding to his "Cavalier" ancestors. It is curious to notice how generally those who deal with the early ingredients of the British American colonies overlook the re-migration, as pioneers presumably with some money, to the Southern plantations, and even to the West Indies, of New Englanders mainly from Massachusetts. Huguenots, too, were a notable item among the South Carolina pioneers, and

[1] Sir George Collinton.

stamped their mark on the country. Here, as elsewhere, too, the Scotch-Irish were in possession of the mountain frontiers.

Georgia, founded by the philanthropic General Oglethorpe in the mid-eighteenth century, growing up as an extension of South Carolina and becoming more or less a reflex of that province, was too new at the Revolution to need more notice here than this brief statement of fact.

I have taken rather a free advantage of the heading of this chapter to overrun in parts of it the period covered by my book.

I trust however, this slight departure from chronology may be overlooked in view of the somewhat widespread misunderstandings it endeavours to correct.

CHAPTER II

THE OUTBREAK OF WAR

BEYOND the notion that George III insisted on illegally taxing the Americans and that the Americans resisted, little, I think, is remembered by most Britons of the rights and wrongs of the question. For lack of knowledge, or rather, perhaps, of interest in the subject, it is generally assumed that the colonists had all the right on their side, and that they were all of one mind in their policy. One may fairly say that the American War of Independence gets nothing like the recognition from posterity in England that its importance would seem to warrant. In a military sense, no doubt, we should be glad enough to forget it. But then the Seven Years' War, the long struggle with France for predominance in North America which ended gloriously in 1761, and left England greater in the eyes of the world than at any period before or perhaps since, is almost entirely forgotten, save for the dramatic incident of Wolfe's death, generally but quite erroneously described as its deciding factor. Of this conflict England, with her troops and money, bore the chief brunt. The colonies reaped far the greater gain. With the capture of Canada, the "French terror" was removed for ever, the frontiers of New England freed from the constant harrying by French-Canadians with their Indians. The vast territories beyond the Alleghanies, from Pennsylvania down to Georgia, hitherto claimed by the French and held by them in lonely forts and villages flying the French flag by virtue of pioneer discoverers and their influence with the Western Indians, were to be formally annexed.

A forward American policy had been conceived by Louis XV, then in the vigour of his earlier years, and statesmen of energy found to push it. The land companies of Virginia with grants beyond the mountains, found themselves confronted by hostile Frenchmen, backed by hostile Indians, in possession. In short, the English were to be hemmed in between the mountains and the sea, and thus confined to their then existing Provinces. The great virgin West from the Lower Mississippi up to the Canadian Lakes was to be French, an annexe of Canada for all time that then counted.

Those English Colonies, whose future and expansion westward was thus blocked, had been slow to recognize the danger. The wealthier class along the Atlantic seaboard were leading comfortable, easy lives in towns or on plantations out of reach of Western doings. The up-country farmers and frontiersmen were absorbed in their own hardish lives. Two or three English Governors first sounded the alarm. Small sums were wrung out of colonial assemblies, and trifling companies of provincial volunteers under young Washington were sent into the trans-Alleghany wilderness to remonstrate with or remove the French, some of whom were regulars from Canada. The French repulsed or captured them, and laughed at their claims. It was obvious that the much disunited colonies were powerless against the French with their regular troops in Canada, and its population trained to arms and ready to march at the Viceroy's word. So English troops came out under General Braddock, and met with the disaster at the French backwoods fort, the key position of Duquesne, that has rung down the ages. The Western Indians, already allied to the French by intercourse and propaganda, now desolated the English frontiers with torch and tomahawk. France and Britain both poured out regular troops to Canada and New York respectively, and roused their respective colonists and Indians to the fact that France and England were to decide once and for all which nation should control the boundless possibilities of the North American hinterland, by this time recognized by all intelligent minds. The war began in 1755.

The New Englanders rallied creditably to the side of the King's troops, partly as more efficient in common action and organization, and partly owing to the fact that

GEORGE WASHINGTON
From the painting by G. STUART *in the National Portrait Gallery*

they and the French had been raiding and scalping one another for generations. The contributions of the Middle and Southern colonies, who had most to gain, were negligible in proportion to their population. They had never met Frenchmen, nor realised the shadow that lay over a future they dimly but still definitely cherished. They were hard to arouse. With the British troops in the Ohio expeditions, marched a few hundred Virginians and Marylanders, mostly backwoodsmen, of whose officers, Braddock at one stage and young Washington at another, had the meanest opinion. But the war rolled northward, and in due course, amid the great lakes and wooded mountains of New England and western New York, and on the wild coasts of Nova Scotia, developed into a struggle for Canada not originally contemplated. It was begun, merely as a protest against the French policy of encirclement. It ended five years later in the expulsion of the French power from the country, and the cession of Canada, with all that Canada then meant, by the Treaty of Paris in 1763. Britain, as already mentioned, then stood at her very zenith as a world power, admired even by her late enemies whom she had stripped of so much territory and prestige. But many warning voices arose, both in and out of Parliament, against the retention of Canada. They were drowned, however, in the exultation of the moment. The colonists, from New England to the Carolinas, lit bonfires, rang bells, and fired off guns in their triumphant exuberance, while orators from pulpit and rostrum celebrated the glorious achievements of the British Empire, and even more fervently perhaps, if less loudly, thanked Heaven for the removal of the French terror and the French fur-traders.

The French had cleared out of Canada, leaving there some 60,000 war-sick peasants and a few hundred priests, seigneurs, merchants, lawyers and the like. Montreal was then the limit of French-Canadian civilization, which clustered mainly along the banks of the St. Lawrence. Beyond this was the great Canadian West, stretching into infinity, probed by daring Jesuit missioners, lay adventurers and fur-traders. They had already penetrated the shaggy Ontario wilderness, to trickle out beyond it on to the Western Prairies, and marked the route there with small trading settlements of Frenchmen living in friendly relationship with Indians. All this, though with indefinite bounds, had been hitherto recognized as in the French sphere. It was the still vaster, and under the conditions of that day, the more attractive wilderness that lay to the southward, roughly the great country known to-day as the Middle West, that had been the *casus belli* of Anglo-French strife.

All this was now open to British development. The Canadian West was regarded as a semi-Arctic country and of small account save for the fur trade. Boundaries were now obliterated. The whole West, but vaguely known and sparsely dotted with French trading-posts down to the Spanish territory on the Mississippi, fell under the administration of the English crown. The entire situation had altered. The decade of 1763-74 forms a unique interlude in American history. The French had gone, the prospects of the colonies were such as they had never been. Some 20,000 persons who had served through part or all of the war had returned to their farms or desks. British garrisons were occupying the seaboard, a situation which in peace time had scarcely ever happened before and was never to happen again. The French-Canadians, who had had more than enough of fighting, were submitting peacefully to a mild and liberal military rule.

But Great Britain, as a matter of fact, was beginning to set her unwieldy house in order. Her Colonial Empire had outgrown the rather easy-going conditions under which it had flourished without any serious hitches, since in 1676 the Virginians had risen in armed rebellion, for no very urgent reason, against their Governor. Two great questions now called for immediate solution. First, the suppression of smuggling. For in contravention of the Trade and Navigation Laws, this practice was flourishing to such an extent as to render active measures imperative. The only alternative was a revocation of the laws themselves, and for this Great Britain, under the ethics and conditions of that day, was not prepared. Hitherto, all efforts to suppress this illicit trading over broad seas had been futile, for lack of endeavour, as were the paltry efforts at home to suppress cross-channel smuggling in Sussex and Kent. But the American smugglers were big merchants and rich skippers, and their influence was great. When, therefore, the British Navy was commissioned to take a serious hand in capturing their ships, and trying their owners in Naval Courts, a great outcry arose, more especially in New England, which was chiefly affected.

The second question was that of a garrison for the Colonies. The recent war had shown plainly, that left to themselves, they were of but small military strength. The New Englanders were far the readiest and ablest to take the field. The other Colonies had made a rather poor show, alike with their untrained militia and small bodies of permanent troops. For all of them still thought provincially. They had admittedly learnt a little more about one another in the late war, but were still far enough from mutual affection and respect, and united action seemed hopeless. There really was a general consensus of opinion that an effective garrison would be required. France was smarting from the loss of Canada. Spain had many an old score to pay off when opportunity offered. Neither France nor Spain would have found the conquest of the Colonies an easy achievement. But both powers were on their south-western borders, while in any lapse of the British Navy their ships could ravage the coasts, where most of the wealth of the colonies lay. The requisite force was approximately estimated at 10,000 men. The need for this number was generally accepted by responsible people on both sides of the Atlantic. The question then arose, who was to pay for them? No vast sum was required, £100,000 being quoted as a rough yearly estimate.

Now the British taxpayer had been heavily laden by the Seven Years' War in Europe and America, and was getting restless. He had borne nearly all the expense of clearing the French out of North America and placing the hitherto hampered colonists in an improved position with a great and unclouded future. The considerable war expenses incurred by the New England States, as well as the lesser liabilities of those to the southward, either had been, or were to be, largely made good by Great Britain. That these colonies should now bear all or part of their own land defence was surely equitable. In truth, they frankly accepted it as such. They could hardly have done otherwise, loth as most of the Colonial legislatures had always been to vote money for any purpose, particularly, it may be noted, the salaries of their Governors. And now began a long wrangle as to the proportions which each of the thirteen Provinces was to contribute, for their own stipulations ran that they were to vote the money themselves without interference by the Crown. Massachusetts at once pointed to the active part she had taken in the French war, the troops supplied and the expenses incurred, compared, for example, with Maryland, who had done little or nothing. But Maryland evaded the point and objected to contributing as much as, or more than, a larger and wealthier Province. This sort of thing went backwards and forwards between the different Provinces, all of them recognizing their share in the responsibility, but in hopeless disagreement as to their respective contributions. It soon became apparent that they would shuffle out of it altogether, and leave the heavily burdened British taxpayer to bear the sole expense of their military as well as naval defences. This, in fact, actually happened. It is true that the defence of the colonies, whose safety without it would not have been worth a month's purchase, was a leading argument for the Navigation Laws. But the late war had given the Americans both a welcome relief from a troublesome neighbour, and an unclouded future. Their own taxation, though much increased, was trifling compared with the burden that the British taxpayer, partly on their account, was called upon to bear. Lastly, the sum of money asked for was not sufficient to defray even the whole cost of the proposed defensive force. It is no wonder that the British Government grew irritable.

In the meantime, the urgent need for a regular force was already being demonstrated, without any threat from European powers. For a great Indian war had broken out. The ablest Indian leader who had ever faced the white man had united, by a carefully prepared and subtle policy, all the Western tribes in one great offensive and defensive league. This was Pontiac, and the war he waged is known by his name, and described under that heading by the American historian, Parkman, in a fascinating volume. It should be noted too, that under the conditions of that time and country, one Indian warrior was equal to one white soldier or frontiersman in battle. The Peace had finally destroyed the belief of the Western Indians in French power. Pathetic efforts were still made by the Western French traders and settlers to persuade their Indian friends that their great Father Onontio would yet return and "drive the English into the sea." But it was no good. The English were inexorably pushing westward, clearing the forests in their path, driving the Indian and the game before them. Quite a different invasion this from that of the French, who merely traded and hunted and squatted among the Indians in friendly, sociable fashion.

General Bouquet, one of those clever and loyal Swiss officers who had served, for linguistic reasons, in the Royal Americans (60th Rifles) since their formation, took with him into the wilds a strong force of British regulars, with some companies of Provincial frontiersmen. Pontiac put up a long and able resistance with a force of picked warriors from all the Western tribes. A tradition, not wholly mythical, had arisen that British regulars were of no use against Indians in their native woods, and that only American frontiersmen understood the game. Bouquet found his colonial Irregulars, though good shots and clever at taking cover, ineffective for driving an advantage through. They were constantly leaving for home, with or without permission, under urgent pleas of seed-time and harvest, and no real headway was made against Pontiac. The general then had an inspiration, and trained his regulars to do the impossible thing, to charge and rout these terrible forest warriors with the bayonet, to pursue them hot-foot from shelter to shelter with a weapon more effective than a tomahawk, thus leaving them scant time for reloading their rifles. In the end, Bouquet returned in triumph, though himself broken in health. Pontiac and his Indian alliance had been shattered, and thus the far West was made safe for the settler and the trader. But in this decade of the seventeen-sixties, more serious things were brewing than even formidable Indian wars.

As before stated, many a clear-sighted Englishman and American, to say nothing of foreigners, had doubted the wisdom of retaining Canada. Proposals had actually been made at the Treaty of Paris for accepting the French West Indian island of Guadeloupe in exchange. Strange as it may now seem, its value to an European power, in tropical exports, was much greater than that of Canada, whose population could barely support themselves, while the Fur Trade, which gave the colony its prime value, enjoyed the monopoly, with the British Hudson's Bay Company at the North, and the now British-American West to the south of it. But the triumph of the moment had been too great for the forebodings of a few.

And now the first mutterings of the predicted storm were heard in the land. Despairing of getting assistance for their own defence out of the colonies, England passed the Stamp Act in 1768 to provide at least a portion of the money. The storm it aroused caused, as we all know, its ultimate repeal, with rejoicings that evoked renewed professions of loyalty in most quarters. Whatever the technical rights of the matter, this should have been a sufficient warning, but unhappily it did not so prove. There had never been a question of the right, however unpalatable, of the Mother Country to regulate the trade of the Colonies and to tax it at the Colonial ports. Parliament's right to impose internal taxes had never yet been brought to the test. But it had been now, and was denounced, not as merely burdensome but as illegal. All the best brains on both sides of the Atlantic then and later discussed this right, and the balance of their judgment, regardless of country, was on the whole in favour of its legality, but against its expediency. These two words probably put the whole of an intricate question in a nutshell. Some trifling internal taxes were now laid on the colonies, though actually for their own support, and the fat was in the fire.

A careless posterity is quite apt to imagine that England attempted to tax the colonies for her own aggrandisement. As a matter of fact, such trifling revenue was merely an instalment of what by all equity they should have raised themselves, and probably would have raised but for their invincible internal jealousies. The distinction made between internal and external taxation seems to the enquirer to-day as indeed it did to many at that day, almost a quibble. That the one should be universally accepted through generations, while the other should start men to their feet shouting "liberty or death," has never yet been satisfactorily explained. It would be doing injustice to a great number of astute men at the top to suppose that there was nothing more than this at the back of their minds, and of misunderstanding masses at the bottom to suppose that such "parrot cries" were more than a means to an end. "No taxation without representation" has rung down the ages as the slogan of the Americans and their sympathisers. But as was shouted back and forth at the time, whole communities in England were unrepresented in Parliament, while it was urged that the colonial merchants were sufficiently strong to protect colonial interests at Westminster. Colonial representation at Westminster had been suggested on both sides, but such a procedure was too impracticable in that day for serious discussion. The fact is that the term, 'Representation' had, in America, a different meaning from its English interpretation. It had there its original significance. Every county, township, or town sent up one of its own people, as a representative to its Provincial assembly after the Old English pattern, upon a popular though restricted vote. In the 18th century, as everyone knows, there had developed electoral eccentricities which gave a quantity of obscure boroughs, and even the ghosts of vanished boroughs, representation in Parliament to the exclusion of large centres of population. Most of these members acquired their seats through favour or purchase from landed magnates or little groups in borough corporations.

Hitherto, the colonies, save for the generally accepted Navigation and Customs laws, had governed themselves and been as happy as prosperous. In truth they had been very much let alone. Duties had been evaded wholesale owing to slack supervision, and now everything was to be tightened up, and the smugglers did not like it. Glass and some other articles were, after all, now taxed partly in deference to a fad of the King, merely to demonstrate his right. After the surprising storm of opposition these taxes raised, whatever this particular King's obstinacy (or conscientiousness), few Englishmen could have imagined that another monarch and another Government would ever again stir up such a hornet's nest. But the Americans lived in a remote atmosphere. They took it differently, and saw, or professed to see, the thin edge of the wedge, and their Provinces bled by tyrannical future kings. That there never would be another king of such autocratic instincts in England, or if there were that he would not be tolerated, Americans could not, perhaps, be expected to surmise, and that was the dreadful pity of the whole business. How, for instance, could Patrick Henry, a half-educated rustic genius in the rural heart of Virginia, realise the improbability of this last kick of a belated autocrat becoming a precedent?

And so the trouble waxed from bad to worse and there followed the tea episode at Boston, and the closing of the port which shook the Colonies from end to end, the sympathetic boycott of British goods by all the Provinces, the angry mobs and pelted, though patient, soldiery. The slowness of communications added to the misunderstandings on either side. With steam or telegraphy there would probably have been no Revolution. Nearly all the Americans who "counted" were of colonial birth. Since the 17th century, there had been comparatively little immigration, but the successive waves of Ulster Protestants already spoken of, and they, though potential republicans, were largely segregated in the "back-country." Englishmen had small opportunities for realising how different from themselves in many respects their collateral relatives beyond the Atlantic had become, how their outlook, even their speech, had altered. The diverse English dialects, bewildering to neighbouring counties and baffling to strangers, had disappeared in the great melting pot of Colonial American-English. This, though by no means uniform, differing indeed in North and South, being harsh or soft, nasal or otherwise, while cherishing occasional archaic words, was, nevertheless, always intelligible. The rare English visitor of those days accustomed at home to associate a shirt-sleeved rustic with some incomprehensible dialect, always showed surprise at the "good English" spoken among ordinary provincial Americans.

The smallest differences in speech, dress or demeanour excited prejudices, almost amounting to antagonism. Every Englishman who has lived in any oversea English-speaking country is familiar with this attitude, something not readily put into words and quite unintelligible to those without this particular experience. It is, or was, part of an atmosphere that accounts for much that is not understood by those who have not breathed it. Practically all the English historians of this war are totally without any experience of what may be called the "American atmosphere." To those familiar with it their works show this plainly, however convincing they may seem to the general reader. To the latter and to the authors themselves, these old Americans are probably just Englishmen living across the seas! When the first congress from all the colonies met, we are told that intercolonial jealousies even at that pregnant time showed themselves. Even slight differences in dress and a little more perhaps in speech and intonation caused irritation. For a majority of the first convention were not from the most cultured class.

At this moment, 1767, when the uproar caused by the stamp duties had died down, Pitt's retirement, through ill-health, for once left Townshend supreme. As the Stamp Act had been resisted on the plea purely of internal taxation, Townshend now proceeded to test the good faith of the colonists by a fresh attempt to get a trifle from them towards their defence funds. He imposed a small tax on certain imports. The legality of such procedure had never been questioned, and indeed had been virtually endorsed by the very stress that had been laid on the nature of the Stamp Act. Townshend, whose great abilities were unchallenged, had laughed at the colonial distinction between internal and external taxation. He must have chuckled when he found the Americans, when their pockets were freshly touched by taxation they had never disputed, come suddenly round to his point of view and oppose his measures with such violence, that all his taxes were remitted save a tea duty of threepence in the pound. The sequence is familiar: the East India tea-ships were boarded in Boston harbour and their cargoes flung overboard, and thus the innocuous drug, legitimately taxed and cheapened by threatened ruin to the smugglers of Dutch tea, became the very watchword of the rising rebellion, and set men shouting of "chains and slavery" and "liberty or death."

New England, headed by Massachusetts, was from the first the firebrand. Never from earliest times had these provinces felt the blood tie with the Mother Country as the other colonies. Their ancestors had left in ill humour with her. Early 18th century officials write home of Rhode Island and Connecticut as virtually rejecting any connection with Great Britain. Except ships' masts, which were crown property in the forest, New England could furnish her with little she could not produce at home, and actually competed to advantage with her in supplying the needs of the planting colonies. The country was more or less self-contained and imported no great share of British goods. It was the planting colonies, providing the Mother Country with luxuries she could not produce, and taking freely of her manufactures in return, that appealed to the statesmen of those days. Barbados, the Carolinas, and Virginia were far more regarded as possessions than the northern colonies, with all their internal prosperity. England did not want mere homes for a surplus population. She had none to spare and had no wish to be "bled" by the colonies. The most desirable possession in her eyes was a community of white men, few or moderate in numbers, employing large quantities of slaves or bonded labour, shipping exotic products to England, and taking her manufactures and even grain, which she was still exporting, in return. In 1700, Barbados, the size of the Isle of Wight, alone exported to England ten times the value of the amount received from all the New England colonies, with their twenty-fold larger white population.

So England, drawing little profit from these prosperous New England shipbuilders, smuggling traders, fishermen and less prosperous but hardy farmers, growing generally poor yields of merely English crops, had for long held them with a looser rein. A disregard of the custom-house and kindred laws was so general that large fortunes had been made. A group of powerful Massachusetts families, much intermarried, represented a sort of smuggling aristocracy. When of a sudden their ships began to be seized, sometimes by zealous young lieutenants, with contraband, and confiscated in maritime courts without the protection of a sympathetic or intimidated local jury, it may be imagined how fierce their local patriotism waxed. The protection of the British taxpayers' Navy against French, Dutch and Spanish privateers and Barbary pirates through all the years was conveniently overlooked, while the ignorant Boston mobs which were harangued into such a frenzy against everything British had doubtless never regarded that side of the question at all. The sense of Empire was hardly a part of the New Englander's creed, whereas with the other colonies, like Maryland and Virginia, it was part of their code, in addition to a latent affection for a Mother Country, whose ideas they more or less shared, and against which they had no elementary grudge.

The New Englanders, on the other hand, were a sort of outlying relic of a 17th century Puritan England, of a bigoted type, long discarded and laughed out of existence in the Mother Country, as in the other colonies. They were antipathetic to the rest of the English-speaking world, including their sister colonies. Even the Scottish Presbyterians, having long ejected their otherwise beloved ministers from political meddling, could not abide the tyrannical New England atmosphere. The many solid virtues, which the New Englanders possessed and of which they were not slow to boast, though toleration was not included, contributed more to personal prosperity than to outside popularity. Still, they had relax. d a little by this time, and a backsliding element had made itself felt. The Church of England had already gained some footing, and was frightening the always republican preachers with the spectre of colonial bishops, a bishop, as with John Knox's Scotland, having horns and a tail. Even amusements, always excepting the theatre, were being winked at. The great magnates of contraband lived bravely in fine houses, wore gold-braided velvet cloaks, drank the best of liquors and drove in fine coaches. All of them joined in active protest against the British measures, though when the hour of parting came many, and among them some of the shrewdest and wisest, rejected the appeal to arms and the prospect it seemed to offer, and were to be found in the ranks of the United Empire refugees.

It is impossible to deal here with the Navigation Act and trade laws, a vast and complicated subject. Most American and English writers, the latter generally following the lead of the former, have dismissed these measures as ill-advised and rather tyrannical exercise of power. They cannot free their minds from modern conditions. No power in the world in those days would have been expected to give their colonies commercial independence. Under such conditions they would not have been considered worth the cost of defending, save as a precaution against immediate capture by a shrewder rival. The Navigation Act, confining all trade from the colonies to British ships, was on the whole accepted as beneficial to both parties, and of vital import to the welfare of the British Navy. With regard to trade, if, speaking broadly, Great Britain insisted on all colonial products being brought to her markets either for her own consumption or re-shipment to the Continent, she gave her colonists the monopoly of those markets and excluded all foreign produce. The Act operated impartially—with over-production adversely, with normal or under-production favourably to the planters.

It must not be supposed, however, that this simple statement, though sufficient perhaps for these pages, adequately expresses the full situation. For most of the colonial period, under various titles, a Board sat in London, watching vigilantly the conditions of each colony, and altering or amending the import or export duties, not selfishly for the good of the Mother Country, but for that of the Empire as a whole. In a masterly and exhaustive survey of the whole question, the American expert, Professor Beer, has once and for all disposed of the fallacy that England's colonial trade laws were framed and run in her own interests alone. He has shown the unceasing interest which the Board of Trade and Plantations took in their work, meeting sometimes two or three times a week for consultations and for conferences with the Board of Customs. Circumstances constantly altered, and endeavours were made to meet them by readjustment of the conditions of inter-colonial trade for the relief of one or other of the colonies, with an honest attempt to be fair all round. Constant reports, too, were received from Colonial Governors, who were by no means the leisurely figureheads of American tradition. Correspondence was kept up with Ambassadors or Representatives of foreign countries concerning colonial ships slipping into their harbours.

The whole story is full of disconcerting details and apparent paradoxes. At one time, about 1700, we find Virginia actually discriminating and without any remonstrance against all ships, English included, but her own, and taxing liquors save those imported in Virginian vessels! New England was a natural trading complement to the West Indies, each supplying the other's necessities. The regulations of trade between them were being constantly readjusted and sometimes altogether thrown open. But all this well-meant supervision did not stop the Free-Traders, particularly the New Englanders, who cared nothing for Empire and were ready to cheat the Mother Country out of its defence tribute at any and all times. "In the eyes of the Statesmen and publicists of that day, England was fully justified in restricting colonial products to the English market. While the enumerated articles could not be shipped to any place in Europe but England, in return, competing commodities of foreign nations were virtually excluded from the home market. The reciprocal nature of the old Colonial system is manifest not only in the scheme of Imperial defence but to an even more marked degree in the preferential features of England's fiscal system." So speaks the first American authority[1] on the subject to-day, though I do not suppose his words will prevent the old Shibboleths from being perpetuated eternally on both sides of the Atlantic. But for good or ill, it was impossible for England to put an effective stop to smuggling on remote and distant seas. Her efforts on her own coasts, though in this case from sheer niggardliness, towards a preventative force, let about four million pounds' worth of contraband through every year![2] In 1768, the sloop *Liberty*, belonging to that Prince of Smugglers, John Hancock, was seized for contraband, upon which the Boston mob raised a serious riot. After this, two regiments, much under strength and quite inadequate to the situation, were brought into Boston. The Boston populace and in truth most of the colonists, hated soldiers. That the latter had freely shed their blood in ridding the former of the French in the late war, was nothing to these folk with the rowdy mob instinct in their blood. That the poor fellows were merely doing their duty, and that in the forbearing manner that has nearly always characterised the British soldier, was nothing. The Boston roughs, rather grotesquely termed 'patriots,' never let them alone. It was quite safe to jeer at and insult them, to pelt them with stones and brickbats, for, being such a trifling force among thousands of frenzied New Englanders, it would have meant destruction had an issue been forced. The loyal, and consequently, though a native, hated Governor Hutchinson, after having his property destroyed by the mob, was removed, to be replaced by General Gage, who as a very young officer had served with credit through the late French war in America.

He had an impossible job to face. In quite good faith, and to help the East India Company, the Government had arranged for its tea to be shipped free of the English tax of a shilling direct to America, with an import duty of threepence at the American ports. This meant a drop of ninepence in the price to Colonial consumers.

[1] Beer.

[2] See two volumes on Eastern and Western Cinque Ports respectively (A. G. Bradley).

Hitherto, Americans had mainly drunk smuggled Dutch tea from the great smuggling depot of St. Eustachius. This legally imported Indian tea at ninepence cheaper spelled disaster to the whole smuggling fraternity on the Atlantic coast. The repeal of the threepenny tax would have finished them. So this last remaining one of Townshend's imposts, served as well as any other for the new cry of "No taxation without representation," and the Boston hooligans were incited to board the East Indiamen and fling their cargoes overboard. All down the coast, as far as tea-drinking was a habit, the word was passed to abstain. The populace were humbugged by the great smuggling houses into boycotting the Indian tea-ships, and if the approaching upheaval had not occurred, the sympathetic public would have continued to line the pockets of these worthy patriots with an extra sixpence over the legal price of tea. Yet by the man in the street whether on this or the other side of the Atlantic, the "Boston tea party" is, I feel sure, generally regarded as an outburst of altruistic patriotism.

The "Boston massacre" also ranks with a careless and credulous posterity as an instance of British brutality. A crowd was engaged in the popular pastime of throwing missiles at an unoffending company of soldiers. One of the latter, in exasperation or by mistake, let off his musket, which gave his comrades the impression that the order to fire had been given, and four men were killed. There was a fearful outcry. The troops were then subject to the civil authorities, who by this time were incapable of treating them fairly. However, for once, the facts being too obvious, the soldiers were acquitted. One instance is quoted by Fortescue of a wretched private who for a trifling theft was fined £70, and sold as a white slave for seven years in lieu of payment—indentured whites and negro slaves being then an important feature in New England economy. Samuel Adams, cousin of the soberer and sounder John Adams, afterwards second President, was the firebrand of this lawless period. A demagogue of the extreme type, he was well-equipped for the part by a narrow experience, an incapacity for business, and a vitriolic facility of tongue and pen. He did yeoman service for the great contrabandists in half a dozen New

England newspapers, which supported what was rapidly becoming open revolution. Adams, who had hated England from his birth, though he had never been twenty miles from Boston, depicted in these journals and on the stump fantastic and coarse pictures of the English King and the governing classes. These travesties delighted the mobs he harangued, and the bourgeois and farmers he wrote for, a public that was in the main as ignorant of the outer world as himself.

The tea affair brought vigorous action from England. The port of Boston was closed until the town should repay the East India Company for its loss. The Charter of Massachusetts was annulled and another framed, better adapted for efficient government, but quite unpalatable to the "sons of liberty," as may be readily imagined. "The archives of Constantinople," declared the widely travelled Samuel Adams, "might be searched in vain for so barbarous an edict." As for his New Englanders, "A godlike virtue shall blazon our hemisphere until time shall be no more." Such wild excesses had converted many substantial Bostonians into Tories, who styled these outpourings "inflammatory speeches by patriots without property or anything else but impudence." To protest against the Government's measures and back their opinion by joining the general boycott of English goods was one thing. But to flout in arms the strongest nation in the world was quite another. Moreover, there were still New Englanders, particularly the Episcopalian element, to whom the ties of kinship with the Mother Country, to say nothing of their oaths of allegiance, meant something. Over a hundred substantial men in Boston signed an address to that effect, a proceeding for which in due course they suffered. Events moved rapidly in Massachusetts. The unfortunate Governor Hutchinson, though a local man, was not only driven out for his criticism of the "patriots," but ruined, while his property, as we have mentioned, was wantonly destroyed. Some private letters of his deploring the state of the Province had been purloined in the post and made public by the otherwise impeccable Franklin.

Hutchinson's place was taken in 1774 by General Lord

Gage—the Commander-in-Chief in America, who was provided with about 1,600 regulars, nothing like enough to quell a serious rising. For many thousands of militia were now drilling throughout the countryside, nearly all used to firearms, adepts at taking cover, and a fair proportion veterans of the late war. Gage's proclamations were entirely disregarded. The colonial governments were still functioning, and he called the Assembly together at Salem, 20 miles from Boston. They met, but locked Gage out, and then appointed delegates to meet delegates from the other colonies which were all moving, though less truculently, in the same direction. From now onward the Government of Massachusetts, outside Boston, went on independently of the Crown. Men were beginning to take sides. Those who objected to the lead of Samuel Adams and John Hancock were indiscriminately labelled Tories or the "friends of Government." They were not yet actually maltreated, but seeing clearly what was coming, hundreds moved to Boston, abandoning their homes, which most of them were destined never to see again.

Already the vituperative tongues of Adams and his followers were exhausting their lurid rhetoric on fellow-citizens who differed from their opinions, objected to the violence that had brought these troubles upon them, doubted whether a tea tax was the prelude to a future of chains and slavery, and considered that the tyranny of demagogues and a mob might be even worse than the problematical taxes with which the imagination of Republican orators terrified simpler folk. Those who held these views were mostly people of education and property. They realised that New England was from their point of view, one of the happiest and most prosperous countries upon earth. They did not feel disposed to turn it upside down to please demagogues and wealthy smugglers baulked of their profits. They were soon, however, forced to choose one course or the other. Committees had been formed in every province, with sub-committees in the counties or townships, in communication with one another, and with appeal for guidance to the intercolonial Congress, by this time sitting in Philadelphia. This last had been on the whole welcomed, even by those of steady or loyal sympathies. It was expected that so much collective wisdom, ventilating soberly the grievances under which the colonies considered themselves suffering would find a way out, and it was hoped that a good understanding with England would eventuate. The loyalists were disappointed, however, at the arrogance, as it seemed to them, of the proceedings. An association had also been formed, with sub-centres in every colony, for the non-importation of British goods. To sign or not to sign now became a preliminary test of patriot or loyalist. Many of the latter, however, signed what only appeared a peaceful procedure.

These committees in New England were nearly always chosen by minorities. Apart from the Tory dissentients, thousands sat upon the fence signing anything that made for peace and quiet, and this not only in New England but through all the colonies. Congress, acting through the local associations, had directed that every non-signer of its enactments should be branded as a Tory, his name posted up and his life made generally miserable. Armed militia, good shots and skilful at taking cover, now swarmed in the country round Boston. Gage, shut up in the city, was anxious to secure a large store of munitions that the rebels had collected at Concord. He had also been ordered by the Home Government to seize the persons of Adams and Hancock. As these gentlemen happened at the moment to be in the same neighbourhood as their collection of stores, he dispatched a force of 1,200 men to make, if possible, the double capture. It was a cold April morning when the soldiers left Cambridge, the roads deep with mud and snow slush. The heavily-clad men, through some blunder of Colonels or Majors, missed their breakfast and fought all day on empty stomachs, over about 30 miles of road, against crowds of sharp-shooters lining the woods and fences. They eventually got back to Boston exhausted, having expended all their ammunition, and achieved neither of their objects, and lost 273 men in killed and wounded. The effect of this may be imagined. "The King's hirelings defeated in the open field by the sons of liberty."

The rebellion at once took an upward leap, the grip on

the loyalists tightened, and persecution soon succeeded mere social boycotting, posting-up of names and the like. The loyalists even in New England were numerous enough, being mainly those attached to the Anglican Church. Their fundamental mistake lay in failing to form counter-associations to those of the Revolutionaries, which would have been possible at the beginning. Had they done so, thousands of waverers would have joined them, and they would assuredly not have fallen so ready a prey to their opponents. But not merely at the beginning of hostilities but for long afterwards they pinned their faith too much on the overwhelming power of Britain and the apparent greatness of the odds. They could not believe, nor can one be surprised, in the ultimate success of the colonists in forcing their demands on the Mother Country, or still less in the possibility of independence being wrested from her by force of arms. So there being no intermediate state, no buffer party, no counter-association for the thousands of potential loyalists, no breathing space, nothing, in short, to choose but British protection or lip service to the rebels, which last would count as treason, they sat upon the fence. In New England, as it so happened, being almost unmolested by British arms, they were enabled to come down from it at the right moment with impunity. "After the Revolution passed the bounds of peaceful resistance," writes Van Tyne, "it was (except in Virginia) distinctly a movement of the middle and lower classes. A new set of leaders came forward, hitherto unknown, less educated, and eager for change. The very public documents became more illiterate. To the aristocratic and cultured class it seemed that the unlettered monster was unchained, and while they waited for British power to restore the old order they withdrew for the most part from what seemed an undignified contest." Social jealousy, particularly in a soil so susceptible to it as New England, undoubtedly played a large part in the Revolution.

Boston was now full of refugees from all over the country. It was also suffering much privation, from the closing of the port, added to the difficulties of getting supplies from a semi-hostile neighbourhood. Gage was now reinforced by Howe, Burgoyne and Clinton, with fresh troops bringing his numbers up to about 10,000. Washington had just been elected to the command of the colonial forces, and was expected shortly to take charge of the rebel army outside Boston, which numbered roughly some 15,000 men. Gage's position was threatened by some neighbouring heights which commanded the town, and the Americans had recently captured a large supply of guns and ammunition by surprising the ill-defended forts of Ticonderoga and Crown Point. So Gage determined to fortify the ridge in question, which bore the immortal name of Bunkers Hill, and lay just above Charlestown, and some half a mile across the water from Boston. His intentions, in such an atmosphere, of course leaked out, and at daybreak of June 16th the hill revealed itself as in possession of the patriots, busy fortifying themselves. The three ships in the harbour then opened and maintained for some hours a, for some reason, futile fire.

Gage, in the meantime, dispatched Howe across the water with some 2,500 men to force the now completed barrier behind which were about as many farmers, hunters, Indians and others, mostly armed with the weapons they owned and could use from covert with deadly effect. The British could easily have taken them in the rear, but despite all the lessons of the late war, they despised these colonial irregulars too much and made those three bloody frontal assaults which cost them 1,250 men in killed and wounded, before they carried the position, and would have cost them more had not the defenders' ammunition run out.

For the next nine months the unfortunate Tories, refugees as well as such natives of Boston as had declared under pressure or otherwise for the King, endured all the privations of a siege. Washington, with about 15,000 men, now rapidly developing into an army, lay outside. Gage had departed, and Sir William Howe was in his place. Howe was a Whig with strong American sympathies. Later on, he lost the war by slackness or bad faith, and has been under suspicion ever since. But at any rate he assisted the loyalists to form themselves into military companies, besides impounding the ordinary townsmen for the cleansing work of the city. Despite short commons, he helped to keep up the spirits of the loyalists by social festivities, while Burgoyne entertained them by writing and acting dramas, to which pastimes he was notoriously addicted. He was even rash enough to write a farce called "The Blockade of Boston," which grim reality turned into its evacuation in the following March.

Washington, with an army augmented by reinforcements from farther south to 18,000 men, now proceeded to occupy and fortify Dorchester Heights, which commanded the town, so Howe decided to evacuate it—to the despair of the loyalists. For they had now no longer a refuge, most of their homes having been destroyed or leased or sold to others. Washington cynically suggested that they had better commit suicide. Howe allowed them to go first, but the transports were scarce and small. They were loaded up with such effects as the unfortunate fugitives could save from the utter confusion inevitable to the evacuation of a town full of a hostile element ready to take advantage of the occasion. The rest of the thousand or more refugees squeezed into such space as was left on the laden-up schooners allotted to them, and went out on to the wintry seas, amid a fleet of nearly 200 sail, and headed for Nova Scotia, the first of the 35,000 who were eventually to find a refuge there. It was a poor welcome they got from a still wild, and to them, unknown country, with as yet but a trifling population, chiefly centred around the new town of Halifax. Still, this first instalment of expatriated loyalists, but a hundredth part of the ultimate total, were possibly less to be pitied than many thousands of their successors. For a fair proportion of these people had held offices under the Crown, and returned to England, where their loss of income at any rate was modified by some sort of post or pension. The Government, from the very first, behaved with exemplary fairness to all victims of their policy who had a just claim.

CHAPTER III

FROM THE EVACUATION OF BOSTON TO SARATOGA

ALL pretence of peace was now over. From North to South the country was in a blaze, while learned men wrote endless themes for or against the right to tax the Colonies—the anti's generally omitting the salient fact that they owed their immunity from foreign attack and the safety of their mercantile marine to the British fleet and the British taxpayer. The most violent still protested that separation was remote from their thoughts, and that they were only contending for bare justice, a return, as some leaders put it, to the "Status Quo" system of wholesale smuggling, prior to the active steps taken to suppress it. The reader who has never troubled himself with eighteenth century ethics and conditions of Colonial trade the world over, will naturally suggest, Why not Free Trade? As before observed, it would have been asking a good deal of a European taxpayer of that day to protect his colonial ships in their intercourse with foreign markets, while on the other hand a system founded on evaded laws was an anachronism.

But what we are most concerned with here is the fierce antagonism that by this time divided the patriots from the loyalists in every colony. The milder measures of the previous year, mere boycotting of intercourse of every kind, social and commercial, and such-like persecution, had given way to cruelties more direct. Those who were not prepared to abandon at short notice the allegiance of their lives for a point of view about which the wisest men then and even yet split hairs, were denounced as traitors. Traitors to whom? To men who on their own initiative, and often with nothing to lose and possibly something to gain, proposed to plunge a singularly happy and peaceful country into war! The town mobs and ignorant small farmers might be deluded with cries of "chains and slavery," but to a large element, almost certainly at that time a majority of educated Americans, such ranting seemed nonsense. In most colonies, except Virginia, the movement had a local democratic flavour, as representing the instinctive grudge of the commoner folk against the more educated and well-to-do, for the Tory Party was naturally stronger in this class. Districts as well as Provinces, however, differed vastly. In some, the loyalists were so numerous they could more than defy their antagonists, and even make themselves unpleasant in return. But the patriot was naturally more active in his propaganda than his neighbour, who preferred things to remain as they were, and to go about his business in peace. He remembered the late war, and the solid benefits bestowed on the country by the expulsion of the French by British arms and the opening of the West. If he were a New Yorker, he did not in the least want to be governed by New Englanders, or Virginians. He hated the one and knew nothing about the other, and the same feelings applied to the loyalist in every colony. He had always looked direct to the Mother Country in every connection with his own, her protective insurance included. Though he had quite readily signed non-importation agreements, and indeed very often could not help doing so, he would sooner suffer a little taxation, which might or might not be equitable, than launch himself into the chaos which the schemes of his more democratic, or hot-headed, neighbours seemed to portend.

Boston was never again in occupation of the British. The four New England Provinces, Massachusetts easily foremost, with Connecticut a good second, homogeneous and of like ideas and origin, remained for the rest of the war the chief stronghold of aggression and resistance. New England furnished as many soldiers as all the rest of the country combined. Her loyalists were expelled or quelled, her luke-warm element reduced to a definite attitude of patriotic sympathy. She had taken the leading part in the invasion of Canada in this winter of 1775-6. That country being almost denuded of British troops, while its French militia refused to fight, Schuyler,

Montgomery and Arnold pushed Sir Guy Carleton within the walls of Quebec. There, gathering a motley force of British regulars, volunteers, sailors and French citizens, he had made a notable and epoch-making defence throughout the winter till the arrival of Burgoyne's ill-fated army relieved him, and drove the Americans out of the country.

New York, both as City and Province, was quite different from Boston and New England. It was in the colonial sense of the word, as already told, distinctly aristocratic in character. It was also the key of the American colonies. Its great river, the Hudson, gave access into the interior, and if held in force cut off New England from the other colonies. The loyalist interest was to prove stronger here than in any other province but South Carolina, and the occupation of New York City for the remaining seven years of the war afforded it a support that gave the struggle eventually the character of a savage civil war. Many counties had gone into revolt, formed associations and committees, and bullied the loyalists and "pacifists" as rigorously as the New Englanders. On the other hand, many districts had no sympathy at all with rebellion, and proved loyalist throughout. These turned the tables on the others with such effect as to convert some parts of the country into a scene of devastation.

Slowness to move, while their opponents were acting and organising, had characterised the loyalists in New York as elsewhere. They had remained too long as passive objectors and individual resisters. This was hardly strange as they were not the party that wanted war. In many parts, too, they had been deprived of their arms by the quick action of the Whigs. As already mentioned, they felt sure of the ability of the British army to crush the revolt, a confidence one can readily understand. Some had organized and helped Gage at Boston, but the strength of their assistance took no concrete shape till the British came and supplied them with arms and stimulated their enrolment into corps. There had been a few sporadic risings of loyalists in some other States, but they had not been powerful enough, and the punishment meted out had been intimidating, prior to the British occupation of New York.

A group of powerful Anglo-Colonial families owned large landed estates, actual manors, in the Province with quite a large tenantry settled on them, who were virtually retainers, a condition of things scarcely known in the other colonies, where the local aristocracy farmed their own land with negro slaves and indentured bondmen from the British Isles. Of earlier origin than these were the old Dutch patroons, who antedated the British annexation, and had received large grants from Holland with manorial privileges, generally on the banks of the Hudson, and had settled on these lands a tenantry mainly of their own race. These two dominant groups had long forgotten any international asperities, and saw eye to eye in Provincial politics and social standards. The Patroons, such as the Van Courtlands, Van Rensselaers, Van Brunts, Cuylers and many others, honoured names in New York to-day, naturally enough had no liking for democratic movements which would doubtless instigate their tenantry to claim their farms and become generally troublesome. A very few took the Whig side, but more of them held for the King and served freely in the loyalist regiments raised in 1776, and subsequently.

Of the great Anglo-New York families there were the de Lanceys, Morris', Phillips', Churches, Beverley Robinsons, Jessups, and many others with descendants still living, mostly in one or other of the Canadian provinces. Most of these had members in the Crown forces, and suffered the penalties consequent on their loyalty. Some idea of the substance of some of these colonial magnates is afforded by the fact that the confiscated landed estates of the de Lanceys brought £120,000, an immense sum for the period and country. The head of the family, Oliver, raised three battalions for the Crown, and going to England at the close of the war, sat for a time in Parliament. Another de Lancey of the next generation was killed at Waterloo on Wellington's Staff. I give these details as an example of a leading colonial New York family, New England had no such types. Merchants of the Hancock sort were different, nor, I think, could the slave-states have produced their parallel. But one picturesque semi-feudal figure in the old Province of New York must be given a word to himself for his influence as a loyalist was great.

This was Sir William Johnson, Baronet, of Johnson Hall, a then fortified stone manor house up the Mohawk Valley. He had come out as a young man to take charge of a large tract on the Indian frontier belonging to a wealthy uncle, Sir Peter Warren, and died in 1774. His grasp of the Indian character, and influence with the tribes, had acquired for him the office of Crown Agent for Indian affairs. He planted many hundred immigrants, too, mainly Scottish Highlanders and Germans, on his large estates, married the sister of the great Indian chief, Brant, and lived amid his dependants of both colours as a sort of Backwoods feudal chieftain. Of fine presence, he could harangue the Indians in their own language and style of oratory, and entertain them with feast and dance for days together, but always as a sort of Grand Seigneur, and the representative of the great King over the water. As these Mohawks were of the famous "Five Nations" who had almost held the balance of power in war between English and French, his services were beyond price. In the French war he had been given command of the New York forces, and for his efficient leadership was made a baronet with a gift of £5,000. The growing trouble between England and the colonies so preyed on him that he died suddenly of a stroke at sixty, and an unfounded report went about that he had killed himself from grief.

His son and nephew, Colonels John and Guy Johnson, carried on his influence and traditions, in their country, which produced several hundred loyalist combatants besides the Mohawk Indians. For nearly all of them, when the valley was overrun by the Whigs, moved up into Canada, and the Niagara country. There, for the rest of the war, they helped to wage a frontier warfare with a degree of ruthlessness not surprising in men who had been expelled from their homes for maintaining their ancestral allegiance. American historians follow one another with rather ingenuous diatribes against the reprisals of Sir John Johnson, Butler's rangers and Brant's

Indians, who had also been burnt out and driven into Canada. Savages under such circumstances could hardly be expected to stay their hands when confronted by their most bitter and ruthless enemies. Both sides freely used the Indians when they could get them. The latter naturally inclined to the King's side as something traditional, a solid figure, whether English or French, in their imagination. But as for these "upstarts," how could they be placed or trusted? To close this perhaps rather parenthetical episode, the Johnson estates were, of course, ultimately confiscated and valued at £120,000. The family papers had been buried on evacuation in an iron safe, but were found after the war so much rotted as to be almost illegible. The plate had been secured from the enforced sale and buried by a faithful slave. In 1780, Sir John Johnson went with an armed party and found it intact, and filling the knapsacks of forty of his men carried it to Montreal. The Johnsons remained mostly in Canada, filling various offices, civil and military.

But to return to the New York of 1776. Apart from these aristocratic groups, the Province abounded in middling and small freeholders. It was mainly these, with some leadership from above, that formed the com mittees which terrorised the indifferent and persecuted the refractory in word or deed over half the Province. Elsewhere, the loyalists were either numerous enough to make the committees ineffective, or in such force as to control their county and make it hot for the "rebels." John Adams thought that New York would have joined the British had not the near vicinity of New England on the one side and of Maryland and Virginia on the other controlled her. Judge McKean, another conspicuous contemporary, believed one-third of all the colonists in America were at heart loyalists. No less a person than Alexander Hamilton declared that not half the people were Whigs in 1775, and that even in 1782 one-third still sympathized with the British. Gouverneur Morris, the most distinguished, though a Whig, of that famous family, thought that half New York colony were in open or secret sympathy with the King's cause. Sabine, the leading authority of the next generation, thought that in New York the Whigs were numerically far weaker than their then opponents. Mr. Flick, the author of *Loyalism in New York*, sums up the colony's condition thus. Out of a population of 180,000, approximately 90,000 were loyalists, of whom 35,000 were active and expatriated, while 55,000 accepted the inevitable, and came down sooner or later in time to save themselves, on the Whig side of the fence. But let us return to the main subject where we left it.

The declaration of Independence in July, 1776, made a clean cut between Whig and Tory. As the labels now ran, everyone who did not conform openly to the new government was a traitor, surely a curious inversion of the term! Wherever committees had been sufficiently supported, Tory hunting and baiting had been for long a favourite pastime. Already, those who had refused to sign on had been deprived of their arms wherever the rebels were strong enough. If this last were doubtful, the provincial militia were summoned to carry the job through. In some cases where this was not feasible, militia from Connecticut or some more Whiggish neighbouring Province were called in. But this was no use in some counties near the capital, where the Tories of all classes were in a majority. Long Island, for instance, running its narrow form northward from New York City for 120 miles along the coast of New England, was cut off from the mainland and its influences by a generally broad stretch of water. It had been settled early by way of New York and by the miscellaneous but generally anti-puritan type of the rest of the Province. Ranging nowadays from the actual suburbs of New York to the country houses of the wealthy with their field sports and pastimes, it was in the days of the Revolution mainly occupied by farmers, tenants or freeholders, of loyalist opinions. Its three counties of King's, Queen's and Suffolk, were a stronghold of the King's cause, though their people were sorely tried by the later food demands and even raids of the British Army, as they had previously been by those of their opponents.

Like the people of some counties in our own civil war,

who suffered equally from both sides, the loyalists of Long Island, and of some of the mainland counties just north of the city who were equally loyal in complexion, were severely tested. Before the British came to New York in 1776, and while Washington was before Boston, Long Island had been so rigorously dealt with by Congress troops, that what Whigs there had been became Tories with alacrity when Howe arrived. But in northern New York and all parts where the Whigs predominated, everyone who was even under suspicion of being a friend to the old order, or "an enemy of liberty," was subjected to treatment which, with exceptions, was pitiless and cruel and sometimes ferocious. The most lenient form was banishment to some other province like Massachusetts or Virginia at the expense of the victim. The forms of law were still running, but taken over by the State Conventions. There was little justice, however, for a Tory either in the Courts or without. The opening for personal spite and private revenge was boundless, as may be imagined. On any suspicion of sympathy with the old order, men were tarred and feathered and carried aloft in mockery through their native town or village. Almost worse, they were made to ride on the sharp side of a rail, with their legs weighted down, to be pelted by the local roughs as they were carried down the streets. No one would buy or sell with them. Their stock was driven off or killed. Heavy fines were piled on them, and when a ruined business made payment impossible, their homes and effects were sold at a forced auction. Old neighbours became deadly enemies, even families were parted. The patriots dreaded the services that their Tory neighbours might render the British, and seemed to lose all sense of mercy and equity in that fear. The others raged at being called on to stake their lives and properties at the call of self-constituted dictators of what they ought to think, say and do. Liberty forsooth! thought the loyalists and thousands who dared not label themselves as such. There was not much of it, they declared, in the Patriot creed. Hundreds were sent to gaol.

The prisons in New York had been crammed, and additions to them made necessary before the arrival of

Howe. Some prominent Whigs criticised much of the inhuman treatment meted out by their zealous followers and officials. Washington, however, on being appealed to, thought it served the loyalists right and that the best thing they could do was to commit suicide! Local committees of perhaps half a dozen persons, established by quite farcical elections, sometimes settled the fate of victims. Some were sent on to the Provincial Committee, which was a shade better. Scores of loyalists, to be sure, asked for trouble by the frankness with which they proclaimed their opinions. But as time went on thousands of quiet people who only wanted to be let alone, but whose private opinions had been betrayed by officious neighbours, or were only perhaps suspected, were expelled from their homes or made to lead miserable lives. Quite early, the idea of confiscating loyalist estates to provide the sinews of war for the Whigs, took firm hold. A conceivable policy in itself, but unfortunately it frequently degenerated into mere forced sales. There was not much money about at such a period, as may be imagined, while the land or effects of a Tory would often be paid for in depreciated, or almost worthless paper money. Worst of all, in innumerable cases, the cunning contrivers of these forced sales acquired the estate for themselves for a mere song. In the discussions on peace terms at the close of the war, one insuperable objection to a restoration of the loyalists' estates was the number that in this, or similar fashion, had passed into private hands.

When the brothers Howe, commanding fleet and army respectively, occupied New York, the Tories in such neighbouring counties as had suffered under the Whigs, naturally enough, now took it out of their former persecutors, who betook themselves to the more northern counties where their friends still ruled. The loyalists, too, with the support of the British Army behind them, now began to organize volunteer forces and raid the Whig districts for the arms of which they and their friends had been stripped by patriot militia. In short, a kind of Civil War raged over large tracts of the country, accompanied by a wanton destruction of property. It was a pitiable business, the more so for the technically slight differences of opinion that had set it ablaze. It is difficult to understand the frenzy with which the popular side regarded opponents for merely refusing to change their allegiance, for this is what it all amounted to, at the bidding of their neighbours. At least half of the so-called Tories had opposed the British measures and committed themselves by voice and signature to that policy, legal enough in itself. But taking up arms to enforce their opinions was a different matter, while as for the more important step of independence, the revolutionaries themselves, as they said, had not hitherto dreamed of it. They had thought that by armed resistance they would show the Mother Country how much in earnest they were and force her to concessions. Many of the higher sort in the popular party saw this clearly enough and expressed it. But it was outside the logic of the mobs and of the self-willed, rather arrogant, undisciplined yeomanry and backwoodsmen of the colonies. It might almost be said that two distinct wars came to be waged in most of the Provinces, that of Washington with his more or less disciplined regular force fighting the British, while undisciplined bands of militia contended with Tory volunteers all over the country. In course of time, the influence of the British Headquarters at New York spread over a wide area, and the loyalists began to enrol themselves in those corps on the pay list of the British Army which afterwards became famous under various designations. But this is anticipating. Till Howe arrived at New York, the Whigs had city and province more or less in their grip. For when the Tory districts demonstrated, soldiers and militia were sent to disarm and regulate them. Howe with his army, and his brother the Admiral with his fleet, had arrived in New York on July 2nd.

It is not my purpose here to follow the fortunes of the war more than is necessary to illustrate the situation of the loyalist in its different phases. It is enough that Howe with 25,000 men, more than half German mercenaries, landed in Long Island, where the American Army of some 15,000 men, mainly ill-disciplined, short-service militiamen, were entrenched. These he defeated and drove back into New York, which Washington hoped to defend, but found himself quite unable to do so. On the contrary, his raw troops made a panic-stricken flight on the approach of the British, and according to General Greene, already Washington's most able lieutenant, were at Howe's mercy—the first, according to Greene, of that General's many opportunities to finish the war. Washington, in one of his fine rages, had ridden among his flying troops, laid about him among both privates and officers with the flat of his sword, cursed them for cowardly scoundrels, and had not an aide-de-camp seized his bridle, might have been captured by the British. He was commanding New Englanders, whose regimental officers he disliked and despised for having been elected by ballot and neither able nor willing to enforce discipline over men who resented the slightest assumption of superiority, and had never been ordered about in their lives.

Howe had come over with a very liberal offer of terms. Failing their acceptance, he was to prosecute the war with the utmost rigour. But the Americans had already proclaimed their Independence, and had moved some way since the latest message from Congress had declared their "attachment to the Empire." The meeting of Howe with the delegates, Franklin, John Adams and Routledge (South Carolina) at New York came to nothing, and only a fight to a finish remained. So Howe sat down in New York to prosecute the war after a fashion that no one at the time, and no one since, has been able to account for, seeing the capable soldier that he was. British and American authorities alike believe that he deliberately threw away successive opportunities of crushing Washington and his army and thereby ending the war. His force was enormously superior in every particular to that of Washington, who never could himself account for his numerous escapes from his opponents' easy grasp. Howe was, of course, a Whig in politics. Still, he accepted a high and critical command from the Opposition with definite instructions. In short, there is little doubt but that he betrayed his employers and incidentally his country. His family had been popular in America. His talented brother had fallen by a stray shot in the advance on Ticonderoga, to the grief of the whole army, regular and colonial. He himself had served through the late war. He had been very anxious to make peace on this present occasion. But the Americans had preferred war, and Howe apparently set himself to make them a present of victory. He pushed Washington about the country, around and south of New York for a time, manœuvring at first with the skill he notably possessed, and winning one or two small but useful victories, but always failing to push home his advantage. His instructions were to seize and hold the line of the Hudson river, and thus isolate the New England Provinces.

Another British force, which had just landed at Quebec and cleared Canada of the Americans, was to descend by the old war route from Montreal along Lake Champlain and Lake George to the Hudson. Yet another and a smaller force under St. Leger was to descend the Mohawk Valley from Lake Ontario, through the Johnson and Tory country to its junction with the Hudson, and there unite with the two larger forces of Burgoyne and Howe. How Burgoyne and St. Leger met disaster, and Howe failed to support them form a notable chapter in history, fraught with disaster to the British and triumph to the Americans. It illustrated the folly of ministers 3,000 miles away, and all that distance then signified, in attempting to direct armies in a country they knew nothing about and could not even imagine, and especially with the kind of minister that was now in control. The scheme in itself was sound enough, but the King had foolishly placed at the head of affairs Lord George Germain, a man who had been cashiered for bad behaviour at Minden, and was hated and despised by nearly all his contemporaries—an attitude which he repaid by a haughty indifference to opinion, a carelessness in official details, and personal spite in military appointments. It is even said that he forgot to apprise Howe of his share in the plan of campaign!

But these disastrous events were yet in the future. With New York in possession of the British, the time of the loyalists had come, while the still more numerous element whom the Whigs had cowed into nominal acquiescence, readily enough swore allegiance to the Crown. Thousands of persecuted loyalists began to pour into the city and its neighbourhood. "From every colony," says the American historian Van Tyne, "they came, by boat, on foot, in carriage or on horseback, thanking God when they passed within the British lines and left behind them the din of persecution. There was in general, however, a loyal spirit and not hypocrisy in the welcome extended to the British soldiers, and the few real Whigs now received measure for measure from the lately persecuted Tories." This, of course, and much that followed, has given the most candid American historian, who admits the folly and unwisdom of the whole anti-loyalist procedure, a chance to animadvert on the loyalist reprisals. There is an order of mind always ready to condone the criminal at the expense of the reprisals he invites. A large element in England deliberately turned their faces away from the most hideous crimes against innocent people in Ireland, but rent the air with their clamour, and filled columns in the Press with abuse of any misdirected zeal on the part of those entrusted with the punishment of the assassins posing as soldiers. To some extent, the American and the English Whig attitude towards the loyalists resembles this, though the murder instinct was not in this case natural to either party. The reprisals of the loyalists were for being treated as traitors to a cause to which they had never subscribed, in short, for a violation of the very right for which the patriots were presumed to be fighting, the right of rejecting laws enacted without their consent.

There is no doubt, however, that the loyalists paid their late oppressors back in their own coin. What else could be expected of human nature? Even those who merely believed that armed opposition was foolish and useless were in effect perfectly right. That a Heaven-sent general like Washington would appear could have been foreseen by no one, and without Washington the Revolution must have failed to an absolute certainty. Nobody approached him in the extraordinary qualities demanded for this particular occasion. Even as it was, could the Americans have hoped for such an ally as Howe in the

British Commander-in-Chief? Imagine Wolfe, or Monckton, or Carleton, or indeed any capable regimental colonel, letting Washington off as Howe repeatedly let him off. The anti-war party had been right. Only two utterly incalculable developments had upset their judgment. And even then, but for the French, the cause would have been lost. Still foreign assistance was vaguely foreshadowed and we may let that pass. But a combination of Washington, an inexperienced colonial major with a gift for backwoods fighting, turning out a great commander with the precise temperament needful for this difficult work, and Howe, a tried soldier, so belying his reputation as to behave like a traitor to his country and his employers, was a conjunction of circumstances utterly outside the shrewdest calculations.

Practically, the whole of New York City, Long Island and the adjoining counties, together with the adjacent districts of New Jersey, now came back to its allegiance. Washington was just across the Hudson in New Jersey with a force now reduced to 5,000 men. His lack of success had brought much adverse criticism, and there were even schemes to depose him. At the root of these, apparently, was his second in command, Charles Lee, an ex-British officer. Lee had fought in the late war and previously all over Europe. He was, however, a vain, plausible, boastful man, who had imposed himself on the Americans, naturally enough, rather inexperienced in such matters. They thought they had found a heaven-born general, and had very nearly given him the chief command. He professed to be a great democrat, and supporter of an American Republic, and though in receipt of half-pay from the British Government, had toured the colonies in favour of armed resistance to Parliament. They showed their gratitude by presenting him with the price of a property in Patrick Henry's county of Hanover in Virginia. Lee was regarded with awe and admiration as he rode by Washington's side to meet the army at Cambridge; but he had himself expected, and had been expected by half the country, to ride at its head, as Commander-in-Chief. He had been a thorn in Washington's side ever since. He had now 7,000 men on the opposite side of the Hudson from his chief, and hoping in this set-back to Washington's popularity to take his place, persistently refused to bring them across. After losing a portion of them in muddling skirmishes with the British, he was suddenly surprised *en déshabillé* in a tavern by a party of British, and carried off prisoner in his underclothes. Instead, however, of being shot as an ex-British officer, he contrived by his persuasive and entertaining tongue to secure the best of treatment and company during his temporary arrest, and later on he was even released on exchange.

At any rate, Washington was rid of Charles Lee for the time, and he continued to retreat southward through New Jersey before Howe's vastly superior and more efficient force. His own army was shrinking daily in numbers. Discouraged by defeat and continued retreat, all the time-expired men went off home, till their chief at last stood on the wrong side of the Delaware River with only 3,000 left, and no apparent chance of ever getting any more! Howe could have overtaken and overwhelmed the little force with ease, but as usual, he contrived to arrive on the banks of the Delaware just as Washington's last boatful had pushed off, and the enemy had seized all the boats on the river. The Americans were now in despair. Philadelphia, which the British were approaching, was filled with panic, and Congress fled from it in haste to Baltimore. The Tories of Philadelphia and New Jersey were lifting up their heads. The Revolutionists had hardly any money. Their little army was half fed, ill-clothed and unpaid. Congress issues of paper money only found takers at a ruinous discount. Patriotic Philadelphia, following Congress in a panic, hurriedly packed its trunks before the dreaded British Army. The Loyalists and Quakers, who were mostly of that colour and represented the substance of the City, remained. The Quakers as a sect had been badly used, imprisoned and mutilated in many of the colonies, particularly by the "Sons of Liberty" in New England. They had small cause for loving them as political bedfellows.

The prospects of the patriots were now generally regarded as hopeless, even by themselves. Washington alone refused to despair, and with Howe's insane connivance, saved the situation. Howe assured the Home Government that all was now well and the rebels at their last gasp. So Philadelphia was left alone, though why he had gone there no one quite knew, and he returned to New York to give its social world, civil and military, a really gay winter, with routs and plays, dinners and balls, and to enjoy himself with the ladies. The future seemed well assured. No disasters had occurred nor seemed likely to occur. Howe had 25,000 men with him and Burgoyne in Canada with another 8,000 was presumably descending the Hudson, finally to sever the New England colonies from their allies. New England could then be settled with. As for the middle and southern colonies, the loyalists and the indifferent would almost keep them quiet. So it was thought at Headquarters.

The great crowd of loyalists now within the British lines almost enjoyed that winter. They could take it out of the rebels in the city, and being assured now of the victory of the King's cause, and of compensation for their losses, they sent grateful addresses of congratulation and devotion to the King and to Howe. But Howe had not done with Washington yet. That resourceful and undaunted man now turned to Congress with some extraordinarily plain speaking. He would have nothing more to say to their driblets of untrained militia from various States, coming and going when they pleased. Nothing, he told them, but a regular army enlisted for a long period could save the situation. The old Anglo-Saxon dread of a standing army was magnified many-fold in the Colonies. But the panic-stricken and sometimes rather absurd members of Congress had now to choose between that and the loss of Washington. They had no one to take his place, and they knew it. The one-time second string, Lee, had given out. General Greene, Washington's able lieutenant, had not yet sufficient experience, even had he sufficient character. Gates, the other ex-British officer in high command, was facing Burgoyne in the north. Though he won the fateful battle of Saratoga, it was rather a "soldiers' battle" on the American side, stimulated by the "Traitor" Arnold, and Gates fell subsequently in estimation.

Congress unwillingly recognized the situation. They had no technical or legal authority for their actions whatever, but were accepted as a sort of chief Committee of the patriot party of the several colonies. It was now decided to raise 60,000 troops if possible, and allot so many to each colony or State, a term we may now for brevity employ. Every State had by this time its own Government, so far as its Whigs were concerned, and the Whigs had seized power almost everywhere. Two States had kept the old Colonial Government, minus the King and his Governor. The rest had formulated new constitutions, more or less on the old lines. Each was now to clothe and arm its quota of men, after which Congress was to pay and support them. "If this fails," wrote Washington, "the game is up." But neither the numbers nor the proportions asked for were secured, and the States individually gave Washington no end of trouble. But now when things were at their very worst, that general achieved a most dashing enterprise, which proved, though a small affair in figures, the turning of the tide.

It so happened that the Hessians of Howe's army were quartered at Trenton, and Washington determined to surprise them. Selecting Christmas Day, which to Germans particularly, was likely to be distracting, he spent all the dark hours of a stormy Christmas morning in conveying some five thousand men over the icy waters of the Delaware. Only half of them succeeded in crossing, but with that force and a ten-mile march before them Washington succeeded in completely surprising the Germans, drove them out of the town and captured a thousand prisoners. These were exhibited in Philadelphia like a circus, a proceeding much resented by the officers, mostly of noble birth. This brilliant affair heartened up the Whigs amazingly, and Washington's dejected little army signed on for another six weeks, though on rather exorbitant terms, which their commander had to pay. For since they would not accept the Congress paper money, he pledged his own fortune, which happened in his particular case to be good security! How often, we may well wonder, did Washington literally save his country? What would have happened to it if an Indian bullet had got him at Braddock's defeat or some other of his earlier backwoods skirmishes? This was, of course, a mere incident in the long roll of his priceless services. But if his army had actually gone home in December, 1776, as it threatened to do, even Howe might have been tempted to leave the fleshpots of New York and see about winding up the war.

As it was, he sent out Cornwallis with 8,000 men to capture Washington, who had entrenched himself at Trenton. Arriving there, Cornwallis put off his assault till the next morning, but in the night Washington, knowing his case to be hopeless, most skilfully slipped away to Princeton, from whence Cornwallis had just come, fought successfully detachments of three British regiments, exposing himself recklessly, and then proceeded to lead his little force on to the heights of Morristown. Had Cornwallis attacked Washington on arrival, he would have ended the war, and Washington knew it. But that usually alert General had obviously been infected for the moment with the deadly sloth of his chief. Again, at Morristown, a portion of Washington's army, their few weeks' extra contracts terminated, went home! They and those who remained were utterly worn out—without shoes, tents or blankets. "A force of 500 resolute men," says Gordon, a contemporary American historian of the war, "could have demolished them." And there were 10,000 fresh troops within a day's march, and as many more with Howe thirty miles off at New York! But this was no mere passing opportunity lost. Washington remained for four months at Morristown with the mere skeleton of what had been his small army—the remnants of five regiments from his own State of Virginia. He poured out his soul in many periods of vigorous language at the apathy of his countrymen. Nor could he understand his own immunity from attack. Every movement was known to the English, for Jersey was full of loyalists. But it had now for no reason been practically evacuated by the British. The Jersey farmers had made lots of money out of the British army campaigning in their midst, but they refused to take Congress paper money and supply the patriot forces. There had been some looting, too, particularly by the Hessians, on the traditional lines of Continental Europe. Contemporary accounts picture them as hung about with household utensils, and each soldier looking like a travelling pedlar! But now the militia, mostly farmers with their long guns, swarmed out. In enfilading British troops moving through the woods they were always invaluable, and took small risks. Washington's soldierly prejudices, however, held them lightly. "The militia come in," he wrote, "you cannot tell how, go out you cannot tell when; consume your provisions, exhaust your stores, and leave you at last in a critical moment." Of their officers in New England elected by the men, he always spoke with profound contempt. Their main object, he declared, was to curry favour with the men by manifestations of almost grovelling equality. Nevertheless, the militia did enormous service to their cause in this war, whenever ramparts were to be manned or wherever the woody nature of the country suited their tactics. Dodging from tree to tree, they potted with small risk to themselves, at the British or Hessian infantry, who hardly professed to be marksmen, and could not catch with their bayonets the nimble and lightly-dressed Colonials.

The loyalists of New Jersey, a small province but otherwise something after the New York pattern, touching that city at its northern and Philadelphia at its southern point, were now handed over to the mercy of the patriot forces. After all his costly progresses through the country, Howe had abandoned most of it. Its farmers had probably been indifferent to the war, but several thousand had taken the oath of allegiance to the Crown. Many had now to abandon their homes for the British lines, though most were let off on taking the Whig oath. It was hard on these peaceful farmers, who had doubtless taken slight interest in the Boston tea-party, to be raided by Hessian looters and then victimised by their own people. Many, it was said, had both certificates in their pocket ready for use as the case required. It was obvious enough to most of them which was the safer for the moment, at any rate, to exhibit.

The reader may be reminded that during this autumn of 1776, while Howe was emulating the noble Duke of York, who in the old nursery rhyme, had 10,000 men and "marched them up to the top of the hill and marched them down again," the British Army in Canada was to capture the strong forts of Crown Point and Ticonderoga, on the Lake Champlain route. From thence, in the following summer, it was to descend the Hudson and there meet Howe's army from New York. This, as before mentioned, would cut off the New England States, and with such overwhelming force as to reduce them by arms or pressure to submission. But many difficult circumstances, irrelevant here, prevented the capture of the forts before the Arctic winter set in. The following summer, with a New England force under Gates, "the hero of Saratoga," in occupation, they were taken with ease by Burgoyne on his fateful march to the Hudson. The rest is a familiar story.

How Burgoyne, with 4,000 British and 3,000 German troops and a few Canadians, loyalists and Indians, got entangled, trapped, and surrounded when at length he had fought his way through the woods to the Hudson, needs no telling. Another bit of good luck had fallen to the Americans. Sir Guy Carleton had been to the last moment in command. A fine and tried soldier, a personal friend of Wolfe, and familiar with American warfare, of which Burgoyne had no experience, he had been removed by Germain for personal reasons and replaced by Burgoyne. Carleton, like many others of the best soldiers, despised the War Minister, and had unfortunately shown it too plainly in his despatches. He might not have got through, but, what matters most, he would never have been trapped. He knew the game of American warfare far too well. Now Burgoyne's surrender was the turning-point of the struggle, for it brought in the French, their men, their money and their ships. Assuredly, the stars in their courses fought for the Americans, yet only a handful of historians among them appear to realise what luck they had. That they did not throw it away is to their credit, but then that again was Washington against Howe, Germain and Burgoyne. Howe, when he ought to have been coming up the Hudson in July to join Burgoyne, was actually in his brother's fleet sailing south for Philadelphia with some 12,000 men. For this, however, Germain seems to have been responsible. A story runs that he wrote a draft of a despatch to Howe ordering him up the Hudson, pigeonholed it and then forgot all about it! General Clinton was in Rhode Island with about 7,000 men. He was outside the scheme of the Howe-Burgoyne junction, and could hear nothing of the latter. His messengers could not get through; they were caught and shot at once. So by late July, Howe, with about 12,000 men was on the sea, and the fleet, says a loyalist who saw it, "presented a magnificent sight."

Howe expected to sail up the Delaware, but when after a month on calm seas, they reached its entrance, his brother, the Admiral, refused to ascend that river for various technical reasons. Washington, who was still about Morristown, had taken it for granted that Howe would ascend the Hudson to Burgoyne's support, and was much puzzled when he heard of him at sea. He assumed Philadelphia to be his object, unless it were a feint! Nearly another month was lost by the Howes in sailing round the Capes and up the Chesapeake, at the extreme head of which a landing was effected 20 miles from Philadelphia. "Where the scourge of God and the plague of mankind is going to," wrote John Adams to his wife, "no one can guess. At any rate," continued this bitter-tongued patriot, "he will lose all his horses." And so he did.

The efforts to provide Washington with an army after his scathing ultimatum to Congress in the winter, had met with some success, and he had now about 11,000 men to contest Howe's approach on Philadelphia. The battle of Brandywine was the first encounter. Here Howe's good handling of his well-disciplined men carried the day. On this, large numbers of Philadelphians fled from the city, preceded by Congress, who again went at best pace to Baltimore after leaving Washington with full powers as a dictator. The militia of Pennsylvania were not active enough seriously to harass Howe's march, and on September the 25th he took possession of Philadelphia. His army was encamped in the suburb of Germantown, and reduced by 3,000 men required for outlying posts. Washington, therefore, made one more bid for victory, and fought the unsuccessful battle of Germantown.

A week after this, Burgoyne surrendered his army to Gates at Saratoga, vainly wondering what had become of Howe. But nobody knows to this day quite what Howe was expecting. Germain, by carelessness or stupidity, had made a fool of him, or rather of Burgoyne. Actually, Clinton, with his force from New York, was coming quickly up the Hudson. He had already sent Burgoyne a cheery message which never reached him. But the latter, with an army reduced to 5,000 men, with the broad Hudson in front of him, out of provisions, and encircled by 16,000 inspirited enemy troops, gave up the game. The terms of surrender were honourable, and the troops were to return to England under the condition of not serving again in America. Congress inexcusably repudiated the terms and retained them as prisoners, marching most of them 400 miles to a camp in Virginia, near Charlottesville, where they were half-starved, not from design but through the sheer incapacity of the casual Virginia planters to grapple as commissars with such an unprecedented demand. The officers were released on parole. Captain Anburey, who has left a most interesting journal of the northern campaign, was entertained at his home near the camp by Colonel Randolph, of the well-known Virginia family. An incident typical of the internal changes at work is given by the English captain. He was sitting on one occasion with his host and the ladies of the family in the parlour, "when two common, boorish countrymen walked into the room from the verandah without invitation, sat down on a sofa with their hats on and made themselves at home." To Anburey's surprise and disgust, Colonel Randolph treated their conduct as natural and conversed with them civilly. On their departure, he excused himself for not kicking them out of the room by the remark that this was the sort of thing they now had to put up with. It may be remarked, however, that his class after the war soon abandoned this inconvenient social toleration of the "common people," as they still called them. But never again after the Revolution, even in Virginia was the word "gentleman" used as it had been to define a class, save in private. It became in truth a mere synonym for a male human being with a white skin, and after the abolition of slavery was even adopted by those with a black one. This is not to say that those who had a logical right to the term accepted such an absurd misuse of it. But they had to affect to as regards white men in public, and invent fresh terms for their own class, assisted incidentally by their slaves, who were always eager to proclaim the difference between their masters and the mass of common farmers, "plain folk" who were also slave-owners. Anburey was quartered for a time with one of these latter. He describes the bare frame house, its owner practically illiterate, and an impossible companion, spending his day between rides round his plantation and sitting on the floor scraping at a fiddle and drinking peach brandy. He made no secret of the fact that many of the little mulatto slaves running about the yard were his own children. I happen to have known a century later the representatives of both these families still seated in the same locality. The Randolphs were, of course, still the Randolphs. The others, in vastly improved conditions, were honestly persuaded that they were a "fine old Virginia family." Thus is social history often made in other places than America. But then they had never read Anburey! Few have, even in England.

Burgoyne's disastrous march down the Western borders of New England, from sympathy shown or assistance given him, had caused another combing out of unfortunate loyalists, about 1,000 of whom found their way to a refuge in Canada, where the Governor, Sir Guy Carleton, and his successor, Haldimand, gave them shelter and maintenance. We need not dwell here upon the shock which Burgoyne's surrender caused in England. At last men felt that they were really up against a difficult business. It was obvious that the Americans could fight, a fact hardly yet realised. Indeed, loyalist refugee groups in London, as shown in the journals of their leading member, ex-Governor Hutchinson, were constantly irritated by hearing their compatriots alluded to as poltroons and cowards. These London loyalists consisted largely of the comparatively well-to-do men who had lost good posts in the colonies. Some were English born, or colonials who had English connections and influence, and despite immediate losses, felt hopeful of getting good posts elsewhere, or still better, a reversion to their former offices in America, when the Revolution, as they all expected it would be, was crushed. In the meantime, many of them were given allowances or pensions. They used to meet together in the coffee-houses and occasionally dine with Cabinet Ministers, or the Generals on leave from America. Their hopes and fears and criticisms of the war as it proceeded are recounted at great length in the memoirs of Governor Hutchinson, already alluded to, and of one or two others. Hutchinson was a native of Boston, and, as already related, his fine property there had been destroyed by the mob, leaving him little but his expectations of a British victory to live upon.

And now there was this bad news from France! The temptation to pay back old scores and take revenge for the losses inflicted on her by England, and by the humiliating peace of 1763, was overmastering. On the other hand, the King was naturally disinclined to assist the rebellious subjects of a brother monarch. It was risky, too. Louis XVI was torn between conflicting interests. His advisers, however, continually urged what a heaven-sent chance was his of recovering both his reputation and former possessions. A whole group of young nobles and soldiers too had imbibed the new liberal doctrines, and had already offered their swords to the gallant Sons of Liberty beyond the Atlantic, struggling in her sacred cause. They went over in shoals with certificates of their military experience, and expectations of commissions in what they conceived to be an army of raw farmers, yearning for military discipline at the hands of professional officers. The American representatives in Paris had scattered promises and introductions lavishly among these enthusiasts.

Washington was greatly embarrassed by them. How could these people, who knew nothing of the country, or the language, or the natives, command battalions of captious and touchy New Englanders, who resented any assumption of superiority, regarding one man as good as another and their officers with slight respect? Despite, too, the profession of these young heroes that no thought of payment was attached to their proffered services, their views on the subject, when it came to the point, were found to have altered considerably. But the support of French ships, regiments, supplies and money was a very different matter. Spain, too, had many old scores to pay off, and was coming in, so the prospects in 1778 were vastly different from the sanguine outlook of the preceding year. The French alliance rather staggered the friends of America, who, in and out of parliament, had regarded the rebels as Englishmen struggling for freedom, and had openly rejoiced in their victories and mourned their defeats. It stiffened the attitude of that portion of the English public which had hitherto been rather luke-warm in support of the war, and intensified that hostility to the Americans already contracted by a distinct majority of the nation. Independence they assumed would at once deflect American commerce to other nations and be the ruin of England. The loyalists were sadly disheartened by the news, both those in exile and those serving in or living under the protection of the British army, to say nothing of the thousands still in their own homes, who in their hearts wished for nothing better than a return to the good old days of peace and prosperity, with freedom of speech and action.

CHAPTER IV

FROM THE FRENCH ALLIANCE TO THE SURRENDER OF YORKTOWN

IN February, 1778, France recognized the Independence of the United States and signed a treaty of alliance with this collection of colonies that were not yet knit together by any definite bond, and as a matter of fact, had no legally delegated powers. But even among the patriots the news of the French alliance was not everywhere hailed with enthusiasm. The French were hereditary foes, but recently allied with savages and lifting scalps from New England heads. The country had just got rid of them, with relief and for ever. They were papists too, and monarchists, with all those personal failings that the Americans in common with the insular English of that day attributed to every Frenchman. What dark design too had they in the background? A recovery of Canada perhaps, or a share in the West, and there would be no British ships and bayonets to help to drive them out as of old! The loyalists made the most of such suspicions and scattered broadcast the most sinister reports of French designs on American soil and American liberty.

This, however, did not stop the ships and men and much needed supplies of the King of France from coming in. In truth, they were needed badly enough. The financial situation was deplorable. The individual colonies had always been rather too fond of issuing paper money even before the war, and generally against the advice of their own experts. It came easy for Congress in their present dilemma to issue paper in such amounts that it was already worth less than half its face value and rapidly sinking. With the British paying in gold for farm produce, which was everywhere most plentiful, all of it went their way. This state of things invited speculation, and led the quickest brains to concentrate on money-making rather than on patriotism, as Washington bitterly complained, "Speculation, peculation, engrossing, fore-stalling," he declared, "afford melancholy proofs of the decay of public virtue." It does seem strange that when Washington could neither pay nor clothe his small army there was material abundance in the background, and that fortunes were being made and lost.

But so it was. Philadelphia was extremely snug and comfortable. Howe was spending a thoroughly enjoyable winter there. The city, shaking off its Quakerism, except in finance, outshone even the social glories of New York in the previous year. Never yet, it was said, had so much beauty, fashion and elegance been gathered in any American city. The Quakers chiefly, and secondly the German merchants, were the main source of Philadelphia's wealth, and though not themselves of a frivolous nature, the lighter members of society no doubt frolicked in the golden rays that emanated from handsome mansions in Chestnut Street and Germantown and warehouses on the Schulkyll. These "warm" people themselves were mostly for peace, quiet and the Crown. There had been an outbreak of Tory-baiting, however, before Howe's arrival. A truculent, patriotic minority had forced the declaration of opinions upon these lovers of a quiet life, and those who held to the Crown were sent adrift, some to prison, some to Virginia. The easygoing, middle element signed anything that came along, under protest or otherwise, readily making their peace by a similar process with the British when they appeared. The self-righteous chronicler denounces these double-faced patriots, but after all, they objected to the whole business and saw no cause for it. It was not a crime to sign a paper that perhaps seemed foolish to them, if the alternative was the loss of property or even life.

It must be said, however, in fairness to the Americans that Quakers were generally excused active service on account of their well-known opinions. Out in the back counties, mixed with Germans, was that strong element of Scotch-Irish Presbyterians, so often alluded to. Still farther back, on the frontier, was an even wider and hardier belt of the same breed. But to a man they were for the American cause and rather truculently so. They and the Philadelphians had always hated one another. The latters' Indian policy, it was claimed, had been one of success and peace till the Presbyterian Irish settled on the frontier and stirred the savages up to war, which cost the province much good money and a few very bad scares. But as for the Scotch-Irish scalps, the Philadelphians let it be plainly understood that they were not interested in them. The Presbyterian pulpits had vied with the New England Congregationalists, much as they detested one another, in fanning the flame of war. In Philadelphia itself the Anglican interest had been fairly strong, and as elsewhere was associated with loyalism. On the whole, the loyalists were not so harshly treated in Philadelphia as elsewhere, though at the end of the war Pennsylvania proved itself the bitterest and most relentless of all the States, probably owing to the increased influence of the Presbyterian element.

To make sure of himself in Philadelphia, Howe had to gain control of the Delaware River, and Washington, aware of this, endeavoured to anticipate it by the battle of Germantown. This was a skilful but desperate attempt to cut the line of Howe's extended position. A thick mist helped to defeat the Americans' attack, which was made in force on October 4th. Three days later, away in the north, Burgoyne was making his last desperate attempt to get through to aid Howe's approach, as he thought, before retiring to Saratoga and surrender.

The rest of the winter passed uneventfully, though gaily, at Philadelphia. Washington and his army were leading a very different existence at Valley Forge. A great deal has been written about the sufferings of his army there. Out of 5,000 men it was said that some 4,000 were unable to go on duty for want of clothes, while scarcely a man had a pair of shoes. As for the hospitals so called, they were taxed far beyond their wretched accommodation, and the money supplied for their maintenance seems to have been frequently embezzled by the patriotic recipients. But Howe, though he had 7,000 sound, well-fed men, did not worry about Washington. He had resigned his command as a protest against tacticians in the War Office, and Clinton now took his place in Philadelphia. The event was celebrated by a grand tournament known as the *Meschianza,* which was said to have been attended by " the most brilliant assembly the New World had ever known."

Soon afterwards, Clinton received orders to evacuate Philadelphia and concentrate all his forces on New York. The occupation of the former had been perfectly useless. It had routed Congress to be sure, but Congress gave no real importance to a city, and moreover had been extraordinarily foolish during its hours of exile, worrying Washington continually, besides treacherously revoking the convention of Saratoga and thus calling down, as the American historian Fiske justly says, " the condemnation of impartial historians to dim the lustre of the soldiers' victory." The evacuation, however, proved the ruin of 3,000 loyalists, who, without the encouragement of the British occupation of Philadelphia, might in part, at any rate, have retained their homes. Now they filled nearly all the ships that Clinton had at command, so the general decided to march his army once more through the fertile and oft-traversed province of New Jersey. Amid all this confusion of departure, Peace Commissioners arrived from England, offering the Americans practically everything they had been fighting for. As usual, however, there was delay in putting into practice what had been decided on. For the King had actually consented to these terms before the Franco-American Alliance, which would have made all the difference to the American attitude. But now that France was in arms and Philadelphia being evacuated, Congress took the loftiest tone. It would accept nothing less than Independence and the withdrawal of the British fleets and armies. Then, it was understood to say, it would do its utmost to prevent any further useless bloodshed.

So, after offering a pardon to all who would lay down their arms and remain loyal to Great Britain, the Commissioners departed, not, however, before warning the Americans that their decision and the presence of the

French would alter the character of the war, and that England would now lose no opportunities of destroying or rendering useless an alliance contrived for her ruin and for the aggrandisement of France. So the English might now say that the Americans had only themselves to thank for the ravage that characterised the coming campaigns in the South and the triple contest between the British, the Tories and the Whigs.

The American army entered Philadelphia immediately on its evacuation. Arnold, afterwards the "traitor Arnold," was left in command. Though a New England trader by profession, he was a born soldier. He had greatly distinguished himself in the Canadian campaign of 1775-6, and had done far more than Gates towards the defeat of Burgoyne. Washington now set out to follow Clinton through New Jersey and worry him. At Monmouth, he attacked and only failed, according to American writers, through the treachery, or slowness of the irrepressible Charles Lee, who had been exchanged and restored to his old rank. Probably the British, during his comfortable captivity, had taken his measure and returned him to Washington with small reluctance, or even with some hope of profiting by the exchange. Having sworn at him till, as the old story runs, "the leaves shook on the trees," Washington had Lee court-martialled and dismissed the army.

With the concentration of the British troops once more at New York, it should be recalled that for two years a British force some seven thousand strong had been posted at Newport, Rhode Island, about 100 miles to the eastward. After the French alliance and the refusal of the British terms, the character of the war altered. It became sterner and more ruthless. A reluctance to damage the country more than necessary had so far prevailed with the British commanders. Now war was carried on as against foreigners, and these last moreover the ancient foe. Raiding parties attacked the coasts, and private property was less respected. Above all, the loyalists had begun to play an actively militant part. Early in the war, as before mentioned, they had lacked combination and initiative. The failure of the rebellion within a short time seemed to them a certainty, while the British commanders had shown little cordiality towards them. As they had despised the rebellious "colonists" as antagonists, so they had half despised the loyal "colonists" as potential allies. If the British officer was not so supercilious towards the Americans as American writers are given to asserting, there is no doubt that, as a type, the two breeds even of the same rank were antipathetic, while with the plainer folk, unaccustomed to be dealt with in the normal European style as inferiors, friction was inevitable. Nor were the young officers of that day in the least likely to adapt themselves to the social ethics of a country they neither could understand nor, probably, cared to understand. It all seems so natural to anyone who has had opportunities of seeing somewhat similar situations in more recent and peaceful times. A great many loyalists, to be sure, had enlisted in British regiments, but they did not like it. And perhaps no wonder. A man even of humble rank who had been independent all his life, must have found the rigid discipline, harsh punishments, and sometimes even the company in a British regiment a severe trial.

But by 1777 battalions and companies of loyalists had been raised, mostly by leading members of the party and under officers, usually of the class that had been their leaders in peace time, or in the last war, and understood them. New York had naturally been so far the largest contributor, since that colony had been for so long the chief seat of the war and also the most divided of any in opinions. But refugees to the British lines at New York City from other provinces had been so numerous that the loyalist corps, now formed or forming, became fairly representative of all the colonies north of Maryland. General Tryon, the Royal Governor of so much of the Province as was not in revolt, had been commissioned to raise loyalist troops. In August, 1776, he had raised 1,300 men on Long Island. Later on, he had invaded Connecticut with 2,000, and had formed a troop of Light Horse of the élite of Westchester county. Jessups' Corps, led by two brothers of that family, had operated continuously with Johnson in the Mohawk valley, then crossed to Canada, joined Burgoyne, and fought with him till his surrender, when not one word was said in his articles of capitulation on their behalf. Another corps, de Peyster's, lost 157 killed in the battle of Bennington during Burgoyne's campaign. Most of these troops, loyalists of New England and northern New York, operated for the rest of the war from the Canadian border. Several thousand non-combatants, with their families, under the harshest persecution, filtered through into Canada, and were temporarily provided for by the Government's orders. In the meantime, several more battalions had been raised and officered in the Province, to the total in all of some 15,000, and placed on the strength of the British Army. Those who did not enlist showed their sympathy in other ways, even out of their sorely reduced circumstances. Staten Island raised £500 for the support of the loyalist troops. The city gave £2,000 in a fortnight, King's County contributed £3[illegible]o for Colonel Fanning's battalion, while Queen's and Suffolk counties collected larger sums. The Quakers furnished clothing and other materials. The loyalist militia paid visits to districts in New York and New England, which had been especially active with tar and feathers, confiscations, imprisonments and hangings, paying their former oppressors back in part at least of their own coin. For that portion of the province which was administered by an assembly tributary to Congress had for its Governor a notoriously truculent Scotch-Irishman, bearing the same name, curiously enough, as the English general opposed to him.

This George Clinton was the son of a man of some substance, who had commanded a battalion of New York troops in the campaigns in the last French war, in which the lad was a subaltern. Later on becoming a lawyer, marrying an heiress and engaging in politics, he developed into a most violent patriot and hater of Great Britain. As a delegate to Congress, he turned his own district when at home into "a very Hell for all who thought differently, as absolute and despotic as the French King in France and as cruel and arbitrary as the grand Turk." He had condemned, imprisoned and punished the loyalists most unmercifully. They were by his orders tarred and feathered, carted, whipped, fined, banished, and in short, endured every kind of cruelty, death not excepted. After going to the second Congress, Clinton returned home more vindictive than ever, persecuting, imprisoning, and, to his own emolument, fining and robbing the loyalists in the most barbarous and inhuman manner. His energy secured him the Governorship of the province, where with renewed ardour he continued to rob, plunder, banish and imprison these unhappy people He declared that "he would rather roast in Hell to all eternity than consent to a dependence on Great Britain or show mercy to a damned Tory." By the constitution of New York the Governorship was limited to a three-year term. Clinton is "still Governor after ten years, now lives in New York and continues his persecution against the loyalists notwithstanding the Treaty of Peace which declares that no man shall be molested or injured for anything done during the war." Thus writes his contemporary, Judge Jones, Justice of the Supreme Court of the Province of New York,[1] and Clinton was a type of scores of lesser Jacks-in-office who thus disgraced their cause.

In 1779, the loyalist ladies of New York presented a privateer, the *Fair American*, to the British as a New Year's gift. The loyalists, too, acted as an armed police, and most of the spies in the British Secret Service came from their ranks. They formed also a marine society, the Government providing them with ships and guns, and made raids upon the coasts of New England and Jersey. Despite much snubbing and unjust depreciation on the part of the military, and, for those in London, the sort of talk one can imagine among the English Whigs, "Great Britain," writes a recent American historian, "had certainly no reason to complain of the lack of helpful activity from the loyalists. Their blood and treasures were freely sacrificed on the altar of Imperial patriotism. Those who sought refuge within the British lines, or took up arms, of course escaped immediate persecution, but generally lost all their possessions. Those who stayed at home, taking neither the British side nor

[1] Also Van Tyne, Fiske, and other modern American historians.

RICHARD (ADMIRAL) EARL HOWE
From a painting by H. Singleton *in the National Portrait Gallery*

declaring against it, and of such there were thousands, suffered almost as much. They were deprived of their votes, and if they tried to vote they were fined and imprisoned. All offices of trust or profit were forbidden them. In the law courts not even the rights of a foreigner were left them. They could not sue their debtors nor have recourse in law for any assault, insult, blackmail, or slander. They could not buy and sell land or make a will. Their deeds of gift were invalid and their property at the mercy of their neighbours, and as lawyers they were denied practice in the Courts. That the rabble should have made all justice impossible for the Tories was an inevitable result of war, but the refusal by the Legislatures of even theoretical justice, shows how deep-seated political hate had become. There must be not a whisper against the patriot cause. It was sacrosanct. Enormous fines, half of which went to the informer, punished the offenders. Imprisonment, and even death, in some cases, was the penalty. Long lists were published in the papers of delinquents who were to be treated as lepers." The local committees kept a strict eye on all these affairs. Sometimes, as the prospects for the patriot side darkened, men would show some inclination to hear what the boycotted loyalist had to say for the King's side. The Committee then pounced on him and confined him to his own house, and on any further breath of suspicion sent him to prison among thieves and murderers. A milder plan was to march loyalists off to another State where things were less threatening, often to the back-country "driven"—so the victims declared—"like herds of cattle to distant provinces," and with much cruelty besides being jeered and hooted at in the towns through which they passed. Those not imprisoned at the end of their melancholy journey found it hard enough to get anyone to lodge a Tory. When friendless and short of money their lot under such circumstances was deplorable.

By 1777 both North Carolina and Massachusetts had introduced permanent banishment. Investigators were chosen in each district to prepare a list of enemies to the patriot cause. They were tried separately and when convicted sent on board a guardship, and transported to foreign lands at their own expense, their property confiscated and the penalty of death without benefit of clergy in case of return. One may wonder how many of these tribunals with all the boasted education of New Englanders of that day had enough of it to recall the different attitude of their Cromwellian ancestors towards delinquents, and if so whether the contrast caused them in after days any qualms. Another cause of torment to the neutral loyalist permitted on sufferance to stay in his home, was his enforced acceptance of the depreciated Continental currency, so all his debtors hastened to pay him in this worthless paper, while the many fines and impositions he was subject to had to be liquidated in gold or material. Though pages might be filled with harrowing details from all the States of the persecution of loyalists, whether outrageous or merely petty, I have said enough perhaps for the moment to give the reader some appreciation of their position, at or about the time of the French alliance, and the re-concentration of the British forces in New York. That they made themselves in return as unpleasant as they knew how, when they got the chance, is surely but human nature? To dwell upon the methods they sometimes adopted would merely be to repeat some of the cruelties which provoked them.

There is nothing strange or unusual about such reprisals. Under the exasperating circumstances they were inevitable, and in truth they lack the interest of the policy which provoked them. American writers are naturally constrained to dwell on the often savage nature of these reprisals, since all who count are at one in deploring the short-sighted cruelty of the patriots to the loyalists, not merely on moral grounds but for the loss of a most valuable and steadying element in the rather crude political atmosphere of the earlier stages of the Republic. Their absence was shown in the inter-State quarrels and chaotic conditions which for a decade preceded the adoption of the Constitution and sent thousands of fresh immigrants on the heels of the loyalists into Canada, where if the climate was rigorous and the conditions hard, there was at least a stable government and a secure future.

And now in 1778, with the French alliance and that of Spain shortly to follow with its valuable aid to French sea power, the war entered upon another phase, in which the Southern colonies became the principal sphere of action. This second stage, 1778-81, resembled the first inasmuch as each side in turn experienced revulsions of triumph and despair. For if not despairing England had cause enough to be despondent. Half Europe was arming, or threatening to arm, against her—for American envoys were busy at many Courts—whilst she had to make war in a vast and rough country over 3,000 miles away. The Americans, on the other hand, seemed on the very top of the wave. Yet before the end came, they were to be plunged in a gloom almost as deep as that which enveloped Washington's army, at Trenton or Valley Forge, and while England and her loyal subjects in America really thought that the rebels were exhausted, unexpectedly and rapidly the end came.

The Americans had, of course, no regular navy, their resources were sufficiently taxed to keep an army in the field. But innumerable privateers sailed the seas, preying on English commerce to the loss of nearly two million pounds annually. That, however, did not much affect the war. And now a superior French fleet, under d'Estaing, set out to catch Lord Howe sailing back from Philadelphia to New York. But they were late, and his fleet was in New York harbour when the French arrived outside it, and d'Estaing, there meeting Washington, it was decided not to attack the British fleet in the harbour, though of inferior strength, but to capture Newport which still had its British garrison of 7,000 men. Washington supplied 1,500 regulars and about 8,000 New England militia, while d'Estaing had with him on board 4,000 French troops. The prospects of success seemed more than good. When all was ready however, Admiral Lord Howe sailed out of New York, upon which d'Estaing with his troops again put out to sea. After much manœuvring both fleets were dispersed by a gale, and d'Estaing considered his damages necessitated a resort to Boston for repairs, leaving the militia lamenting, as not equal alone to coping with the British forces.

Expostulations and recriminations were now bandied about, and the New Englanders, always just a little mistrustful of the alliance with their ancient foes, broke out here and there in hostile demonstrations. For to their disgust d'Estaing now sailed away for the West Indies to capture peradventure an English island or two! Good business for France, but cold comfort for Boston. Now the seas were clear, Sir Henry Clinton, Commander-in-Chief all this time, shifted the war to the South. He withdrew the Newport force to New York to help secure that city and the ports outside it against Washington, who always hovering in the neighbourhood had made occasional dashes on the British outposts. Then just before Christmas, 1779, he sailed away with Cornwallis and about 7,000 troops to recapture Charleston, which had repulsed him three years previously. The whole south, from Maryland downwards, had been singularly happy and prosperous before the war. The English Chief Surveyor of Customs for Maryland, William Ellis, wrote a series of extraordinarily interesting letters between 1768 and 1777, when he returned unmolested to England. The different points of view from the Maryland historian writing a century later and this gentleman who witnessed the rise of the revolution at close quarters, even allowing for their respective prejudices, are interesting. The former describes the public and committee meetings as unanimous and spontaneous expressions of the inhabitants. The latter, a highly-educated man and devoted friend to Maryland, writes of these same committees: "An infinite number of petty tyrannies called Committees, in which a few despots lord it over the calm and moderate, inflame the passions of the mob, and pronounce those to be enemies of their country who presume in any way to differ from the creed they may impose. There are too many individuals who from interested or ambitious motives embrace every opportunity to foment the seeds of division by artfully delineating the miseries of that arbitrary system which they assert will be the inevitable consequence of submission to magisterial mandates."

Virginia alone of the Colonies made the Act of Separation and the fresh Oath of Allegiance apply simply to herself as an Independent Commonwealth. In Virginia alone, too, the Revolution was carried through by an overwhelming majority of the aristocracy or planting oligarchy, backed by the "common people," to whose democratic notions they for the moment rendered much lip service. They had no Rousseau dreams or belief in social or even political equality. All they wanted was to get rid of King George, his governors and taxes, and then govern Virginia precisely as they had governed it before. So though all were agreed as to Independence of the Crown there were two parties as to the form of government that was to take its place. The Conservatives and the Progressives led by democrats like Henry and Jefferson, in short the old East against the new West in voting proportions of about 45 to 60. The latter shook the old Order rather badly for a time, but in the end after the war the aristocracy renewed with much fresh blood, which flattered by the delusion that they too were "aristocratic," got back most of its own, before the Civil War and the abolition of slavery brought all to an end.

As previously mentioned, there were fewer avowed loyalists in Virginia than in any province, which seemed unnatural. But the very spirit of a landed class used to authority, not feudal, but one merely of superior education, manner and property, resented encroachments on it more touchily than even a more democratic community, while they had behind them a backing of democrats who saw in revolution as propounded by orators a chance to score off their own oligarchy. They were just strong enough politically with the help of some liberal members of the opposition to prevent Virginia deliberately assuming the *status-quo-ante*, minus only the Royal Governor.

Previous to the Southern campaigns of the British, little need be said at all vital to these pages of the course of the Revolution in Virginia or the South. The same elaborate methods of Tory hunting by committee were adopted as in the Northern provinces, but there was apparently not so much cruelty in executing them. The trade of the country extending from mercantile houses, in Norfolk, the only port and town of importance, to the country stores had been mainly conducted by Scotsmen. These were loyalists almost to a man, and were mostly deported. A great deal of money was owing to them, as to the Colonial merchants in London, which they never got, though after the war that perfervid democrat, Patrick Henry, who in later days reverted to natal type and became almost a Conservative, thundered against the dishonesty of the repudiation which disgraced Virginia. His collected speeches on the subject are eloquent and sound.

Early in the war, Virginia had driven out its Governor, Lord Dunmore, who for a time waged futile strife with a motley following around Norfolk, which held out for some months as a loyalist centre with British ships in the harbour. Encouraged by the Scots merchants and Dunmore's presence, small forces on both sides being engaged, the patriot troops in the end sacked and pillaged their own town and burned two-thirds of it. The rest was destroyed by order of the State Convention, and a town of 6,000 inhabitants, important for the time and place, was temporarily wiped out in January, 1776. Nothing else of real importance occurred in Virginia till Cornwallis swooped down in '79. But as regards the expulsion and treatment of loyalists, says Professor Eckenrode, the most complete and scholarly of recent Virginia historians, " The year 1779 saw the saddest and to us after the long lapse of time, the most regrettable feature of the Revolution—general confiscation. Estates in all parts of Virginia, comprising many thousands of acres, had been left vacant by their refugee owners. These estates were now condemned by escheators and sold for amounts of depreciated currency representing a very small value in specie. The forfeitures, as in the case of almost all seizures, brought in little to the State but greatly benefited purchasers, and there can be small doubt that much corruption and injustice were practised, and that many estates were wrongfully condemned and sold." Numbers of small farmers bought these for a song and acquiring a small breeding stock of slaves, became, eventually, in many cases, under the curious conceit afterwards current in that country, " Old Virginia families," at any rate in their own estimation. This is only typical of what on an even larger scale happened in nearly all the States. Some favouritism was shown to loyalists of prominent families, Byrd of Westover, for example, "the first gentleman in Virginia" was allowed to remain quietly on his estate, also Ralph Wormeley, a late member of the Council, also the Corbins and the Fairfaxes. There was little mob violence in Virginia as in the northern cities. Farmers are not the material for mobs. White slaves and white bondsmen did not count as an element. Out of a population at that time of 600,000, 300,000 were negro slaves, approximately the numbers in about equal parts, owned in Maryland and the two Carolinas combined. Virginia was mainly of unalloyed English blood save for the Scotch-Irish belt upon its mountain frontiers, and a few German Lutherans.

North Carolina was a weaker, less populous replica of Virginia, its planting and slave-owning class along the eastern shore a less definite oligarchy, and at the back a larger and stronger element of common farmers, more mixed in blood than its equivalent in Virginia. Germans, Swiss, Dutch, Scottish Highlanders and a few Huguenots, more fractious and less loyal before the war than Virginia, but in the actual struggle providing a rather larger Tory element, mainly Germans and Scots, with Whig Scotch-Irish borderers in the rear, but speaking generally too remote to translate their republican sympathies into action. South Carolina was even more Tory than New York. The least move of the pendulum would have kept it a royal province. A wealthy planting oligarchy occupied the coast belt, not wholly rural in habit like its Virginia equivalent, but concentrating in the handsome and attractive capital of Charleston, then in trade importance almost a rival to Boston, New York and Philadelphia, and in social amenities quite their equal with a southern atmosphere superadded that even then gave it special attraction to all visitors.

Indigo and rice plantations, however, meant wet and malarial lands, for cotton was not yet, and for most of the planters at least a partial residence in Charleston, and with a more direct mercantile interest in shipping their produce. All this made for a more gregarious and less provincial society than in Virginia. Plantations heavily stocked with slaves managed by overseers, and treated less considerately than in the other Provinces, were the rule near the coast. In short, South Carolina approached more to the West-Indian model, and like those islands maintained a closer social connection with the Mother Country. The upper class was mainly of English or Huguenot stock. While the people of the higher, back-counties, as in North Carolina, were of mixed blood, but strong in Germans who had been snubbed by the coast Oligarchy and cared nothing for Revolutionary theories. The Colony had doubled in population and wealth in the twenty years preceding the war, and was amazingly prosperous. Its planter class, though more recently established than in the neighbouring States, was individually as wealthy or wealthier and less indebted, while its yeoman farmers in the upper country, at least half of them immigrants from Europe, and on still fresh land, were equally flourishing. In no province could a prosecution of war have seemed a more deplorable measure. The influence of Virginia alone brought the colony into it, with results, for a generation at least, disastrous to her welfare. A strange reversion of what happened eighty years later when Virginia in turn was practically forced by South Carolina into the, for her, yet more disastrous War of Secession. Georgia was too young and thinly populated to be much interested in the struggle. She took some part in it, but of hardly sufficient consequence to detain us here.

Charleston in June, 1776, was by way of being revolutionary. She raised a force sufficient to repulse a rather half-hearted attack on the city by Admiral Parker and General Clinton, and was then left alone till the Southern Campaign of 1779, that we are now concerned with. All these Southern States had forwarded contingents to Washington's army, but South Carolina, with her large proportion of negro slaves to whites, could not afford to denude herself of defenders, even had she remained as Revolutionary in sympathy as at first, which she did not. However, when Clinton and Cornwallis invested the city with a force increased by an addition under Prevost, who had been dealing with Georgia, the American General Lincoln surrendered with nearly 3,000 regulars from Virginia. Clinton himself now returned to New York to hold it against Washington on the Hudson, and the French force which was in alliance with him, but nothing worth recording in these pages occurred there.

The arena of fighting was now vastly extended. The war in the North had been concentrated on a comparatively small area around New York and Philadelphia, save for Burgoyne's attempt to join it from Canada and the partisan warfare along the Canadian frontier. Arnold's treachery had staggered his chief and his friends, and he now came south with a British General's commission and 1,500 men to raid Virginia. For war and rapine soon raged over much of that State and the two Carolinas. With long marches and counter marches and cavalry raids, the tide of battle swept back and forth over the three States for some two years. Gates and then Greene were in chief command of the Americans, together with the foreigners, Baron Steuban and Lafayette. Cornwallis, with Phillips, and under them Lord Rawdon and the dashing young partisan, Tarleton, were responsible for the British leadership. Virginia was invaded from various points, but though the most solid Whig State her resistance was not, and could not be, effective, and the spirit of discontent with the patriot cause grew apace now the horrors of war had reached them. Jefferson was Governor, and having fled, together with the Legislature, from Richmond, and sought refuge in the back-country at Charlottesville, was very nearly trapped there by the ubiquitous Tarleton and a force of loyalist cavalry he had trained. They escaped by half an hour!

Tarleton, who wrote a history of the war, is a long-forgotten name in his own country. But not so in America. Within easy memory at any rate there was not a countryman in Virginia and possibly in the Carolinas, unfamiliar with it. He was the ogre of their nursery tales. In effect he was a perfect partisan, and it is to be feared, was none too squeamish. The best horseman in the British Army, young, handsome, and a *beau sabreur*, a leader of men and burning with ardour, he returned to

England at the Peace a popular hero, crowned with laurels. But he fell into the Prince Regent's set, and never drew his sword again, though he lived to old age, a non-combatant through years of war, and died a Major-General, a strange, nay, I should imagine, a unique career. The engraving from Reynolds' portrait of the handsome young dragoon, apparently about to leap on his impatient steed may be still occasionally seen in curiosity shops.

But Virginia did not suffer anything like the Carolinas, above all, South Carolina. After the burning of Norfolk by the first rebel militia, when the Governor, Lord Dunmore, was making a stand against them, there was little serious domestic strife. Virginia produced no loyalist troops to speak of, and the disaffected and war-sick element created by Cornwallis' invasion did little more than grumble. Through these two years there were many minor battles, nearly all favourable to the British, and many skirmishes, some of which, if this were primarily a story of the war, would demand notice. The biggest pitched battle was fought at Camden, an important inland post in North Carolina, where Rawdon and Tarleton, commanding a force mainly of disciplined loyalists, inflicted a disastrous defeat on the chief American army operating in the South. This was commanded by Gates, the dubious hero of Saratoga, summoned by public clamour from his retirement, against the will of Washington. He is blamed for the catastrophe, and incurred much ridicule by arriving in safety, as a fugitive without his army!

The Whigs had some compensation in winning the battle of King's Mountain, an outstanding spur of the Alleghanies in North Carolina. Numerically a small affair, its rather dramatic nature made it memorable. Ferguson, a sort of infantry Tarleton, was marching a Tory battalion, a thousand strong, on a fighting and recruiting tour through North Carolina, when the extreme frontier men and Indian fighters, who could not easily leave their district, were stirred on this occasion to come out into the fighting zone by a challenge from Ferguson, couched in a language they understood and resented. They broke out of their valleys a thousand strong, all mounted as usual on their own horses, which they tied to trees on going into action. They were all sharpshooters, and scattering to the bayonet charges of the Tory militia who held the hill, as constantly returned and finally shot half their opponents and captured the rest. Ferguson at the head of his men incited them to a prolonged and brave struggle, sounding, as was his custom, a piercing silver whistle, heard above the tumult as a token of his presence and encouragement. "When the silver whistle ceased to sound and its gallant owner lay shot through the head upon the forest slope," says President Roosevelt,[1] in his spirited account, the fight was over, and there was only the prisoners to be gathered and the dead collected." The Borderers then rode home. They had repaid the dreaded Ferguson's taunt and that was about all these half-savage men were out for, though they heartened the Whig cause far more than they knew.

South Carolina was now almost ripe to return quietly to the loyalist fold. The patriot element would have sacrificed much for peace, and life would have been resumed as before. But according to American writers, the British made the mistake of demanding specific declarations of allegiance, which set the whole country once more agog. More than anything, it broke up families. Brother was against brother, father against son, particularly in the upper classes. For the rest, there were Germans and Scottish Highland loyalists, and Scotch-Irish Presbyterians Whigs almost to a man. The British and American forces marched and countermarched, each practically forcing the oath of allegiance to its party on the non-combatants of the districts occupied. When fortunes shifted the unfortunate inhabitants were treated by either side as traitors; plundered, burnt out and often murdered. So ferocious was the hatred engendered between Whig and Tory, that apart from the main struggle between British and American forces, a sort of vendetta prevailed throughout the land and threatened to become a war of extermination. Ordinarily decent, even more or less God-fearing, peaceable farmers on both sides, became like demons. Outrage and reprisal were indistinguishable

[1] "The Winning of the West."

in their ferocity. Tory militia acting independently, fought small but bloody actions with Whig militia all over both South and North Carolina. Tarleton with his cavalry, swept backwards and forwards, travelling with uncanny swiftness, often swooping down on Whig camps or magazines that had no thought of him. Houses were burned, and crops and stock seized remorselessly by both sides. Along the coasts of Virginia and the Carolinas, privateers manned by American loyalists, added to the miseries of the interior by raiding and looting the seaboard plantations.

An intimate account of all these bloody doings in the Carolinas was written by the noted Tory partisan, David Fanning, who was in the thick of most of them, and by his own testimony, as ruthless as any. Of common farming stock, he turned out at the age of nineteen for the six years of the war, a born soldier and leader of men, though the bloody scenes through which he hacked and shot and burnt his way were those of savage partisan warfare. It is impossible not to admire his courage, endurance and pertinacity in upholding the loyalist cause. In the varied fortunes that befell him, this extraordinary man suffered every horror but death, which he had inflicted on others, chains and imprisonment, under horrible conditions of unrelieved festering wounds, or as a fugitive in forest solitudes. He raised and commanded later on with His Majesty's commission of Colonel, several troops of horse and companies of foot. He survived, however, to record his career while still but thirty years old, and comfortably settled in New Brunswick, where he died in his bed some forty years later. The simple unvarnished account of his doings is candid enough and extraordinarily illuminating. But contemporary evidence is unanimous that the worst is glossed over, for Fanning's reputation had been as black as his services were conspicuous, so much so that his Crown pension and annuity after the war had to be granted *sub rosâ*.[1]

Inland Virginia, though not nearly so distressed as

[1] Flora Macdonald's husband Alexander Macdonald together with his two sons, held commissions in the North Carolina Highland Regiment. The old couple returned to Scotland and in due course died there. The elder son after serving throughout the war died ultimately in Scotland.

the Carolinas, since no Tory party had remained in operation, began to show an increasing discontent with the Revolution. The gaols were packed with men awaiting their trial for treason, and many counties were reported as full of malcontents.

The best Virginia regulars were mostly absent with Washington in the North; 3,000 had surrendered with Lincoln at Charleston. The thousands of militia were short of arms, clothes and ammunition. There had been Indian troubles too upon the Border. On that account, and also from their number of slaves, these States found it difficult to contribute large forces of men for distant service. Depression on the American side was now, in 1781, as deep as at any period. Congress too had become a mocking and a reproach. In the close of the year 1780, Ramsay, the contemporary historian of the war in South Carolina, writes that the United States appeared to be in nearly the same situation as they were at the close of 1776, but with this difference, "In the first crisis of American affairs, the spirits of the people were high and the paper currency had credit equal to gold and silver. In the last the inhabitants of the United States were thoroughly tired of the war and their bills of credit would scarcely defray the expense of printing them."

The French troops so far had been offered no opportunity of effective action, for the opposing armies in and around New York had done little more than watch each other. The French fleet, however, had more or less broken the British blockade and oversea trade had to some extent revived. As for England, she was now confronted with the three next strongest naval powers to herself. For the inevitable friction with neutrals as to contraband of war had brought in Holland, and added another foe to the triple alliance against her, the recovery of Gibraltar and Minorca, and the invasion of England herself being its objective. Further reinforcements for America were now out of the question, and the drain by death, disease and desertion, the last always tempting in America, even to offers of land grants, had been so great on the armies of Clinton and Cornwallis that about half of those now serving were American loyalists. But both combined were not much inferior to the French and the Americans still with the colours. Cornwallis, who had now invaded Virginia, had only some 5,000 men, while Lord Rawdon with a still smaller force had been left in South Carolina under the fiction that both Carolinas were conquered and brought into the King's Peace.

Lafayette, with a force of militia, retreated before Cornwallis into the back-country, but gathered there such large reinforcements that his opponent was compelled to fall back on the coast expecting to find there the English fleet. Washington, with the French under Rochambeau, had been intending a combined attack on Clinton and New York, for the French, mainly stationed at Rhode Island, had chafed bitterly at their year of inactivity. But news now reached Washington from Lafayette of Cornwallis' position, and an express from de Grasse, commanding the French fleet in the West Indies, intimated that he was sailing for the Chesapeake. Rodney, commanding in the West Indies, knowing of this move, sent Hood with reinforcements to Admiral Graves at New York. Hood, hearing *en route* of the approach to Virginia of de Grasse's fleet, apprised Graves of the critical situation. The latter sailed south at once, encountered the superior French fleet but was out-manœuvred and Cornwallis thus cut off from relief by sea was left at the mercy of Washington, who by a masterly stroke, had arrived overland from New York on the scene with a Franco-American force of 16,000 men. Cornwallis made a brave but hopeless resistance, till the inevitable and historic capitulation on October 19th, 1781. Even so, the fiery Tarleton had protested against the surrender. If Cornwallis would only give him 2,000 men he undertook to cut his way through the Franco-American army and join the British forces still in being.

It was a knock-down blow to England, and virtually ended the war. Savannah, Charleston and New York were still in British occupation, and partisan fighting still dragged on in the Carolinas and the South. But the Whig Government now succeeded to power. The King, who had actually inspired the policy pursued, which

Engraved from an original drawing by T. Prattent

whether right or wrong only failed through the incompetency of his generals, was brushed aside, and in February, 1782, a Whig Government came in, with the intention of making a speedy peace. The nation, too, which on the whole had been with the King, was now sick of the war in America, particularly in view of the dangers on all sides threatening at home. Though the preliminaries of Peace were not settled till the autumn and the Treaty signed till the beginning of 1783, the practical certainty of the triumph of the American cause made the year 1782 a lull as regards any serious military operations. Both sides were marking time, save for unimportant skirmishing affairs and some bloodshed in localities where loyalists and patriots were so balanced as to keep their quarrels burning. But so far as this story is concerned the war may be regarded as ended, and its main object, war's aftermath, alone to be considered. It is impossible, however, to conclude this portentous businesss, whether as reader of its many and differing chronicles, or as writer of the brief summary I have here attempted, without indulging in that alluring dream of what would have happened if a wiser or more pliant government had controlled the affairs of the Empire, or even if war had been inevitable, the luck of it had not been so cruelly adverse in producing a Washington on the one side and a Germain and Howe on the other. For the pity, if it was a pity, of the whole thing lies in the original absence of any intention to sever connection with the Mother Country. Even in New England, much the least in sympathy with her, no fraction of responsible opinion appears to have harboured such a thought. John Adams, the very embodiment of New England dissatisfaction, writes that when the quarrel began such a thing as secession never crossed his mind. Franklin's declaration that no one in the colonies harboured such a thought is a classic utterance. It is sad that two years of growing rancour so absolutely changed the attitude of the colonists.

CHAPTER V

THE EXPULSION OF THE LOYALISTS

SAVANNAH was evacuated by the British in August, 1782. The loyalists collected there went mostly to Florida and the West Indies, both hopeless countries for the penniless white man, though a few may have saved enough from the wreck to buy some land and negroes in the Islands. Georgia was still in British hands, but soon to be taken and for a short period held by Spain. The more important evacuation of Charleston, though long announced, was not carried out till December. It contained a great crowd of loyalists, both of the City and Province, whose sole remaining hopes now centred round such terms as the British Government might make for them in the coming Treaty of Peace. Some of them had anticipated the evacuation by sailing for Florida, the West Indies, or England. Of these and their varied fortunes, doubtless mostly sad ones, no available record exists. The remainder sailed with Leslie, now in command, for New York, to swell the throng of refugees which had been accumulating there for the past seven years. It is in New York from now onward that the interest of the loyalists' story mainly centres. A fairly unanimous estimate places the total number that left the country at 100,000, about half of whom scattered to various destinations overseas, while the remainder went north to the British provinces, either in groups or as individuals, through the war, but some 45,000 at the lowest estimate were now to take part in the final transportation there, which so profoundly affected the future of North America.

Clinton was recalled, and it was rightly felt that the task of carrying out such arrangements as the Treaty of Peace might entail, including the withdrawal of the British forces from America, demanded the wisest and best commander at the Government's disposal. There was little doubt as to their choice. Sir Guy Carleton, whom Germain's petty spite had removed in favour of the hapless Burgoyne, was obviously the man for this difficult but rather inglorious task. He alone had not yet failed them, and furthermore, by his spirited defence of Quebec, in 1776, he had saved Canada from the Americans. Rather magnanimously, for he did not like it at all, Carleton accepted the command. He had served for years both with and against the Americans, and they had a curious liking and respect for him. Indeed, their extremists were none too well pleased at his appointment, fearing that this very fact might weaken the demands of their negotiators. They need not have worried, for he proved absolutely rigid in defence of such poor rights as were left to the exiles.[1]

General Haldimand had succeeded Carleton as Governor and Commander-in-Chief in Canada. He too was an admirable man, one of those Swiss officers originally selected for the 60th Rifles or "Royal Americans," which on their formation some years before the war were in large part composed of German-speaking colonials. He had shown great sympathy for the loyalist refugees who for three or four years had been streaming intermittently into Canada, and had worked untiringly in finding them quarters and maintenance, and later on in building houses and allotting lands, prior to the great influx expected after the Peace. Carleton arrived at New York in May, 1782, invested with extraordinary powers as Commander-in-Chief of His Majesty's Forces between Nova Scotia and the Floridas, and as Commissioner for carrying out the conditions of peace, when these should be formulated and signed. All the loyalists who had abandoned their homes and all the troops, British, German and loyalist, were now, or were soon to be, collected in New York.

Those who had been operating from Canada under Butler, St. Leger and the Johnsons, along the borders of Pennsylvania and New York, were still intact and active. The remains of some twenty loyalist regiments were now with Carleton. Chief among them were

[1] See "Life of Dorchester."

battalions of de Lancey's brigade, three more of volunteers under Skinner, Pennsylvania loyalists under Allen, and New Englanders under Chalmers. The "Loyal Americans," with a company of Guides and pioneers, were under Beverley Robinson, while Fanning of South Carolina commanded the King's American regiment, and lastly there were the Queen's Rangers, raised and led by Simcoe, with Tarleton's own noted light horsemen. The pay rolls of these corps are among the forty stout volumes of correspondence which Maurice Morgan, Carleton's indefatigable secretary, preserved for us, and now lie in the rooms of the Royal Society. All the refugees were recommended by the King to Carleton's "tenderest and most honourable care," a trust which he faithfully performed.

The position was curious. Of the two armies, that of the British was in and around New York, that of Washington and the French mostly on the Hudson above the City. A sort of mutual understanding existed that all hostilities should cease while peace propositions were in the air. It had been left to Carleton to decide during this interlude on his attitude towards the enemy. New York was the last foothold of British rule and occupation. All outside was under the nominal supervision of Congress, but actually governed by the several State legislatures, all busy passing Acts, for the most part of democratic tendencies, and of filling the cup of vindictive legislation against the hapless loyalists who still braved persecution, rather than fly they knew not whither from their hearths and homes. The naval position had been for a time precarious, with only Digby and a weak squadron at New York; but Rodney's victory over the French in April, 1782, had relieved the situation.

Carleton was well off both in money and supplies, but his cares were legion. More refugees kept dropping in, either those who, with peace in prospect, had ventured to test the social atmosphere of their old homes and found it hopeless, or those who could no longer stand the persecution practised by their neighbours, often by savage and cowardly methods. While full admiration is due to the endurance and valour of that fraction of colonial manhood who, often half-starved and seldom paid, held the field so long and stubbornly against the King's troops, one cannot think that the non-combatants and large portions of the militia are entitled to any great share of such admiration. The latter were always the most forward in Tory-baiting. Some of them fought bravely, but others only came out to shoot at the soldiers from safe covert, and run away when it became dangerous. One need not criticise these simple farmers, whose heads had been filled by fiery orators with the most amazing fictions about England and King George, which, naturally enough, were believed.

Expresses were constantly passing between Carleton and Washington, the former with characteristic warmth urging consideration for the loyalists, and receiving in return merely non-committal replies. Washington, as we have seen, had given his opinion that suicide was the loyalists' proper course! Adams wrote that they all ought to be hanged. They were regarded as the vilest of traitors. Yet their treachery had consisted in their refusal to forsake the allegiance in which they had been born for an upstart authority, as it seemed to them, established by discontented neighbours, and promising disaster which, but for astounding luck, would have inevitably occurred. All wars are demoralising; but a mass of the available evidence and contemporary testimony to the condition of the provinces seems to indicate moral deterioration almost everywhere conspicuous. Most certainly this was the case with the rank and file. That simple farmers whose previous lives, one assumes, ran on more or less kindly and normal lines, and often with much religion both professed and genuine, should so change their outlook as to suffer, if not to practise, such outrages on humanity, argues some great reaction to barbarism. It is useless to fall back on the weak argument of Tory reprisals. However brutal, they are not relevant and never were under similar conditions of which we have had examples nearer home in modern times. Again, there is overwhelming evidence that the dollar was already a god, at least in the northern provinces; that greed for it and sharp practice in acquiring it were prominent traits is noticed by every single traveller of that day. How much of this passion for gain entered into the patriotism of the New England merchants, for instance, is an interesting speculation. On the other hand, the prompt response in sympathy made by Virginia and the South to the disciplinary treatment dealt out to Massachusetts, a province they heartily disliked, is noteworthy.

The loyalists, crowded into New York, spent a weary and anxious time awaiting the first hints of the terms of peace. An active publisher named Rivington had consistently buoyed up their hopes with a journal pitched always upon the top note of optimism. This intensified the crash when it came, for they never for a moment anticipated that the British Government would let them down. In the meantime, there was frequent correspondence between Carleton and Washington as to the exchange and treatment of prisoners. The Americans had no money and were short of supplies. Their own army remained unpaid and even ill-clad, and it was not surprising that loud complaints came from the various groups of British and German prisoners, detained mostly in Pennsylvania and Virginia. There were constant efforts to make farm hands of the private soldiers under the indenture system in vogue in the colonies[1]. An English visitor and intending settler in Virginia, caught in the meshes of war and detained on parole, witnessed a company of Highlanders making a comrade who had succumbed to such an offer, run the gauntlet of cuffs and blows. A most curious petition was addressed to Carleton (among whose papers it has survived) by a group of Germans, non-commissioned officers and privates, imprisoned in Pennsylvania under wretched conditions. They were offered their liberty, they declared, if they would serve in the American Army, or again if they would consent to sell their services for three years to farmers, who were prepared to pay eighty dollars into the American war chest. These poor fellows are always written of as mere hirelings and slaves of their prince, without the honour and feelings of ordinary free men. But one gathers from the indignant attitude assumed by these much despised mercenaries, when approached with the aforesaid terms of freedom, how strong among them was the pride of the

[1] Cresswell's journal.

military caste. Some of these encounters with the American officials are vividly described by the soldiers in this petition to Carleton from "men following the glorious trade of war." They scorned the very idea of doing "menial work as slaves to an American farmer." When approached by recruiting sergeants of the Continental line with the offer of liberty and a bounty, these simple people found their duty to their own Prince and oath of allegiance to King George an insuperable obstacle. "Though we are treated not like prisoners of war but like wretches fallen into the hands of barbarians, we replied that every word was thunder in our ears and were struck dumb with such barbarous proposals." The address is signed by about twenty men of all non-commissioned ranks, annexing the service record to each signature. The number of privates, corporals and sergeants with fifteen and twenty years' service is remarkable.

There lies before me, too, a long list of outlawed loyalists, filling many pages of Judge Thomas Jones' exhaustive record of his own times and his own province. The judge had been Justice of the Supreme Court of New York, and had an estate on Long Island with a handsome mansion, still standing, and was himself a victim of banishment and confiscation. His personal loss was estimated at £44,000, though he was ultimately consoled by the Crown with high office in the Maritime Provinces. Particulars of the lost estates of all leading New Yorkers are here exhaustively set forth. Attorney-General Kemp, for example, lost £98,000, and 26,774 acres were confiscated from the Mayor of the city. It is curious to find almost all the wealth, considerable for the times, based on territorial property, a standard of means and position that the Revolution in great measure destroyed, not merely by individual confiscations but by the wholesale sub-division and resale of the big estates as freehold farms. The head of the de Lanceys, the most powerful family in the Province, lost estates to the value of £140,000. Sir John Johnson's confiscated estate in the Mohawk Valley, of 50,000 acres, represented £100,000, and Guy Johnson, his cousin, lost £25,000. Frederick Philipse, of another semi-feudal family, lost

£160,000, while the Morrises, Bayards, and Beverley Robinsons of the still conspicuous Toronto family, were each deprived of almost half that amount. These are but a few of the leading cases cited, and in estimating the scale of loss, the greater value of money at that time, particularly in America, must of course be remembered. Of the compensation ultimately granted by the British Government more will be said later. Enough for the moment that nearly one-third of the estimated losses was paid in cash to many hundred applicants. In most cases this proved a fairly reasonable settlement.

I have quoted New York as an example of facts and figures which are more or less applicable to the other provinces, partly because they are here very completely set forth, and further because at least a third of the total loyalist exodus came from that Province. All through this year, 1782, when the loyalists were anxiously awaiting the terms of the coming Peace, parties had drifted away from time to time to Nova Scotia, Canada, and occasionally to England. But the bulk of them waited in suspense to hear their fate. Unfortunately, an unwarranted spirit of optimism and a pathetic belief in the power and will of the British Government to right their wrongs, combined with a flamboyant local Press pitched upon that note, had not prepared them for the shock which was to come. Carleton had more than enough on his hands through this busy and anxious season. Already arrangements were being pushed forward in Nova Scotia for the reception of the loyalist emigrants. Petitions from them streamed in upon him. "If we have to encounter," ran one of these, when a rumour of the acknowledgment of complete independence reached New York, "this inexpressible misfortune, we beg consideration for our lives, fortune and property, and not by mere terms of treaty." Carleton's always warm heart was wrung by the situation of these unfortunate people, "many of them," as he wrote to England, "of the first position in these provinces."

A swarm of negroes, too, had found their way to New York, some of them with their masters, others runaway slaves. The latter embarrassed Carleton greatly. By law they should be returned to their masters, but Carleton adopted the principle that when a slave reached the British lines he was free. However, he kept a careful list of them, with their names and descriptions. There are many columns of Pompeys, Cæsars, Jupiters, Princes and Dianas, labelled "likely lad" "stout wench," "stout fellow," "incurably lazy," and "worn-outs," with their master's name attached, so that should there be later any case for compensation there would be data to act upon. These slaves, who had got away with the British forces, were made a grievance later on by the Slave States, and worked into a claim against Great Britain. These States had mostly repudiated their debts to English merchants, a course condemned by leading American writers as "without precedent among civilized nations." Professor Fiske[1] holds that the defaulting States were so conscious of their flagrant dishonesty that they trumped up this abducted or runaway slave question as an attempt to salve their conscience, or rather extenuate their conduct before the world.

The preliminary terms of peace were discussed at Paris, with America and France separately. The chief British Commissioner for America was not a diplomat, but an able merchant credited with special knowledge qualifying him for the task. He, Oswald, and Dr. Franklin had virtually settled the question by February, and the news reached America in the following month. The opposing generals complimented one another, and Washington issued orders for an absolute cessation of any hostile acts. But the loyalists learned to their dismay not merely that independence was conceded, but that any hopes they still cherished of getting reasonable guarantees in the Treaty were dashed to the ground. The British Government made every effort to make reinstatement of the loyalists a clause in the treaty, but in vain. It was replied that Congress had no power to legislate for the several States, which, however disconcerting, was certainly true. All they could promise was to recommend the States each and all, to deal leniently with their loyalists. This was, of course, hopeless, and everybody in America, including Congress, knew it. The loyalists, at any rate,

[1] "The Critical Period of American History" (John Fiske).

had no doubt of its futility. The news came as a fearful shock. Hitherto, they had been supported by hopes of a good time coming, when they would recover their own, and possibly something more than their own, in return for all their sufferings. In the constant presence of a powerful British force and the mutual encouragement of a large sympathetic body of fellow-sufferers, that hope had been fed with too much doubtful fuel. Every favourable item was exaggerated, and *Rivington's Gazette*, run in the loyalist interest, dealt far more in fancy than in fact.

Henceforward, the scramble to get within the lines from inland districts, and for those that were there to get away by sea was frantic. Many of the latter had made brief personal experiment of the recommendation by Congress to the States, and found it futile. It does not make the American case much better that a restitution of the loyalist estates was by now a practical impossibility. Many had been long disposed of by the State Governments to private owners, often in sections, and were now occupied by various people. Many had been dishonestly "jumped" by greedy neighbours or purchased by them at forced sales and paid for in almost worthless currency. The money realised by the estates had all been spent, the American soldiers still lacking their pay, and sometimes even boots and clothes. The mischief was done, the injustice perpetrated, and continued to be, for confiscation went on for some time after peace had been actually signed. The French protested against the treatment of the loyalists, urging that as they had brought victory to the American cause, it was only right they should have a voice in such an important clause of the Treaty. The British Government, of course, protested with all their might. But there was nothing to back their protest up. For the country would not continue the war, though, as a matter of fact, American affairs were actually in a very bad way, and the French were already showing signs of weariness. Nearly half Europe, however, was in arms against England, even though it was finding her an unexpectedly formidable foe, and still able to hit out right and left with disagreeable effect.

BENJAMIN FRANKLIN, LL.D., F.R.S.
From a French painting. Engraved by T. Wright

This is what Mr. Jay, American representative at Madrid, and one of the ablest and soundest of the earlier American statesmen, thought of the confiscation policy. In a letter to Governor Clinton, of New York, already mentioned as one of the most rabid anti-loyalists, he writes :—" An English paper contains what they call, but I can hardly believe it to be, your Confiscation Act. If truly printed, New York is disgraced by injustice too palpable to admit even of publication. I feel for the honour of my country and therefore beg the favour of you to send me a true copy of it, that if it be false, I may by publishing yours remove the prejudices against you occasioned by the former." Contrary to Jay's belief, the copy seen by him was authentic. He never changed the opinion here expressed to Clinton.

By this time, there were already over 3,000 loyalists in Canada. They had been supplied with food, beds, household goods and clothing, not lavishly, but sufficiently. Sometimes they were allotted small pensions. A Board elected by Governor Haldimand supervised the business. Ever since 1775, when Revolutionary mobs began to harry loyalists in New York, Boston and elsewhere, there had been a small but steady movement of refugees into England, many of them civil officials or those too old or infirm to bear arms; a certain number, too, of Anglican clergy, hounded from their cures, with some of the wives and children of those serving in arms for the Crown. Among them also were professional men, lawyers and doctors, whose opinions had cost them their livelihood. To all of these relief and help was extended either in temporary instalment or in pensions of from £50 to £200 a year. Some, again, had friends and relatives in England and were absorbed into English life. How these mostly forlorn refugees fared on pensions or doles just sufficient to support life, we may gather from the voluminous letters of ex-Governor Hutchinson, Curwen and others.

They were characteristically chilled by the indifference with which they were regarded by the great world that amused itself as usual, ate, drank and went on its way, to their rather ingenuous surprise, as if no Empire were at stake. They writhed at the contemptuous fashion in which the Americans were often spoken of, and encountered at every turn that curious insular superciliousness towards the colonial, aggravated by the blank mind towards his country for which the most colonising of nations has always been and is even yet in a measure distinguished. They were shocked, too, to find one party in the country rejoicing in the defeat of its own armies. They discussed all these strange things together in the London taverns and coffee-houses which the refugees particularly affected, and the sentiments preserved in their journals are illuminating. About £40,000 a year was expended on the loyalists in England before the Peace.

But with that event, came the great migration and its accompanying and subsequent expenditure, which dwarfs all the former figures. By the terms of the Treaty, the British were to evacuate New York, the only spot in the country, except the far western frontier posts, which they still held, with as much despatch as possible. Nothing was actually said about the loyalists accompanying them, but Carleton, to his honour, determined, despite opposition, to interpret the clause that way. The Americans contended that their deportation was not in the agreement, and continually importuned Carleton to name an early day for the evacuation of the city. He replied firmly, but civilly, that he differed from them in his interpretation of the treaty, that he was as anxious as they were for the evacuation, but that it was not a matter of will but of ships. As soon as Carleton could, he collected sufficient craft, no easy task when only ships averaging from 30 to 100 tons were available, and they far from easy to come by. But we must go back a little and speak of the destiny awaiting those thousands of expatriated people, for so long herded together in the city and outskirts of New York. It need hardly be said that the Opposition in Parliament, which had been responsible for the war, assailed the Government's failure to get justice for the loyalists in bitter and scathing terms. As a matter of fact, the Government had been powerless. Short of carrying on the war, which they had come into office to terminate, there was no alternative. But if Society had been chilly to the loyalists the Government was determined to be generous. It was urged too, and not unreasonably, that further war, to attempt reinstatement of the loyalists, would cost more in a few months than any sum necessary to compensate them liberally. Their scheme, apart from pension and donations, was to offer free grants of land to all and sundry in the still almost virgin regions of Nova Scotia and Canada outside the French settlements.

Nova Scotia had been a British Province since the Treaty of Utrecht, 1713, but had only been developed by promoted immigration, chiefly of ex-soldiers and sailors, and the creation of Halifax in 1748. In this old Acadia, too, were the non-exported remnant of the French Acadians on the Bay of Fundy, a thin sprinkling of New England settlers, 2,000 Germans and Swiss, and some very troublesome Micmac Indians. Only about 14,000 in all, and a poor community to boot. It was said that there was not a thousand pounds in Halifax! But there had been a Lieutenant Governor and a Legislature this long time. Cape Breton, the north-western corner of Nova Scotia, was in effect an island and a separate Province containing the remains of the once important fortress town of Louisburg, the key of the St. Lawrence, the "Dunkirk of North America," captured from the French in the late war and dismantled. Just off the north shore, too, was the long, narrow island of St. John, afterwards and still known as Prince Edward Island, with already a sprinkling of settlers.

Nova Scotia, more particularly, at this moment, was being prepared for settlement in various selected spots of its sparsely-occupied surface. Crown surveyors were busy laying off tracts and town lots against the impending influx. Field officers were to have 5,000 acres, captains 3,000, subalterns 2,000 and privates 200. Stock and implements were to be provided by Government with rations for the first three years. Boards and timbers, for house-building, were provided and even houses were erected in certain places. Thither it was intended to transport the larger body of such loyalists as were willing to go, and in truth most of them were. There was no choice! "Hell or Halifax," the cant phrase ran. The alternative country opened for settlement was the fringe of what is now the great and wealthy province of Ontario. Surveyors were already busy about Cataraqui, afterwards Kingston, thence along the north shores of the Upper St. Lawrence, west of Montreal and the French country, and again along the shores of Lake Ontario. Governor Haldimand, as already stated, had been actively concerning himself with some 3,000 Canadians of earlier importation, but in the main these had been only temporary squatters, and came into the general scheme in 1783-4. Surveys were also made in the West about Niagara, more particularly for Butler's corps that had operated from there in the war, and now made applications for land.

When Carleton knew that Independence was to be granted in the Treaty, he had resigned, but the Government protested that he was the only man capable of carrying through the thorny and difficult task of the military and loyalist evacuation. Several associations had already been privately formed in New York for the purpose of facilitating emigration to Nova Scotia by the less sanguine among the loyalists. The first party, of 500 prospectors and pioneers, sailed in October, 1782, under competent leaders. They explored the country from Halifax, covering the ground from there to the Annapolis Valley, and thence ascending the river St. John from the Bay of Fundy. The result of their published report, a glowing one, much cheered the loyalists in New York, and in the following spring, on April 26th, 1783, the first big shipment sailed in a fleet carrying 7,000 persons, men, women, children and servants. Half of them went to the mouth of the St. John river, soon afterwards to be in New Brunswick, and the remainder to the south-west corner of Nova Scotia.

At the former place little or nothing had been done for their reception. A wild and lonely shore faced them where the brush had to be cut before they could even pitch their tents or build their shacks. Nothing before them but a shaggy wilderness, behind them a grey sea, chill with the drifting icebergs and floes from the frozen north. The women and children, accustomed though they were to the rebuffs of fortune, could not restrain their tears. The grandmother of Sir Leonard Tilley, the well-known statesman of later days, used to tell him, "I climbed to the top of Chipman's Hill and watched the sails disappear in the distance, and such a feeling of loneliness came over me that though I had not shed a tear through all the war I sat down on the damp moss with my baby on my lap and cried bitterly." The large city of St. John now covers the site of this slight but pathetic incident typical of the part that the loyalist women were to play in the founding of British Canada.

Altogether about 10,000 people arrived that year in the St. John's district on the Bay of Fundy. Among them came what was left of thirteen separate corps, namely de Lancey's first and second battalions, the King's American Dragoons, the New Jersey Volunteers, the Maryland Loyalists, the 42nd Regiment (a fragment of the Black Watch), the Prince of Wales' American Regiment, the New York Volunteers, the Royal Pioneers, the Queen's Rangers, the Pennsylvania Loyalists, and Arnold's American Legion. With them came a great number of wives and children. This large group formed the foundation of the Province of New Brunswick, which was created in 1784, much against the wishes of Parr, the Governor of Nova Scotia, and his little coterie at Halifax. Parr had made himself unpopular by the confusion and lack of prime necessities that the refugees encountered on landing at their various destinations. He could hardly, perhaps, be greatly blamed, for no less than 35,000 more or less destitute people poured into the Province in successive batches during the year 1783, and were still arriving in the bitter month of January, 1784. Never had a Government, particularly one of very limited resources, to handle such an unprecedented business. The numbers, for one thing, were much greater than anticipated, and the continuous rationing of such a multitude at various points was a Herculean task, for the Province itself did little more than feed its own small population, and the main supply came over sea. Great numbers of these people had only the clothes they stood up in and those too often worn out. Clothing and blankets had to be supplied to many thousands. Though it is hardly fair to blame Governor Parr and his agents for their shortcomings in such a stupendous undertaking, one can understand, nevertheless, the bitter complaints that at first found their way back to the old Colonies and the satisfaction with which the citizens of the New Republic heard them. They jeered at it as "Nova Scarcity," and apropos of its broken coast-line, declared that it gave them the palsy merely to look at it on the map! Nova Scotia is "patchy" in character. In such a wilderness as it then was, the fertile and infertile districts had hardly been identified. Upon the whole, however, the refugees were better fitted to cope with the difficulties than similar crowds direct from the Mother Country, though many, of course, both men and women, were from the upper classes and unused to manual labour. There were many townsmen amongst them too, but the majority were used to handling axe and plough, and had behind them all the resources of American farmers even of the old settled districts. All the first settlements had to be on the coast or the transport of supplies would have been impossible. The passage from New York to Halifax averaged about a week.

Owing to pressure, the surveys often turned out inaccurate, nor were there enough surveyors. The country, too, was densely wooded from end to end, which vastly added to pioneering difficulties. Mosquitoes and black flies, with all the vigour of a first attack in primæval woods and swamps, proved a real torture, even to those who had made acquaintance with these dreadful pests in the more modified fashion common to the older settled districts. The largest settlement and the most interesting experiment, as exhibiting the errors of the organisers, was at the south-west corner of Nova Scotia, where some 10,000 souls gathered beside the beautiful but not otherwise commendable harbour, known as Port Rosemary. This venture, however, was promoted and carried through by some sanguine loyalists themselves, who had made a preliminary visit and obtained a grant from Governor Parr of as much land as was necessary, also a promise that a surveyor, carpenters and ample lumber for building houses should be supplied them besides the usual provisions. Some Halifax people warned them of the unsuitability of the spot for an agricultural settlement. But the leaders of the enterprise, carried away by enthusiasm for the harbour and the scenery, turned a deaf ear. In May, 1783, four thousand settlers, as first arrivals, laid out the plan of a town and adjacent farming lots. With the carpenters and timber forwarded by Governor Parr, a great number of houses were run up in a short time, and a town came into being.

The Governor sailed down in his sloop and formally named the place Shelburne, after the statesman most responsible for the Peace, which so dashed the loyalists' hopes. The irony, apparently, was not noticed, nor the more vital fact that the land was poor and stony. Then followed a procession, firing of cannon, two grand dinners on the Governor's ship, and a ball. Parr had obviously no eye for practical colonising. He wrote to Carleton, "I have no doubt but that in a short time it will become the most flourishing town for trade, and the district for agriculture, of any in this part of the world." By the next year it contained from eight to ten thousand souls, with shops, churches, inns and all the ingredients of a flourishing town. Soldiers, too, were quartered there, and the band played on the promenade. A brisk trade in fish and lumber sprang up, newspapers were published and spirited elections held for the Provincial Assembly. A shipyard was built, and all seemed going well. Shelburne became actually larger than Halifax, and as populous as were Quebec and Montreal at that day, with their approximately 8,000 souls apiece. But Shelburne proved, in modern parlance, a "boom town." The neighbourhood was barren. Trade for various reasons utterly failed. There were undesirables and incompetents among the loyalist immigrants as among all such communities, and Shelburne, with its premature glitter, seems to have attracted an undue share of them. At any rate, in a very few years, it collapsed. Most of the houses were abandoned and fell into decay, while some were carried away bodily to more promising surroundings. Thus the largest town for the moment in British North America became in a few years a city of the dead.

The famous Nova Scotian author, Judge Haliburton ("Sam Slick"), visited Shelburne many years later, and wrote:—"Some of the houses had been taken to pieces and removed to Halifax or St. John, others converted into fuel. The rest had fallen a prey to neglect and decomposition. The chimneys stood up erect and marked the spot around which the social circle had assembled and the blackened fireplaces ranged one above the other. In some places they had sunk with the edifice, leaving a heap of ruin, while not a few were inclining to their fall and awaiting the first storm. Hundreds of cellars, with their stone walls and granite partitions, were everywhere to be seen like uncovered monuments of the dead. Time and decay had done their work, and those numerous vaults spoke of a generation that had passed away for ever and without the aid of an inscription, told a tale of sorrow and of sadness that overpowered the heart." An episode only, to be sure, but a strange one at such time and in such a place, and so far as I know without a parallel on such a scale in our colonial records. Assuredly, it was not typical of the loyalists' fortunes generally in their new homes, and we can afford to record the rise and fall of Shelburne, as a bit of drama in the otherwise steady progress made in converting the wild Canadian woods into a smiling and pleasant land.

I must not linger here over the details of other settlements effected in Nova Scotia. They were first made near Halifax, the capital, also at Annapolis, Digby and Port Moreton. But place names will mean little to most of my readers. The conditions were much the same everywhere, land to be cleared, log shanties to be built,—for there were at first few saw-mills,—burning, logging and breaking up the land between the charred stumps that rose black amid the crops for years before the era of "stump extractors." The population of the province had been trebled in a year or two. Nearly all supplies and provisions for the newcomers had to be brought overseas by Government ships, and continued, for the most part, to be terribly inadequate. It could hardly have been otherwise. Among other groups of immigrants to Nova Scotia, the late Mayor of Albany led over 3,000 to Cape Breton Island, then under a separate Government. Many Dutch and Germans and Highlanders from the much-harried Johnson-Mohawk country were among them. Later on, at the clearances in the Scottish Highlands, thousands of the clansmen were settled in Cape Breton Island, by that time included in Nova Scotia, of which province, but for a narrow channel, it is geographically a part, and to this day the old people there speak Gaelic. Prince Edward Island, too, then St. John's Island, just off the north coast, 100 miles in length, 10 to 20 in breadth, and of good soil, attracted thus early a few settlers. It too became a separate government and remains so to this day within the Canadian Federation.

The ten thousand or so refugees who entered the St. John river and spread up its "interval lands" had not long to wait before they were deemed worthy to form a sister province to Nova Scotia. The First Council of New Brunswick, 1784, is significant of the quality of the settlers, including as it did two distinguished American Judges, two Colonels of Colonial Corps and late owners of large estates, a Colonel of Regulars, a Winston, a Beverley Robinson, an old personal friend of Washington, and one of the larger landowners of New York, and lastly, Judge Saunders, of a well-known Virginia family and a Bencher of the Inner Temple. Naturally enough, many of the immigrants to these Maritime provinces did not stay upon the ground where they were first deposited, or even on the original surveys. They pushed farther on in search of localities more suitable to individual requirements or of better land, and ultimately found both. Of these 35,000 Nova Scotian loyalists, a proportion, as was inevitable, proved discontented and drifted away, often to Upper Canada, the alternative goal of exiles. A few went to England and quite a number in course of time crept back to their old towns or districts in the Republic, when the bitter feeling had toned down, more particularly towards the obscure and unimportant. But we must leave the story of these Eastern Provinces for the present. The hardships and sufferings particularly with the gently nurtured among the pioneers were for some time intense. But in due course better times came to them, the clearings spread wider around the log-houses, more fields were opened and fenced, and food crops grown and saved.

The half-pay of the officers, small as it was, went a long way in the back-woods. Halifax, about half-way down the Atlantic Coast, was a good distributing post for all supplies. The farthest points in the Province were rarely more than 100 miles from it by land or sea, and many of the new settlements less than half that distance. There were plenty of coasting craft at work, and land transport became more available. Of the money compensation for losses granted by Parliament to the loyalists, and of such vital assistance to them in their new homes, I will speak later, as it was some time before this could be generally distributed. The promise and the expectation of it, however, helped to keep the exiles in good heart during the few years of hardship. Even these were somewhat mitigated by the abundance of good fish in the sea, with trout and salmon in rivers and lakes. There were deer in the forests to be shot, or at any rate procured from Indian hunters, and in the autumn clouds of wildfowl in the marshes. Even more, perhaps, to some of them, as they have themselves testified, was the consolation of being free from the persecutions of their ancient neighbours and under the protection of the British flag.

To return, however, to New York, and to Carleton, who had worked incessantly at getting all these people safely shipped to their destinations. Their alternative refuge to Nova Scotia was, as I have already indicated, Canada. Some three thousand, as we know, had already gone there, probably without any definite ideas of settlement, though many had actually settled; but in 1782 a definite scheme was put in train. Now Montreal, together with the neighbouring junction of the rivers Ottawa and St. Lawrence, formed the western limit of French occupation. Thus far the colony was French, and well occupied all along the St. Lawrence down to Quebec, and thence for about 80 miles below it. The system was semi-feudal, and the British, after the conquest in 1761, in deference to the prevailing wish of leading Canadians, let it remain so. It had been Louis the Fourteenth's scheme. Under this the country had been divided into *seigneuries*, or large tracts of forest land, allotted to men of birth, officers and such-like, and an immigrant peasantry mainly from Northern France settled on them to clear the land in small farms at a nominal rent for ever of about a penny an acre. There were also established on these estates feudal or manorial dues, or fines, after the manner of many European countries, England included, the details of which I need not elaborate here. The *seigneurs* constituted a sort of aristocracy, though some were actually plebeians who had purchased their *seigneuries*. Nearly all, however, were very poor, and few could maintain the outward position of a noble. But the framework of the system was rigid.[1]

The Government had been an autocracy in the form of a triumvirate, composed of the Governor, the Intendant, and the Bishop, all subject to direction from the King. The *noblesse* had no political status whatever. The Church was intensely ultramontane, and the priest representing it in each parish was a power. Beside him was also a captain of militia, generally, but not necessarily, a *seigneur*. All the men between sixteen and sixty had to serve and, when called upon, to march at the word of command against Indians or British in any direction. Such, briefly, was old French Canada, since the conquest, governed by a British Viceroy and nominated council on the whole benignantly and with a view to encouraging loyalty to the Crown. The fact that the Quebec Act of 1774, passed in the British Parliament during Carleton's government, granted the Canadians their religion as established and perpetuated their semi-feudal land laws, was one of the formal indictments against the Crown promulgated by the United States. I have sketched thus briefly the position of French Canada, which contained about 100,000 souls when the great immigration of loyalists flowed into the country, to show how impossible it was that the latter could settle among the French *seigneuries* or be subject to their laws. There was plenty of room outside however, even in the Province of Quebec, and how it was utilized will be shown anon.

But in the meantime, west of Montreal and along the northern shores of Lakes Ontario and Erie, the primæval

[1] In 1854 a law was passed enabling the censitaire (tenant) to purchase the freehold of his farm at about twenty years purchase of the rent—a penny or two an acre.

forest still densely covered what became the Province of Upper Canada, and in due course the great and powerful Province of Ontario. At its western ends, at Niagara and Detroit, there were old-established French trading posts, and that was all. Nobody in the American colonies knew anything about this dark region. It was popularly supposed to be a land of almost perpetual winter and Arctic severity. The war along its edges, however, had already opened the eyes of a few people to its value and possibilities. So, when the emigration of the loyalists became a Government project, experts were dispatched to examine this unknown country, and their report was wholly favourable. Following this, in the summer of 1783, Governor Haldimand got busy, and before the snow fell had made rapid progress in laying out lots and townships along the St. Lawrence, west of Montreal and farther on again to the Bay of Quinté, at the outlet of Lake Ontario. All through that summer, Carleton was resisting the importunities of Congress to fix a day for the final evacuation of New York. But to these he replied shortly, though courteously, that he was doing his utmost and if they did not believe it he begged them to send agents to see for themselves. Moreover, as the harsh measures against the loyalists still in their homes grew steadily harsher, more prospective exiles kept dropping in, and he was determined not to embark his army till he had seen the last one of them safely out of New York. He reminded Congress that the more they persecuted their loyalists the longer he would be compelled to remain in the country, anxious as he was himself to leave it. On November 29th, Carleton wrote his last despatch on board H.M.S. *Ceres*, anchored in the harbour. It supported a final petition of loyalist widows for pensions, and concluded with this significant paragraph:

"His Majesty's troops and such remaining loyalists as chose to emigrate were successfully withdrawn on the 25th inst. from the City of New York in good order, and embarked without the smallest circumstances of irregularity, or misbehaviour of any kind."

Thus dropped the curtain on one of the most fateful and pregnant struggles in the world's history.

CHAPTER VI

THE LOYALISTS IN UPPER CANADA

IN addition to those refugees gathering, or already gathered in Canada, whom chance had to some extent directed there, four or five thousand others, attracted by the promise of land grants and assistance, headed direct for the St. Lawrence—mostly by sea from New York. Seven ships full of disbanded provincial regiments, with their families, went this way. Others travelled by the old war route up the Hudson, and thence up Lakes George and Champlain and by the Richelieu River. Others again came up the Mohawk Valley to Oswego, and thence across the extreme eastern end of Lake Ontario to Catraqui, or old Fort Frontenac, now renamed Kingston. This became the official town and centre of the new surveys, stretching thence westward up the Lake shore and eastward down the St. Lawrence to the French country at the mouth of the Ottawa and Montreal. Five townships in the former district and eight in the latter, had been surveyed in the wild woods. A few of the New Yorkers came all the way on foot, others again from Pennsylvania or even more distant North Carolina, laboured for months along the woodland trails in two-horse wagons, and sometimes driving before them their few head of stock with such effects as had perchance escaped confiscation. Among these were the neutrals who had somehow avoided trouble and were out for a quiet life. This desideratum seemed more attainable under the King's government than amid the rather chaotic conditions of the thirteen republics struggling amid constant disagreements into uniformity. Among the North Carolinians came one son at least of the famous Flora Macdonald, who had settled there with her husband, a retired captain in a Highland Regiment. The old couple had returned to Scotland as related and eventually died there, but the sons had fought all through the war.

The surveys were ready for settlement by the summer of 1784. The bulk of the intending settlers were on the spot or within easy reach. There were nearly four thousand, mostly disbanded soldiers and their belongings, persons of all ages and both sexes, to be planted on these particular townships, each consisting of 36 square miles. Haldimand was ever active and kindly in supervision, while the local management was in the hands of Sir John Johnson. The first battalion of his own corps, the "New York Regiment," was here, including many Germans or Dutch of the Mohawk Valley with their women and children, and were planted on the five townships extending to the French border. Next to them were settled "Jessups' Rangers," while the "King's Rangers," also Anglo-New Yorkers, under James Rogers, had the adjoining tract. These corps had mainly operated from Canada, and been recruited from the loyalists near the borders. James Rogers was a brother of Robert Rogers, the famous leader of Rangers in the French war, whose portrait had been all over London, where he had been received at Court. His younger brother, James, had commanded a detachment of these same Rangers, who had won for themselves and their commander such fame on both sides of the Atlantic for deeds of daring and endurance. This brother James, founder of the Canadian family, still well known there, was developing a property of 22,000 acres in Vermont when war broke out. This property went by confiscation and was valued at £30,000. Near by, too, was settled Major Van Alstine with another large band of New York loyalists who had come by sea, and Colonel Macdonnell with further parties of disbanded soldiers, which later on were reinforced by some bodies of Hessians that had been stranded in French Canada. Along the good wheat lands of the Richelieu, again, and around the foot of Lake Champlain, many other refugees, soldiers and civilians found a home. But settlement was at first discouraged in the unoccupied southern portions of French Canada, as it bordered on the State of Vermont, peopled by a roughish breed of frontier farmers with whom the risk of future friction was obvious.

There yet remains to be mentioned, as of great importance, the loyalist settlement in the Niagara district at the extreme western point of Lake Ontario. This was the western, though lesser, wing of the whole movement, and was started by the men of Butler's Rangers, who in their raids through Northern New York have given the American writers so much material as a set-off to the persecution of the loyalists. Unfortunately for their record, they had the Indians as allies, and to control them was on occasions impossible. Yet in Montcalm's victory, known as the "Massacre of Fort William Henry," on Lake George in 1757, his Indians murdered nearly a hundred of the garrison in cold blood after capitulation, including women and children. Montcalm and his French officers endeavoured to stop it but could not. His Canadian men and officers looked on indifferently. Yet nobody calls Montcalm a murderer! He is held, and rightly so, in particularly high honour. Butler's Indians only once broke loose from control and fell on unarmed settlers. That was at Cherry Vale, and they killed nothing like so many as did Montcalm's allies at Fort William Henry. The Wyoming affair, more notorious through Campbell's poem, will be spoken of presently, with its second destruction during the bloody Border quarrels in 1784 between Pennsylvanians and New Englanders. The Americans did their utmost to engage Indian warriors, and, as we have seen, to some extent succeeded. There is no question as to this, but the red man did not recognise what merely seemed to him a bunch of politicians as his Great Father. So those "Five nations," having nearly always sided with their English Sovereign, as against their French Onontio, both, of course, great and mysterious potentates, saw no cause whatever to set up a strange God without any qualifications for playing the part. Besides, Sir William Johnson had long ago captured their hearts, and the spirit of that great backwoods chieftain had not long passed away and still lived in his son and nephew. So Colonel Butler, the Johnsons and others who had been burned out by the patriots, were not, it may be imagined, too particular in the reprisals they made in force from the Canadian frontier. With headquarters at Niagara they had all enjoyed opportunities to sample the land and see that it was rather more than good, and the two corps, speaking broadly, that had forgathered there, had permission to settle and were given the same terms as the rest. The spot was more accessible too to some of the later loyalists straggling up from Pennsylvania and the settlement soon numbered about 2,000 souls. The method of land selection everywhere was to group the settlers on the township assigned to them, and then draw lots for each farm. There are still owners of pleasant homes to-day in the "Garden of Canada," who owe them to a slip of paper drawn out of a battered hat by their ancestor. The officers in Canada, as in Nova Scotia, had usually 5,000 and 2,000 acres respectively, according to rank, the privates 200 acres. When the township was assigned to a civilian group some similar scale was observed.

We have now, I think, landed all the first instalments, the original United Empire Loyalists, as they and their children after them were proud to style themselves. Carleton and the British Government seriously proposed that the two letters U.E. should become an hereditary attachment to their names. The formal adoption of the scheme fell through, but this has not prevented the perpetuity of the honour being cherished to this day by every family that could claim it.

As regards numbers in this first great exodus to Canada, the figures may be fairly set down as about 10,000, including certain independent and immediate followers. Many, too, of the ex-soldiers sent afterwards for their wives and families, who were probably suffered at least to exist unharmed, so long as their departure was imminent, and the head of the family, the chief criminal, had relieved the "virtuous" community of his hateful presence. For with curious lack of humour certain Revolutionary orators and writers, headed by Jefferson and the Adamses, were wont to apply that epithet to the entire population other than loyalists!

Before dealing with what are generally called the "later loyalists," an uncertain number whose motives all but defy analysis, something must be said of the loyalists of another race, namely the unfortunate Indians. Now the remnants of the Six Nations, a combination who by their valour, discipline and ability had been the dread of all tribes to the North and West, and had at times actually held the balance of power between England and France, were now chiefly represented by the Mohawks, who were mostly seated on their hereditary lands in Northern New York to the southward of Lake Ontario, and between the Genesee and Mohawk rivers. One of the three outstanding Indian chiefs of history, Joseph Brant, was at this time their leader. He was a brother of Sir William Johnson's admirable Indian wife, and had been educated and received into the Anglican Church in Connecticut. He was a warrior first, however, though by education and associations partly weaned from the savage ethics of the Indian code. As a boy, he had fought with his tribe under Bouquet against the Great Pontiac. When the War of Independence threatened, he had risen by merit to be head chieftain of the Six Nations. In July, 1774, Sir William Johnson, then sick unto death, had received grave despatches from England urging him to keep these Indians faithful to the Crown. He at once called their leaders in council to his bedside and adjured them at all hazards to stand by the King. That night he died. His son, as we have seen, succeeded to his estates, and his nephew, Colonel Guy Johnson, who also owned a stone manor house and large estate on the Mohawk, was made Controller of Indian Affairs with Joseph Brant as "secretary" or Agent. Brant visited all the Indian settlements in the interests of the Crown, and though little over thirty, by his weight and eloquence, persuaded them to stand by the Treaty that for a hundred years had held good between the Six Nations and their "Great White Father." So when the time came, the Indians went upon the war-path, led effectively, and sometimes too effectively, by Brant. He was himself as little bloodthirsty as one of his race amid the clash of war could be. On the other hand, with the American backwoodsmen, above all with the Scotch-Irish Borderers along the base, and by this time often over the top, of the Alleghanies, the only "good

Indian was a dead Indian" as the saying went. Both sides used the Indians when they could. In truth, between white and red engaged on the frontier in this sort of warfare there was not much to choose.

The Indians looked on the encroaching white settlements as destructive of their hunting-grounds, otherwise their livelihood. Many colonies had done pretty much what they liked in the Indian question regardless of treaties. The Valley of Wyoming, so famous in story, had been formerly in possession of the Six Nations, but in 1754 they had been deprived of their inheritance by a colonizing company, and when the war came; its settlers developed anti-British proclivities so violently that they almost asked for trouble from their savage predecessors. The "Monster Brant," as the poet calls him, and his followers, were not there at all, nor was anyone "massacred" but men with arms in their hands. Campbell's idyllic picture of an American frontier settlement cast in a mellow, leisurely, old-world atmosphere, the happy valley, the frisking peasants, and innocent pipe-playing swains, with some stage backwoods accessories, is, of course, grotesque. Far from having naught to do but "feed their flocks on green declivities," the Wyoming settlers had been extremely busy arresting all those suspected of loyalist sentiments and dispatching them to prisons in Connecticut. Such of his "poor Highland countrymen" whose peace the poet pictures as so ruthlessly shattered by Butler's Indians as had escaped a Connecticut prison, were probably with McLean's Highland Corps at Quebec or fighting under Butler himself, or the Johnsons. But *Gertrude of Wyoming*, published in 1809, made quite a sensation in England, was taken at its face value and wept over by three successive generations. It even served its turn with a public just then working up for the war of 1812 and another struggle with the loyalists, which was to end so differently. Though Brant was not at Wyoming, he was at Cherry River, where his men broke away from him and murdered fifty souls, about half the number massacred, as I have mentioned, by Montcalm's Indians at Fort William Henry, with even less excuse. When Brant's son was in England in 1823, he convinced

Campbell that his father and his Mohawks were not at Wyoming at all, and that his poem had been based on false information. It is not surprising, considering all things, that in 1779 a campaign of vengeance was waged by Congress with a large force under General Sullivan. Brant, assisted by some loyalists, made a brave and skilful defence, but in the end was thrust back by an army of 5,000 men, which destroyed the Indian settlements and every living thing within them. But I must not linger over the bloody raids and reprisals that swept backwards and forwards over this once peaceful land.[1]

When the terms of Peace were known, and it was found that the Indians had not been so much as mentioned in them, there was dismay and indignation among the tribes. When they heard that their country had been granted away by Great Britain to the New Republic, they demanded with just logic, by what right the King of England had handed over lands that were not his to give. There was, of course, no answer to that. Up to the end, moreover, Brant had been fighting forces disloyal, as he regarded them, to the King. His services were not unrewarded. When in 1775 Haldimand had appealed to the tribes to assist the King, he promised them that any losses of territory they might suffer should be made good. Carleton, at a later date, repeated the assurance. The promise was now to be honoured, though not perhaps in the form originally understood. Most of the Mohawk nation at the close of war, driven for ever from their old abodes, were camping on the Canadian side of the Niagara river, and expressed a wish to settle on English ground. Indeed, they had no alternative save to fight the Americans, which was now impossible.

So Brant made the long journey to Quebec, and took counsel with Haldimand, who assured him that a tract of land should be reserved for his people. After some discussion, the Grand River, which flows southward

[1] In 1784 there was a strange sequel to the Wyoming catastrophe of 1778. In Pennsylvania territory, it was resettled and rebuilt by immigrants from Connecticut. The Pennsylvanians, in the interests of a Land Company and actuated by violent inter-state jealousies, burned down the settlement again and imprisoned half its wretched occupants. Ultimately troops were dispatched from Philadelphia to restore order though without success for many months.

into Lake Erie, to the west of the Niagara country, was decided upon, and here a tract six miles wide on either side of that stream, extending upward to its source was selected for the grant. Brant obtained the title-deeds for the Indians in the autumn of 1784, under the seal of Royal authority, as a gift to the Mohawks and others of the Six Nations, with their posterity. It was a fine country in the most fertile portion of what is now Ontario. Among the newcomers were many from their kindred tribes south of the border who were being worried by the Americans and were anxious to remain subjects of the King of England. And there, peacefully cultivating the soil, their descendants may be seen to this day, while, though not of their contriving, the neighbouring town of Brantford, known for its exports of agricultural machinery the world over, immortalises the name of the great Indian chief, and in the heart of it stands a noble monument to his memory. Brant himself was given a large tract on Lake Ontario, where he built a good house and lived in comfort, served by a pair of negro slaves whom he had captured in war. In later days, he travelled in the States and was entertained by many of the officers who had fought against him. He was distinguished for his abiding interest in the care and religious uplifting of his people, and the church he had built for them is still standing.

The process of settling down in the wild woods of "Upper Canada," as this country came to be called, was much the same as that followed in the Maritime provinces, though the less accessible situation of the former entailed even harder conditions. The same supplies of food and clothing were served out, for numbers had only the much-worn garments they stood up in. The supplies included Indian blankets for coats and rough cloth for trousers, all of which had to be made up on the spot. Boots were contrived locally out of skins. No boards for building purposes were delivered, and as there were no sawmills for a long time, axes and handsaws, in limited numbers, were provided. Unfortunately, the axes were of the wrong kind for felling timber and there were no grindstones! A set of tools, too, was given to each group of five families, a rather scant allowance when everything, including furniture, had to be made upon the spot. No ploughs were supplied as there were few horses or oxen to draw them, but only hoes and mattocks, which caused vast inconvenience in breaking and cropping the soil. Indeed, even with these rather meagre supplies, Haldimand seems to have exceeded the intentions of government, and taken upon himself the responsibility of going beyond his instructions. This shorter measure of supplies to the Western settlers is unaccountable. The fact that they were less accessible to sources of supply should have been a stronger reason for generosity in first instalments. But certainly the British government used no intentional parsimony. The only line of transport was up the St. Lawrence from Montreal, on which there were several rapids to be negotiated, and this meant unloading the *bateaux* at the foot of each and portaging the cargoes through the woods to smooth water again. Livestock also was but meagrely supplied, the first allowance consisting merely of a few cows. The settlers, indeed, had a very hard time for many years. It was long before saw-mills and grist-mills were introduced, and even then there were no teams to haul the logs to the mill or the sawn lumber away from it. Log-houses were inevitable and indeed serviceable enough. For grinding wheat and corn hand-grist mills were served out, though through failure in transport or breakage, much of the grain had to be pounded between stones and sometimes, we are told, between cannon-balls swung from saplings.

The primæval forest of Upper Canada was always formidable, as anyone may see to-day in its still uncleared backwoods. Oak, beech, maple and other hardwoods, together with huge hemlocks and firs, reared their lofty trunks out of the tangle of undergrowth and the wreckage of trees fallen and rotted through the long past years. Clearing is a slow business to the skilled axeman with a sharp blade. Many of these refugees must have been quite unused to swinging an axe, particularly axes unsuitable for the purpose and blunt into the bargain. Supply convoys coming up the river frequently miscarried, capsized in flooded waters, or else were snowed up in the wintry woods, while in hot weather their cargo was liable to turn bad. Settlers were unavoidably far apart, for 200-acre farms, mostly forest, involved isolation. The French-Canadians built their houses along the road or river near together, their 50 or 100-acre farms running back from it in long narrow strips. This made for sociability and safety, but it also meant a long walk to meadow, grain field or timber lot with some waste of time and effort.

But with all the hardships inseparable from their primitive situation, the smothering snowstorms, the fierce heat, the swarms of stinging flies, the absence of most things that had been essentials in the former life of almost all, one consolation at any rate must have cheered the hearts of the settlers and helped them to carry on. That was the assured promise of compensation. Already the ex-officers among them had half-pay. It was of no immediate use in the wilderness to be sure. There was nothing as yet to buy, and from the pensioners in Upper Canada, even this seems to have been held back for a time, though doubtless credited to the payee. Now, however, with the ready consent of both political parties, and that of the King, compensation was to be granted to all who had fought for the Crown or had suffered any loss for their adhesion to its cause. A good deal had been done in a haphazard way, as we have seen, but now a Commission was to be appointed to examine in detail the claims of every loyalist and deal with them not grudgingly but frankly and fairly, and a vote went unopposed through Parliament to that effect. It was a difficult business, and the openings for fraud were, of course, great. The loyalists would not have been human had not a sense of their wrongs and losses sometimes caused an estimate of their money value greater than strict equity and the resources of an over-taxed Mother Country warranted. They could not all claim to be virtuous, as was claimed for the nation that had expelled them, by Jefferson and his friends. Committees had sat from time to time in London for the immediate relief of loyalists in England, and, as already noted, certain disbursements had been made in Canada by Carleton and Haldimand. No time was lost on the passing of the Act. The Commissioners were appointed in July, 1783, and began their enquiries in October. They were empowered to examine persons under oath, send for papers and use the testimonies of loyalists in England and America to determine the validity of the claims. Most of the loyalists were frank and honest in their statements, but some were not.

The details of this long and complicated business are preserved by Wilmot, and reproduced with notes and comments by contemporary chroniclers. They are of extraordinary interest to those for whom names and districts have reality, but for my purposes here must be reduced to the briefest summary. To give the main fact precedence, somewhat over three million sterling was ultimately paid in cash. Besides this, vast tracts of Crown land in British North America were freely granted. These last, of course, cost the Government little, and that little was repaid many times in the prosperous colonies thereby founded. Then there were the supplies and maintenance for from forty to fifty thousand people for a term of years varying according to district and circumstances. There was also half-pay to about 500 ex-officers in the Colonial Corps, and a certain number of war widows. Lastly, there must be added the considerable sums of money granted to the destitute loyalists in England and the Colonies before the Commission of Claims began to disburse the three millions it ultimately expended. The claims covered not merely the loss of property real and personal, but also that of situations and professional incomes.

Speaking broadly, about thrice as much was claimed as was ultimately granted. This does not imply that the claimants opened their mouths quite as widely as this difference represents, but rather that due regard was had to the "Treasury" point of view and the exigencies of high taxation which British governments seem no longer to take into account. Opinion generally has agreed that the Mother Country behaved as generously to her faithful and suffering American subjects as could be reasonably expected at a time when her own fortunes seemed to be at a low ebb. Her total expenditure is estimated at nearly six millions. I do not know whether it is quite fair to compare her conduct with that of

Congress and some of the State Governments towards the impoverished and ragged warriors who had brought them into being. But if it be so, the comparison would not favour the Americans, and we know for a certainty that Washington and all his officers would have said so. Great numbers of loyalists came over to London to press their claims. This was a tedious, expensive and most uncomfortable process in those days, involving, say, ten weeks in a hundred-ton schooner laden with tobacco from Virginia or masts from New England. This is how the best families from the South had usually paid their very rare visits to what they still called "home." So likewise went opulent Bostonians or New Yorkers on their rather more frequent trips to what the former, at any rate, did not give the same endearing term.

To save all this, it was soon found desirable to send Commissioners overseas to examine claimants on the spot. In this capacity Colonels Dundas and Pemberton went to Halifax, and Mr. John Anstey to New York in July, 1785. They had the same powers as the Commissioners at home, and sat at Halifax, St. John and Montreal. That there was much grumbling by the loyalist applicants need hardly be said. They had not been accustomed to keen and searching enquiries by legal experts into their private affairs. One can imagine a colonial planter, farmer or tradesman of that day, unaccustomed before the war to any such inquisition, getting restive under the rigid assessments. The modern income-tax official was in the womb of the remote future. The courts of the Commissioners sat till January, 1789. Of the entire amount granted to the loyalists nearly one-third went to late inhabitants of the Province of New York. South Carolina, in proportion to her smaller population, came next. Professor Flick has set out for us the entire details of the New York compensations actually paid, from Sir John Johnson's £45,000 and the two de Laneys' £65,000, about two-fifths of their actual loss, down to small amounts of ten or fifteen pounds. The money seems to have been paid over within reasonable time of the endorsement of the claim. No doubt in the Maritime Provinces it more generally brought with it immediate relief, but in the prodigious isolation of Upper Canada such moneys as were due could have been of but little use for the first two or three years.

Fertile as the soil was proving, there was no mercy in the wild woods which had to be so laboriously cleared. Through the summer months, stock could live on the bushes and weeds, but for six frozen winter months there was no bite for horse or cow. In the contracted clearings, bristling with stumps, the limitation of the earlier grain crops was marked enough. There was small room as yet for growing fodder for stock. For three or four years, the settlers depended on the food supplies sent up from Montreal, 180 miles beyond Kingston, which was about the centre of the long string of settlements, and I have already mentioned the difficulties and irregularities of the transport. As there were no ploughs the land for wheat had to be prepared, as we have seen, by hoes and mattocks, and even for want of clothes there was for a long time great suffering. The women became extraordinarily resourceful, reclothing themselves and families from the products of the wild woods around them. They learned the Indian method of tanning, spun thread from the fibres of the bass wood bark, and made clothing of deerskins—trousers, smocks and petticoats that would withstand for years the rough usage of backwoods life. There were, as yet, no stockings. Most of the children had to spend the first winter indoors for lack of covering for their feet.

Looking forward to the raising of wool, flax and hemp, the settlers fashioned hand-looms and spinning-wheels in the winter, and when the materials were forthcoming linsey-woolsey took the place of buckskin. Save in Kingston itself, where the requirements of a small garrison advanced things more rapidly, the townships were a long time in struggling out of the homespun and log-hut stage of existence. Some bricks had been shipped for the purpose to the coast settlers in Nova Scotia, but up in this "back of beyond," the chimneys had to be laid on boulders and built of sticks and clay, like those still seen in the log cabins of the poor whites and negroes in the Southern States. While in their old homes they had basked through the cold winters by warm stoves, as in truth the French Canadians were already doing, these loyalists had to huddle round open fire-places, cheerful and sufficient in a Virginia winter, but sadly inadequate in the below zero temperature of the Canadian backwoods. Still, firewood, at least, was plentiful. Of furniture the pioneers, save for a few odd pieces brought with them, had nothing but what they could fashion for themselves with axe, chisel and knife. It was a strange existence for such of them as had been lawyers, professors, doctors or landowners with plentiful slaves or servants, as had been the case with many of them.

But the hard bush life of Upper Canada had not quite the same prospective terrors for the great numbers of these settlers that came in from the United States through the years following 1783. These are generally known as later 'loyalists'. They were mostly people whose hearts had perhaps been on the loyalist side, but who had somehow succeeded in disguising their sentiments, and were now glad to escape from a condition of things that did not promise too well for the future, and to settle where their sympathies lay. All of these at first were subject to a searching examination of their conduct and principles before they took the oath of allegiance and were allotted land. It must be admitted that drinking, as everywhere in North America at that time, was heavy, rum being cheap and abundant, and the "Bees" for raising new log houses or barns, a frequent and worthy motive for social gatherings, often ended, we are told, in an orgy and occasionally even in a fight!

For a long time grain markets were out of the question. The settlements were satisfied to be self-supporting, and taking the modest produce of the harvest to the mill, when mills materialised, seems to have been one of the year's adventures. For even that often meant a journey of days by pack-horse along blazed trails through the woods, or by canoe over restless waterways. The only news which penetrated the wilderness came by Yankee pedlars or itinerant preachers, who gave their own versions of what was going on in Europe or the States.

In 1784, General Haldimand had retired to England

and a well-earned rest. A more conscientious servant Great Britain never had, nor the loyalists a truer friend, and history has never done him justice. The coming of the loyalists was to decide the fate of British North America, and the success of the movement owes to Haldimand more than it is possible to convey in these pages. There was then an interval of two years filled by the Lieutenant-Governorships of Hamilton and Hope successively. The former had endeavoured, through the war, to hold the far western posts in the Ohio Valley against the assaults of backwoods levies under the famous Border partisan, George Rogers Clark, who in the end captured his stronghold at Vincennes and Hamilton within it. He was badly treated by Clark, and still more so in the Virginia prison to which he was afterwards sent. A good soldier and leader of soldiers, Hamilton made an indifferent Governor, and was soon succeeded by Hope, who a year later went home, and Carleton came out again as Governor-General of all the Provinces, with the title of Lord Dorchester.

The thud of the axe and the crash of falling trees were now resounding through all the Canadas, and thousands of acres were opening to the sun. The Nova Scotians and New Brunswickers, though still in the rough, were faring better than the Upper Canadians, for they had river and ocean transport at their doors. The others had lake and river at hand not far off, but these waterways led, as yet, nowhere save to other settlements as poor and straggling as those from which they came. The Government's sometimes "rotten" pork was all the meat the Upper Canadians had, and even that not always, and in 1787 their meagre crops of grain failed totally through drought, and the following winter and spring of 1788 proved a time of stark famine, long remembered as "the hungry year." Sheep had been just introduced to provide wool for spinning and weaving clothes, but it was impossible under the circumstances to protect them from the wolves and bears. Those not seized by wild beasts were greedily devoured by their owners in that dreadful winter and spring, and so too were most of the milch cows. One family, which managed to keep and feed a cow, have left it on record that otherwise they would have died of starvation. Men offered a thousand acres for a bushel of potatoes. Hungry children devoured the buds of the bass wood tree, and eagerly plucked the first heads of rye and barley, while tradition tells of beef bones passed from house to house to be boiled and reboiled.

A group of Mohawk Indians had been settled near these Kingston townships, and their knowledge of wood-craft and of supporting life under primitive conditions proved most valuable to the settlers near them. They also killed deer which had got too shy within range of the settlements for such pursuit of them as these settlers had time to give. It seems strange to read of such things happening not 200 miles from civilization, above all in the warm days of spring when nature was bursting into bloom and leaf. But the blossoming of the Canadian forest was deceptive. Not for a long time yet would it produce anything to relieve the wants of man, and there was no livestock left to pull at the buds or bite at the little patches of beaver meadow. The effects of the "hungry year," however, were not actually fatal except to the stock, which with better times was gradually replaced. From now, indeed, things improved rapidly. Common hardship produced goodwill and helpfulness instead of the gossip and scandal of civilization. The women were constantly experimenting, and every new discovery that lightened their hardships was duly shared with their neighbours. The 200-acre farms, to quote the average size, were mostly still strangled in thick woods. It was still, as always with backwoodsmen, like living in a pit, with no changing scene but the racing clouds or glaring blue skies. The sole communications were by narrow trails "blazed" through the forests. This proved, however, no obstacle to social gatherings, which their rarity made all the heartier, the men turning up in buckskins, to be replaced later by homespun, the women in linsey-woolsey. Weddings especially were occasions of great jollity, and gatherings of distant friends packed into the two or three-roomed log-houses. There were no doctors, and even drugs were sometimes hard to come by. But the women grew amazingly skilful with herbs. In the autumn, we are told, when the moon was in a favourable quarter for the enterprise, the housewife, or maybe a grandmother, would organise an expedition into the woods to replenish the family medicine chest. For coughs and colds a syrup was made from the roots of the spikenard. Tea was concocted from catnip, and poured down the throats of children suffering from stomach-ache, or for affections of the chest. Tansy tea was a popular tonic, likewise hop tea for indigestion and cherry bark for the blood. The favourite prescription for scalds and burns was black alder lard, resin and beeswax. Smartweed steeped in vinegar was applied to bruises and wormwood to the legs of horses. A healing ointment for open sores was made from the leaves of the garden bean mixed with hot lard. Even the roots of the burdock were dried and utilized as a tea for dyspepsia, while the mandrake was used in a concoction for gargle. The roots of the nerve-vine were chewed for the purpose indicated by the name. The roots of elecampane steeped in hot lard formed a popular lotion for both man and beast. These are a few of Nature's remedies which were necessarily forced on a people who for a generation had to be their own physicians. The lore thus gathered and passed on, it used to be said, made the practice of medicine among the Canadian farmers for a very long time after they had come out of the woods an uncommonly poor business. Many hints, too, were taken from the Indians, who had their own remedies proven by time-honoured custom.

But the land so laboriously cleared for the most part, proved rich beyond all expectation. Beneath the dense forests of Upper Canada lay a country as good as the best of New York, the Jerseys or Pennsylvania, and far better than most of Maryland, or Virginia, or North Carolina, even in their virgin prime, which by now was a very old story. This fact, in itself, was a constant help and stimulant to the pioneer. The ownership of 200 acres of good land, for example, though but a tenth of it might yet be opened to the daylight, gave no slight promise for the future and compensation for the endurance of present evils. To the younger generation of that day these last probably signified little, and invaluable training was afforded in those simple arts that tame a wilderness. Lastly, the climate, though hard, proved healthy. Education, save for such scraps as a parent might impart, went by the board.

About 1790, as the clearings spread and sufficient food was raised within them, things got better. Saw-mills and grist-mills appeared, and here and there a country store, stocked from Montreal with all the simpler needs of settlers. Already their numbers had been greatly increased by newcomers from across the border, and by the birth-rate itself, which was high, despite the almost complete absence of the usual amenities associated with the bearing and rearing of children, while new townships were opening out westward along the lake shore. There had been little time, so far, to think about forms of government. These people were all within the limits of the old Province of Quebec, and theoretically liable to the French laws and customs recently codified for the French-Canadians under the Quebec Act of 1774, which had so irritated the American colonies by its official recognition of the Catholic Church. But these isolated communities had felt nothing of this. A few local justices had been appointed who heard such simple cases as came before them in some settler's log home. They had as little idea that they were creating a future political difficulty as that they were laying a foundation for the saving of a great country from the clutches of the people whom at that time they had such good cause to dislike. But some settled government was becoming necessary for this new Canada. Its occupants were nearly all Protestants and all English-speaking save for some few of the German and Dutch loyalists, who were otherwise in full agreement with their British co-refugees.

It was decided, therefore, to form Upper Canada into a separate province. Both geography and racial reasons favoured the scheme. Lord Dorchester, who was now Governor-General, thought it premature, but gave way in the end, and his long colonial experience made him of great service in the framing of the new Act. Since the shock of the loss of the American colonies, Parliament had taken a little more interest in those that were left. Its members always gave trouble, however, in their rooted inability to realise the conditions of a new country and its people. Even now this obtuseness crops up at times among the party of more limited experience and the cocksureness which ignorance breeds. In those days it existed in higher circles. The new Act was introduced by Pitt in 1791. Even he was a victim to the common Parliamentary delusion that hereditary legislators should be created in a new colony. They could not realise colonial conditions with their fluctuations of individual fortunes and instability of personal position. There was always, too, a passion for loading a new country with quit-rents and making the men who carved it out liable for ever to these payments for no service rendered, small charges, but always irritating and generally applied to no useful purpose.

Sometimes, indeed, grants of quit-rents were made to private individuals in England, and their descendants as a mere favour. Dorchester, though unable to be present personally at Westminster, had provided against all this, while Chief Justice Smith, of Quebec, who had held the same post in New York, even went so far as to draft a scheme of Federation for the five Canadian and Maritime Provinces, a measure which would have forestalled the great Act of 1867, under which the Dominion is now governed. While the House was in Committee upon the new Act, Burke and Fox, obviously bored with the subject in hand, drifted off to the more congenial one of the French Revolution, and over it had their famous quarrel. Not, however, before Burke had found opportunity for some rolling periods on the Canadian scheme, in which he described a country of rich land covered by heavy timber as a bleak and barren waste. In short, Upper Canada in 1791 was constituted a Province, covering very much the area now occupied by Ontario. Its constitution was virtually similar to that of the Maritime Provinces, and indeed of all the old American colonies, namely a Governor, with a nominated council and elected assembly. It now only remained to decide on a seat of Government and to instal a Governor. The little village of Newark at Niagara was selected for the former, while to the latter office was appointed John Graves Simcoe, Colonel of the New York Rangers through the late war. This last recommendation alone would have assured him a welcome, and he was further graced with the temperament of a most enthusiastic coloniser.

Since the departure of Haldimand, settlers prepared to take the oath of allegiance had been crossing the line in some numbers into Southern Quebec. As a constitution was now being granted to the new British Province, it was impossible to deny the same privilege to the French. Not that the majority cared anything at all for votes and elections, but the small educated class in the towns did, and made the illiterate peasant echo the demand. We are not immediately concerned with the French Province here except for the British within it. These consisted in the first place of traders in the cities of Montreal and Quebec, perhaps with their connections some two thousand in number. A few loyalist immigrants, too, had settled in one or two *seigneuries* bought by the Crown, and the much larger wave of British immigration was beginning, as stated, to cross the line into Southern Quebec. As soon as it was known that Upper Canada was to be a separate province and that both it and Lower Canada were to have representative Government, immigration set in more strongly from across the line, and when the Act of 1791 was passed it rapidly increased.

In Southern Quebec, below the French *seigneuries* and bordering on the State of Vermont, the beautiful and fertile country known later as the Eastern Townships, was already attracting New Englanders, who for various reasons were ready to live under the British flag. Active as an apparent majority of Vermonters had been on the patriot side, there was now a strong reaction and much discontent with the prospects of their future under the new Republic. Indeed, one faction in the State were intriguing to get it back under British rule. An interesting episode this, though it does not concern us here further than as a probable stimulant to the numbers who now crossed over into the Eastern townships, applied for land and took the oath of allegiance. This picturesque region of fertile hills and valleys and clear streams, bordering in parts on noble lakes and backed by lofty mountains, had been surveyed for settlement on the square mile and township system that prevailed in the other provinces. At first freely settled by Americans, in later years it attracted a substantial element from Great Britain and became an isolated but English block in the French province. Their representatives, with those of two other small English districts, in the Quebec House of Assembly, were for many years at odds with the French majority in their views on the administration of a province. The British were intent on roads, canals, harbours, and other measures necessary for the development of a colony. The French, after generations of political suppression, now gave rein to their tongues and indulged in orgies of futile oratory, and later on, in sheer ignorance, claimed similar powers to the British House of Commons. Unlike colonists of British race, they could not understand the difference between Representative Government, with which the Canada Act of 1791 had endowed them, and Responsible Government, for which these young Provinces with their crude conditions and small populations, were not yet ripe, but were to achieve in all good time. To-day, the "Townships" have, in a measure, relapsed into French occupation, and the vigorous stocks who for nearly a century made them blossom, have in great part disappeared into that insatiable drainer of older provinces, the Canadian North-West.

In 1791, John Graves Simcoe came out as the first Governor of Upper or British Canada. To be precise, he was Lieutenant-Governor under Carleton, now Lord Dorchester, and Viceroy at Quebec of all the British provinces. He had sat in Parliament for a time, and as a successful leader of colonial troops was freely consulted at Headquarters. With him was now sent out a newly raised regiment, named from his old corps, which had long ago exchanged their swords for Nova Scotian ploughshares. With his soldiers and three of his Councillors, he set out from Quebec for the West in June, 1792. After a brief sojourn in the Kingston Settlements, he sailed up Lake Ontario for Niagara, where, amid the clearings on the British bank of the river, at the point where it flows into the lake, stood the capital, the little town of Newark. Here, from a Government House extemporised out of a modest Freemasons' hall, Simcoe met the first elected members of the Province that twenty years later was to hold the door of Canada against the American invader.

The new Governor showed a pretty imagination, and a quite prophetic sense of the importance of the occasion when he met his legislative Council of ten, and elected Assembly of sixteen in the improvised Government House at Niagara. They arrived in boats and canoes from the various parts of the forest-clad province that their, as yet, limited endeavours were opening to the daylight. Simcoe's own corps, in their green uniforms, were marshalled about him, a red-coated company from the fifth regiment at Kingston added colour to the scene, and with their fifes and drums drowned the faint roar of the great Falls but a few miles distant. The cannon thundered from the neighbouring fort which looked across the river to the American shore, and from the little ships which protected British interests on the great international Lake. Simcoe made an eloquent speech, congratulating the members on their representative form of Government, and the vast area of Crown lands granted to them by the King in return for the energy and hazard with which the inhabitants, in their former homes, had defended his rights in the American war. The natural advantages, he declared, of Upper Canada were inferior to none on their side of the Atlantic. The spot on which Simcoe stood with his handful of loyalist pioneers was then but a belt of clearings on the hilly bank of the river, stretching away towards the distant column of mist that marked the mighty cataract.

In the rear of this the primæval forest stretched interminably northwards, covering many hundred square miles of the finest land in the best Province of Canada. If Simcoe could have seen it, as it was a century later and yet more as it is to-day—studded as thickly with flourishing farms and country homes as any English shire, and as closely knit together by good roads and railroads, he would realise how amply his pioneering enthusiasms and his forecasts had been fulfilled. His Welsh wife, a Gwillim, was as ardent as her husband in this admirable cause. A township on the noble lake called after Simcoe commemorates her own maiden name, while three more adjoining it have immortalised her three pet dogs, a fact of which I greatly doubt whether the horny-handed farmers and axemen who occupy them are the least aware.

The future capital of the province was still in dispute. Simcoe urged the site of what became, by his naming, the town of London, deep in the woods and far to the west of Niagara. But Dorchester, of longer experience and cooler judgment, decided on the site then barely occupied, where Toronto subsequently arose, though at first named York, after the loyalist fashion of commemorating every member of the reigning family. There was still a big gap along the 120-mile length of Lake Ontario between the Kingston townships to the east and the Niagara settlements on the west. The site of York, with its fine natural harbour, lay forlorn for a time, about midway in this unsettled stretch. Counties, including townships, were now surveyed along the whole water front, duplicating the names of several English and Scottish shires. The British settlers of all times had an incurable reluctance to perpetuate the mellifluous Indian names, but at least the Canadians did not saddle on their descendants the egregious place-names that their American neighbours imposed on theirs. The rude pioneers of Canada had generally some official or equivalent check on their primitive instincts for such incongruous place-names as may be culled at random from the rich nomenclature of the neighbouring frontier of western New York.

Simcoe was always hankering after a colonial aristocracy, and endowed every county with a Lieutenant, hoping thereby to assist his plans. But a territorial gentry was a hopeless dream in Upper Canada. Nature herself was against it. Simcoe, however, need not have worried. In less than a generation the leaders among the U.E. Loyalists were to come out of the woods and develop an oligarchy as close as any that had ever dominated Virginia or Maryland. The "Family Compact" that had the province under its heel in the next century would have done Simcoe's heart good had he lived to see it. Yet, despite some Tory tendencies not adaptable to a new country, the new Governor was the very man for the moment. His social theories for the future mattered nothing at this primitive stage. The country wanted development and population, and Simcoe strove hard at the first and effected the second. He found about twelve thousand settlers in Upper Canada and left it five years later with about thrice that number. In 1794-5, under a canvas house he had purchased from the celebrated Captain Cook, with his beloved soldiers, whom he liked best to see making roads and felling trees, Simcoe took a personal hand in the founding of York (Toronto). Here he cleared woods, erected sawmills, and a few log houses, and traced the line of future streets amid the raw stumps.

Through summer, autumn and winter, travelling himself great distances on foot and by canoe, up "Yonge Street" of still famous use and name, to Lake Simcoe, and thence across to survey potential harbours on the Georgian Bay, the Governor rested little. Neither mosquitoes, nor black flies, neither snow, hail, rain, heat nor tedious portages nor laborious cruises with oar or paddle upon stormy lakes seem to have mattered much to this energetic soul, nor did his own health, which was thereby permanently injured. There is always a flavour of romance about Simcoe's rule in Upper Canada, with the meeting of the first little parliament in the backwoods station of Niagara, the long uncertainty whether a small military out post on the shaggy banks of what Simcoe characteristically named the Thames, or a couple of shanties on Toronto Bay, were to be the capital of the new country; with his own journeys through wild woods, now replaced by familiar domestic landscape, or along stormy, solitary bays now lined with wharfs and houses and crowded with shipping. Scenes change rapidly and history marches apace in a new country, and provides abundant food for retrospective dreaming. It is not the number of years in the century that gives the old log-house its pathos within sound of the motor-car, but the prodigious changes it has seen, the making of whole nations, the wiping out of others. There is something about the old associations of Upper Canada, or Ontario as it is now called, that with its memories of eighteenth-century devotion to the Crown and the struggles of its loyalist founders with intolerable hardship that assorts well with the name of Simcoe. His devotion to his mission, his single-mindedness and honesty, even his militant Georgian prejudices, will always present him as an altogether felicitous figure to this earliest chapter of Anglo-Canadian history, an epoch that, let us hope, will always be duly treasured in memory by the descendants of the men and women who made it.

Simcoe had importuned the Home Government to promote emigration, but was curtly told that to send people out of the country was the very last thing that was wanted. So he turned his eyes southward over the U.S. boundary line, inviting by proclamation all and sundry to come in and take up the good lands he would allot to them. The loyalists objected to this and made general complaints. So far, every immigrant from over the border had been the subject of fairly rigid enquiry. By now there were probably some 20,000 original and later loyalists with their offspring in the country. The doubtful subjects were still in a negligible minority. But this notion of flooding the country with the detested people from whom they had so recently shaken themselves free was altogether too much for these U.E. loyalists. The Republican principles they abhorred were quite certain to be insidiously introduced. Another war with America, too, was always in the air. For the English debt question had never been settled according to treaty. So the British Government had retained occupation of the frontier posts as security. Moreover, the French Revolution was now at its height, and though the Quebec ultramontane church, which held its people tolerably firm in its grip, detested the whole business, French Republican envoys were not wanting to stir up the old hostility. Flattered by the notion that the downtrodden French were following their example, the Americans ignored, or possibly refused to credit, the horrors by which the former were achieving liberty. That England, who knew all about it, was arming in hostility to the monster was another grievance.

Simcoe, however, threw his new surveys open to all and sundry, welcomed the newcomers, sometimes actually in person, and congratulated them in genial fashion on "preferring good King George's government to the Republic." Several thousand from the New England States and even from New York and northern Pennsylvania responded, coming in sometimes with their wagons and farm stock. They were, of course, admirable, regarded as settlers. Many, too, were honestly disheartened at the confusion that seemed to be abroad in their own country. The convention of 1787, to be ratified with infinite labour and opposition into the Constitution of 1791, though so welcomed by the more intelligent well-wishers of their country, spread no little alarm through the still rather discontented States. Men flinched from the possibility of their old State government being overridden by a Federal administration armed with the powers their fancy dreaded. They might as well, some declared, have King George and the British Parliament back again as tax-collectors from such a mixed-up and irresponsible government invading their homes. What, after all, had been a tea tax? They seemed to have jumped out of the frying-pan into the fire. And now they had a chance to make another jump into a country where there was better land than in their own to be had for the asking, and neither taxes nor hostile Indians, and as much freedom as they had enjoyed in the good old peaceful Colonial days, which to the ordinary farmer had seemed complete till the Revolution had got at him and brought the country, as thousands now honestly thought, to a pretty pass.

Most of these people had the makings of contented Canadian folk. Furthermore, they would be too busy in the woods for years to worry much about politics and their children would grow up, no doubt, to be thankful for the move. There was another motive, too, in favour of Canada with the generation of Americans that would naturally be now moving west. The American North-West, represented by the country south and south-west of Lake Erie, was unsafe. It was still the scene, or the possible scene, of bloody wars between the Indians who had been driven from their lands and U.S. troops. To step across the line or over Lake Ontario into equally good land and a quiet life in Southern Quebec or Upper Canada was, nationality apart, so obviously the better thing to do.

That the loyalists protested was natural enough. In case of war, these American immigrants would be an ever-present danger. The Canadians would have foes behind as well as in their front. If war had come quickly there might have been much in this argument, but it did not come for twenty years. A certain small number then, it is true, did prove false to their oath. But the mass, the potentially disloyal generation, had grown up in their Canadian homes and by no means regarded themselves as the slaves and victims of tyranny depicted in the absurd American proclamations of 1812. They came, moreover, in such numbers, and were usually so expert in backwoods science that they materially hastened the opening and development of the country, thereby increasing the value of loyalist property and the amenities of life.

Simcoe, delighted with his success, worked unceasingly at his task, and expended his superfluous energies in writing voluminous reports to the Home Government, who being now at war again with France apparently scanned these documents with some boredom. Dorchester, his superior, did not wholly approve of Simcoe's enthusiasm for American settlers. He was perturbed, too, by signs of danger among the French Canadians. He knew that in case of war at the moment Canada was quite impotent to resist. He remembered the shock he had had in 1775 when the French-Canadian Militia had left him stranded at Montreal with the enemy at its gates and he had made his midnight dash alone in a canoe down the St. Lawrence to reach Quebec and prepare it for the attack by Montgomery and Benedict Arnold. Officially, Simcoe was certainly rather tactless, and in his zeal a little petulant with his superiors, occasionally corresponding direct and behind Dorchester's back with the Home Government. In 1796, when the veteran Viceroy went home, after, in all, twenty years of invaluable service to Canada and his country, the friction between the two gave a note of bitterness to his departure. The American Government had been bombarding Dorchester for retaining the western posts, but as nothing had been done in the matter of the English debts, some Americans saw the equity of the situation, though they could hardly proclaim it abroad. Dorchester was accused of stirring up the Indians then at war with the United States. He was not a madman, he wrote home in his defence, to provoke a war that must be disastrous to Canada. And war, with the activities of French and American propagandists among the ignorant masses of French-Canadians, seemed through these years always imminent. Dorchester had just 2,500 regulars with which to confront it. The French-Canadian militia, long unaccustomed and opposed to military service, and corrupted by hostile emissaries, might as in 1775, he thought, prove useless, while their loyal upper class was numerically negligible.

Jay's Treaty, however, in 1795, to the rage of the Jeffersonians and to the satisfaction of the Federalists and the British Government, saved the situation, for the time at any rate. In the following year, Simcoe left for home in ill-health on sick leave and, as it happened, never to return. While but half recovered, he was sent to quell a negro insurrection in the West Indies. Invalided again to his home in Devonshire, he was later on appointed to the chief command in India. While awaiting the return of his predecessor, Lake, he went to Lisbon on a diplomatic errand, and there contracted a fatal illness of which he died soon after reaching home. A monument in Exeter Cathedral, erected by the County of Devon, commemorates a man "in whose life and character the virtues of the hero, patriot and Christian were so eminently conspicuous that it may be justly said he served his King and his country with a zeal exceeded only by his piety towards his God." The eulogy is, I think, in this case really justified.

Fortunately, Washington, Hamilton and the Federalists were all for peace. They were supported by the Northern

States, chiefly interested in shipping and overseas trade, while the Jeffersonians of the middle and Southern States, raving against England, and half-crazy French Envoys, dancing round Liberty poles with Southern slave-owners to the edification, one may fancy, of their own negroes, kept at bay. Washington's view of the Indian question and western posts, written to a friend at this time, is interesting. "Land jobbing, intermeddling of States and disorderly conduct of the borderers, who are indifferent to the killing of an Indian, are in my opinion the great obstacles in the way of settlement. Yet these very men who shoot Indians at sight and plunder them or their lands, are the first to cry out for aid when war, brought on by their own violation of the Treaties of the United States, was upon them." Jay's Treaty, with the temporary passing of the war cloud overhanging Canada, and the subsequent departure of Simcoe in 1796, is as convenient a moment as any for leaving the two Canadas and turning to some further account of the Eastern wing of the loyalist immigration in the Maritime Provinces. We may note as regards the condition of the two Canadas, now midway between the U.E. loyalist influx and the war of 1812, which opened a new era of immigration from the Mother Country, that the population of the Upper Province was quoted approximately as about 30,000, the U.E. loyalist portion being in numbers and undoubtedly in influence the greater. It had been, moreover, recently increased and strengthened by dissatisfied groups from Nova Scotia. Simcoe had caused a list to be made under oath of all those who, having suffered for their allegiance to the Crown, were entitled to special distinctions, their sons and daughters to land grants, and so forth. This was known as the U.E. list, and definitely fixes the right of succeeding generations to claim descent from an order that Simcoe and Dorchester both wished to make hereditary. But this, as we have seen, was not considered advisable. In Lower Canada there were about 150,000 French, including 20,000 in the two cities of Quebec and Montreal, together with the smaller town of Three Rivers, and 10,000 to 15,000 British, mainly from the U.S., but still coming in and including, probably, about 3,000 merchants and trade workers of older settlement in the cities. Statistical precision is neither possible nor necessary. But this will approximately represent the then strength of Canada to all such readers as can translate figures into realities.

CHAPTER VII

THE LOYALISTS IN THE MARITIME PROVINCES

WE have already landed the 35,000 U.E. loyalists in Nova Scotia and have given some details of their first efforts and hardships. The newcomers spread gradually to all the more eligible portions of this peninsular province, which runs N.W. into the Atlantic for over 200 miles (including its extremity, Cape Breton Island), with an average breadth of about 50 miles. On the west, the Bay of Fundy pushes a long arm between the seagirt province and the Continent, ending in the narrow connecting isthmus of Canso. It was mainly the coasts of Nova Scotia, the more rugged and exposed one facing the Atlantic, and the more sheltered and more generally fertile strip on the Bay of Fundy, that attracted these earlier settlers. It would be futile to particularize the drifts of their settlement in a country almost certainly unfamiliar to most readers. To deal with the hardships which most of the pioneers suffered would be to go over ground already sufficiently, if briefly, covered in our account of Upper Canada. Conditions were not quite so bad here but for most of the exiles they were bad enough. That the preparations were in general miserably behindhand and inadequate, supplies short and surveys incomplete, was hardly surprising, seeing the weakness in resources of the government of such an infant province. New England for the time was closed. Europe for such a purpose was too remote. Still, the winters were not so severe as in Upper Canada. The harbours in the Bay of Fundy, and elsewhere, were never quite blocked. Such supplies as might come along could reach the settlers easily by water. Over two thousand Acadians, the remnant of those expelled thirty years earlier, and the subject of Longfellow's famous, but unhistorical poem, "Evangeline," lived in their old haunts, the dyked-out marshlands at the head of the Bay of Fundy.

There was much discontent, and not without cause, among the new settlers. There was also much courage and even optimism. "We knelt down on landing," says an Anglican clergyman from New England, "my wife and I and the two boys, and kissed the dear ground and thanked God that the flag of England floated there, and resolved that we would work with the rest to become again prosperous and happy."

The most careful computation places the total number of loyalists to arrive in these maritime provinces at that already given. Of these perhaps the 10,000 souls, civil and military, who arrived during the year 1782 on the western shores of the Bay of Fundy and at the mouth of the St. John river, may be specially mentioned, as they created the Province of New Brunswick. Some had come there previously and were already settled both on the bay and up the St. John. A dozen loyalist regiments had sent two agents from New York to report on the country. Colonel Edward Winslow, Muster-Master of the Colonial forces, was one of them. He has left an interesting correspondence on the subject and the settlement, published during that century. It appears that Governor Parr, who showed such deplorable judgment in regard to the ill-chosen and ill-fated town of Shelburne, was again at fault in discouraging settlement on the St. John River. Winslow accuses him of doing so from a consciousness of the backward state of his preparations there.

Parr's government had indeed prepared a pretty confusion and much dispute between soldiers and civilians. A detachment of the King's American Dragoons, for example, very early arrivals, had settled on the present harbour of St. John, and made considerable improvements under Government surveyors. They were now given notice to quit, move up the river to unsurveyed tracts, and hand over their land to newly arriving civilians. Protests were useless and general indignation was caused among the immigrants. Houses had been promised and none had been erected. "I saw," writes Winslow, "all these provincial regiments, which we have so frequently mustered, landing in this inhospitable climate in the month of October without shelter and without knowing where to find a place to reside. The chagrin of the officers was not to me so truly affecting as the poignant distress of the men. These respectable sergeants of Robinson's, Ludlow's, Cruger's, Fanning's, etc., once hospitable yeomen, were addressing me in language which almost murdered me as I heard it. 'Sir, we have served all the war. Your Honour knows how faithfully. We were promised land. We expected you had obtained it for us. We like the country—only let us have a spot of our own and give us such regulations as will hinder bad men from injuring us.'"

The earlier settlers in Nova Scotia were provided with materials to build their own homes. But all subsequent ones who were sent to surveys, or projected surveys up the river St. John, had to build without assistance or spend the winter in tents till they could do so. Their privations were extreme. Many of the weaker members, women and children particularly, died of exposure and lack of sustenance. For the transport of supplies failed here, as it did in Upper Canada, but with far less excuse. The great number of immigrants dumped on to the Nova Scotian littoral far exceeded the expectations of the Halifax Government, and it could not keep pace with the demand. Nothing like enough grants had been surveyed, but the area already allotted to in-comers was so large as to cramp the grants for later arrivals, which naturally provoked much discontent. Governor Parr was certainly not a popular person on the west shore, or, to be accurate, the north-west shore of the Bay of Fundy. He sent a deputy, an Irishman, to try and smooth matters down, but he only made things worse. The Governor had called the settlement Parrtown, impelled thereto, he himself declared, by the vanity of his wife. The occupants changed it to St. John, represented to-day by a populous city and splendid harbour. Parr was not a bad sort of man, but merely unequal to the heavy calls on his administrative talents.

The old Halifax people too had no love for the new

arrivals, who had swamped their province with new blood, including not a few likely candidates for office and honours. This coolness brought about a desire on the part of the St. John settlers to cut off their country from Nova Scotia and make it a new province, for already they saw it carrying in the future a large population. Geography, too, was in favour of the scheme, and with the consent of the British Government, the Province of New Brunswick, being all on the mainland and only united to Nova Scotia by a narrow neck, was formally established. It narrowly escaped being called "New Ireland," which, as a Canadian province, would have proved singularly infelicitous for reasons we need not labour.

Colonel Carleton, Lord Dorchester's brother, was the first Governor, and even when he arrived, in the autumn of 1784, the loyalists, in an address of welcome, described themselves as the victims of ill-treatment. But their discontents and hardships gave way, for in the following year St. John was incorporated as a city, though the settlers were once more agitated by Carleton's fixing the capital of the new Province at St. Anne's, about a hundred miles up the river, and renaming it Frederickton, in honour of the Duke of York. This made some amends to the old loyalist regiments settled there for the cavalier treatment that had ejected them so unceremoniously from their first quarters at the river mouth. But, as a matter of fact, the whole valley of the St. John proved most favourable for colonizing. Its "interval" lands, as they came to be called, otherwise its rich bottom lands, ever gathering fresh fertility from recurrent, but not too destructive, floods, made a fine distributing centre for the peopling of a province. The administration was established in Frederickton in the autumn of 1785, with representative government on the model of Nova Scotia, and Governor Carleton, with the family aptitude for handling Colonials, presided over it successfully for thirty years. Numbers of settlers shifted their homes from one district to another; many went to Upper Canada on reports of its extreme fertility, many too who failed to make good returned to their native State, when the old bitterness was relaxing. A few who could went back to England, but enough remained to push the province steadily along the path of prosperity. The half-pay of the officers, the compensation money paid all through the later seventeen-eighties by Commissioners sitting at Halifax and St. John, greatly helped to smooth the path of the pioneers to simple comfort, and by degrees, among the better sort, to the old luxuries. This, of course, applies to both provinces, but more especially New Brunswick remained, and still remains, pre-eminently the *terrain* of the U.E. Loyalist. In Nova Scotia, the old element, military and civilian, seems to have been rather more submerged by later waves of immigration than in the younger Province, which was less accessible, or at any rate less favoured by European immigrants.

Several large parties of Highlanders, shifted by the gradual effect of landlordism upon the old clan system, were deported to Nova Scotia, with a strong bias for Cape Breton. Their industry from the first was notable in a people whose whole past was a negation of it. The Highlander who at home had seldom seen a tree, and as a clansman had mostly watched his womenfolk sow and reap his miserable crops, became an accomplished axe-man when confronted with Nova Scotian forests and an industrious tiller of the soil he had cleared. When two or three generations had passed away, Highland names, owing to the Nova Scotian and Canadian importations, were to figure largely as those of captains of industry and finance. It was as if through centuries of semi-barbaric life qualities uncalled for and untapped had lain dormant, having been brought over from some previous existence of which history has no record. In Cape Breton, Gaelic is still spoken by the old people. Other immigrants, too, from Great Britain, besides some Swiss and German groups, in due course, joined the Loyalists in all parts of Nova Scotia.

It was not, however, till after the war of 1812 that here, as elsewhere, a systematic movement set in from the Mother Country. U.E. Loyalist blood has been so mingled with later incoming streams as to disconcert all but keen genealogists, of which there are, unfortunately, very few on the spot. Nova Scotian chroniclers have been rather chary of family records, and have contributed almost nothing beyond occasional fugitive papers valuable enough but buried in the pages of local Societies' collections. I am free to say, however, that I have rarely met a " Blue-nose " who has not claimed to be of U.E. Loyalist stock! The anxiety to claim this ancestry is a sufficient proof of the esteem in which it is still held.

These people had lumbering, shipbuilding, trade, fishing and farming for the exercise of their energies. As the compensation money dropped in, development in many directions moved apace. It must not be supposed that there was no grumbling about the delay in payment and kindred matters. Complaints sometimes were loud and long, and harrowing pictures, no doubt true enough, were drawn of the suffering of those in the woods with nothing to eat but " rotten pork and mouldy flour." Most of the three million pounds had been distributed by 1790, while the half-pay had actually been granted to many civilians with the nominal title of " officers."

The Maritime Provinces were spared the after-dangers and trials and bloodshed of the Canadas. Protected by the British fleet, they were practically safe from attack by the United States. To them, alone of all countries concerned in it, war came, not as a curse but as a positive advantage. What with shipbuilding, privateering, victualling and refitting fleets, together with ocean trade under the British flag, it lifted them into a position to absorb with profit the rush of immigration from Europe that followed the close of the American and Napoleonic wars. Liable to sea fogs, less generally fertile, and more generally broken than Upper Canada, these provinces, including the adjacent island of St. John (Prince Edward), had, nevertheless, in their fertile districts far more than sufficient for any present demand, besides the future asset of great deposits of coal and iron on the north shore of Nova Scotia. A practically boundless supply of timber, including masts for the British Navy, had ready access to the Atlantic trade. Finally, these people were nearer than any to the great fishing-grounds around their own and the Newfoundland coasts. The " Blue-noses " became traditionally amphibious, since such a large proportion of them could sail a boat, guide a plough or fell a tree with equal skill. They were at home, in short, both on land or afloat.

Yet, after the first half-century from 1782, during which all the provinces shared about equally in rapid development, these Eastern provinces, with all their advantages, began to fall behind Upper Canada in the race. In a century they had practically dropped out of it, and with less than a million of population between them settled down into the almost stationary condition of an old country, sending its surplus population into new fields of enterprise, and receiving little fresh blood from outside. In the euphonious American phrase, the Provinces were "side-tracked," and they have been asking themselves why ever since. It does seem hard, on the face of it, that Ontario, with its partner the great North-West, should have gone "bounding along from million to million," while Nova Scotia and New Brunswick stand comparatively still. It is the contrast, of course, that irks them. Denmark is an old and stationary country, but is probably quite as happy as Manitoba and individually as intelligent, possibly more so. The Nova Scotians are quite as happy and as reasonably comfortable as the Ontarians on very similar hundred-acre farms of old occupation, with snug homesteads embowered in prolific orchards. But, *cæteris paribus*, the land is only worth about half of its Ontarian equivalent, merely because it is in Nova Scotia and not in Ontario!

The ordinary Nova Scotian farmer probably thinks, possibly knows, little of this. But the Provinces in an articulate sense do, and I merely give it as a fair example of the general situation. The Dane or the Norman does not worry because there is no unearned increment probable, to double the freehold value of his land. But the atmosphere of North America breeds an impatience of stationary values and conditions, and the maritime provinces are sore because Halifax, once so important, is hopelessly outdistanced by Montreal and Toronto, while the country towns persistently remain of negligible size. The chief cause of this stagnation is that European immigration has given these provinces the go-by for generations. Why should an immigrant, with a whole continent to choose from, select a province that offers certainly no more advantage than any other, and no apparent prospect, save in special spots and special directions, of sharing in the rise of a progressive country? There are, it is true, great spaces of uncleared land of perhaps secondary fertility, but since the prairies were reached the labour of hewing farms out of forests, save under special conditions, has been quite out of favour. But these old Provinces, so proud of their U.E. Loyalist origin, have nothing to complain of save that ever rankling comparison with "boom" countries. Perhaps the individual does not feel this comparison so much as his more eloquent representatives. The farmers, the country folk, of these provinces are, as is perhaps fitting, intensely conservative and old-fashioned, though of democratic manners and usually more simple and unsophisticated as regards the outer world than their fellows in Ontario and the West. But if these communities do feel, in the American sense, a bit "side-tracked" this does not affect their considerable local industries, their mining and shipping and trade. Always, too, their educated class has produced an exceptional number of men who, in the larger sphere of Dominion politics, law and letters, have made their mark. This may surely be credited to the amount of good Loyalist blood that settled in the Maritime Provinces.

But if European settlers of to-day overlook these provinces, American tourists and sportsmen love them. Lastly, Halifax, though not now so commercially flourishing as St. John, and for long practically at a standstill, has always been a city to itself in all the Canadas. Its long association with ships and regiments has imparted to its politer classes a traditionally English atmosphere and English speech on which they greatly pride themselves. The speech of the rural folk, however, as in New Brunswick, is of that provincial type brought over from the American colonies by the loyalists and imparted to incoming generations as inevitably happens. That they are out of the main stream which flows up the St. Lawrence to Canada, with its big cities and populous towns, and thence to the great North-West, gives the Maritime

Provinces a touch of romance. The American imagination particularly, always susceptible to any flavour of the past on its own continent, sees something idyllic in these long-occupied homesteads, whether amid the gleam of orchards and meadowy vales, or by the broad lakes or rushing salmon and trout streams of these Acadian backwaters. Here, amid the descendants of those old Colonial loyalists whom their ancestors drove into exile, and of those much older Acadians whom they had scattered all over the continent, the modern New Englander or New Yorker makes high holiday, with small thought on one side or the other of the bitter hatred that once parted them. But I must now put back the clock and return to those Upper Canadians who, if fewer in number than their neighbours, were the heralds of more vital events and the unconscious agents in a struggle for Empire in which the Eastern Provinces were little more than spectators at home and profitable rovers on the high seas.

The story of Upper Canada, and indeed of both Canadas, from the departure of Dorchester and Simcoe in 1796 for the next ten years, was one of steady progress and development. Sufficient accommodation for the Governor and the small group of legislators that met him in session at the embryo capital of Toronto was erected. Throughout this decade, Upper Canada was mostly administered by deputies of non-resident Lieutenant-Governors. But its interest mainly centred in the settlement of immigrants and in land allotment and land speculation. The leaders among the Loyalists had now emerged from the woods and by Crown appointments to offices, by fortunate land speculations or sheer ability, were steadily acquiring chief powers in the province. They controlled the Executive and the legislative council, and usually the Governor himself, and were already laying the foundations of that powerful clique known as the Family Compact, a group of families which later on practically ruled the country for two generations in the teeth of democracy and its elective assembly. In a sense they came to represent the Crown in its extreme and loyalist sense. They did not profess to be democrats. They had seen enough of democracy, and in truth the condition of their Republican neighbours at this moment was the reverse of encouraging to imitators. The little oligarchy was not yet consolidated. But they looked with suspicion on the recent American immigration, and for the present were supported by the rank and file of their own people still for the most part too busy fighting the forests and establishing their homes, to be much interested in public affairs.

All international troubles and anxieties fell, of course, on the Governor-General at Quebec and his council. The machinations of the French Republican envoys to Washington and their spies and agents in Canada, had brought about a conspiracy which occasioned the arrest of some forty French-Canadians. This plot, however, was directly inspired by the French with a futile hope of recovering Canada, a project that the Americans, with all their tenderness towards France and indifference to her insults, would never have tolerated. But Republican France understood Republican America as little as the latter understood France. Adet, the third French envoy to flatter and delude certain sections of the people into Jacobin demonstrations utterly repulsive to Washington and those in his confidence, had now addressed the even simpler French-Canadians. France, he assured these guileless folk, having now conquered Austria, Italy and Spain, would soon serve England in the same way. He had arranged that himself for a certainty. Lafayette, too, had flirted with the French-Canadians till Washington had snubbed him. Vermont, though an acceding State to the Constitution of 1791, was involved in this plot to bring France back and, led by Ethan Allen, highly esteemed among American patriots, was prepared to attach herself to that power in the event of success. Vermont flirted with both the French and British Governments for years, being actuated entirely by motives of trade, for which her natural route ran northwards to the St. Lawrence. During that troublous decade, when the several States, often most reluctantly, were being brought by the genius of Alexander Hamilton, with the steady support of Washington, into the Constitution of 1791, Vermont was still a Territory under the jurisdiction of New Hampshire. This was disputed by New York, with Massachusetts also putting in a claim, Vermont in the meantime pushing forward its own interests. Troops from each State went to the frontier (1735), and civil war was only averted by the interference of Washington. Vermont was inclined to the course which profited it most. But after some years of curious intrigue between local leaders and rather unwilling British officials [see Canadian archives], she followed her natural destiny as a State in the American Union.

The public lands in Upper Canada, vast forest tracts already within sight of a financial value, were all in the hands of the Crown, otherwise of its officials and their friends. Every member of the Legislative Council was allotted 6,000 acres as a gratuity, but the areas dealt with in a fashion tolerated at the time all over the world, but which a later day would have condemned, were immense. It was possible for those with influence to get large grants of Crown lands free of taxation, and saleable later to speculators or settlers. At the worst, large blocks could be bought at a dollar an acre, and 320,000 acres in Upper Canada had been already granted to legitimate settlers. By these means and by superior talents a little oligarchy arose, establishing itself comfortably as a governing power in the State, securing at once the plums of office and a wide selection in land grants. The dominant clique in many American colonies had done this in the old days as a matter of course.

In the meantime, Genet and others of his kind, who had come out to embroil the United States with Great Britain, and to seduce Canada, only succeeded in further alienating the Northern States and helping to secure the defeat of his patron, Jefferson, at the Presidential election of 1796. There were now only about 2,000 regular troops in the Canadas. In Upper Canada the Queen's Rangers, 600 strong, with the Militia, represented the fighting force. Prescott, as Governor-General, was seated at Quebec, and his chief domestic troubles were land-grabbing in high places, and the continuous flow of American settlers into those parts of the Lower Province south of the French occupation, always so far ahead of the surveyors and map-makers as to create delays and much consequent confusion in the allocation of lands and title-deeds. The loyalists of Upper Canada viewed all this with profound distrust, and if their leaders were somewhat high-handed in fastening their grip on their own province, it is idle to blame them, as some writers do, because their methods did not accord with twentieth-century democratic standards, which, if put in practice then, would probably have lost Canada to the Empire. Prescott, however, maintained that these immigrants would make loyal and contented settlers. His own Council at Quebec, apart from the opposition of the French Catholic Church to this incursion of heretics, did not think so, and there was much friction. He himself considered that they would form an antidote to the French, the French Catholics and the New England Puritans being hereditary and irreconcilable enemies. They formed, at any rate, a strong opposition minority in the Quebec legislature, and represented the British interests in material progress, as opposed to the debating futilities of the French-Canadian in his first exuberance of political freedom.

At the beginning of the century, during Prescott's long Governorship, there were about 160,000 souls in the French Province, a sixth of whom approximately were British. A majority of these last were American farmers from the Border States with a proportion of 'old Loyalists'. A strong minority, however, were, by this time, helping to form the new bourgeois class, British and French, that was rapidly arising in Montreal and Quebec, and was to count for much in Canadian life. About seventy *seigneurs* had remained after the French evacuation in 1761-3. Half of these, writes Prescott, had sunk into the material condition of their own peasants. By no means all of them had been originally of the officer or *petite noblesse* class, for many *seigneuries* under the old French régime had been purchased by traders and *roturiers*. All save a handful, from special causes, were quite poor. Their tenantry or *censitaires* paid the fixed quit-rent their forebears had paid for the virgin forest lands which they had opened out into farms, a penny or two an English acre. A *seigneury* of several square miles, therefore, did not imply a lordly rent-roll! But there were also manorial rights and fines on the same scale. The *seigneur* was a vassal of the Crown, nominally "on good behaviour." He could not sell his land, but his tenants could sell their farms, subject, of course, to the rents and dues of their lord.

Several *seigneuries* had lapsed, or appertained to corporate ownership, colleges, monasteries, Jesuit bodies, and the like. All this old landed system, somewhat modified, had been maintained by the Quebec Act of 1774, mainly in deference to the wishes of the French, just as the Catholic Church had been left to them as established, to the great indignation of the revolting colonies. It will be readily seen how impossible it was for British immigrants of any kind to settle in that portion of Lower Canada which was virtually locked up in the seigneurial system, so the British from all sources were confined to those districts outside its boundaries, and now available for grants in free and common soccage. To the British residing as merchants in Montreal and Quebec, and naturally anxious to acquire landed property in the neighbourhood, the seigneurial system was a hindrance and a grievance, just as the power left to the Roman Church was in their eyes a still greater one. But the rural British of the Lower Province, forming a compact body between the French area and the American frontier, felt none of these things, unless it were their impotence in the Legislature to push through measures they considered vital to the development of the country. As for their religious needs, those were practically left in their own hands, subject to the Governor and to a certain recognition of the Church of England, then automatically the nominal faith wherever the British flag flew. For apart from some provision by the Church for its members, all the various creeds brought across the frontier were free to look after their own souls.

Though the English and French in the country were thus absolutely apart, those in the two, now growing, cities were of course face to face. It is not in order here to relate how friction arose and ill-feeling grew up between them, whereas in the years following the conquest there had been comparative harmony. Faults of tact, judgment and demeanour on both sides were partly to blame, temperament, no doubt, still more so, and political troubles already alluded to, most of all. At any rate, acerbities waxed so sharp that in this decade, drifting towards a war which threatened both equally, the upper sort of either nation would scarcely speak to one another in the street. A small aristocracy of the seigneurial class such as had means and education enough to support social amenities were on one side, British officials and officers with their wives on the other. Then there was the British mercantile class, not qualified in the estimate of these others for social recognition, but full of resentment and also nourishing a rooted dislike to the Quebec Act of 1774 and its concessions to the French. A three-cornered business, one may say, and too paltry for notice here.

Yet these racial and social asperities, at the moment sharper than they had ever been, or were again to be, might well prove of vital moment to the Empire when the blow that was coming fell, and the French of Quebec held the safety of Canada in their hands. In the former attack of the American rebels on Canada in 1775, the French, as a body, and without provocation, went wrong, and the country was only saved by Dorchester. In the crisis of 1812 the situation was far more formidable, the French attitude more important, their spirit far less cordial and their nerves on edge; but they went right! It is often said in after-dinner speeches and the like, with a curious disregard of the simplest facts of history, that the French twice saved Canada for the Empire! In 1775 the territorial militia, on whom the government had largely depended for defence, refused to march. Ignorant and indifferent, they had further been exposed to an active American propaganda. On both occasions the upper class and the Church were loyal. But in 1775 they were numerically too insignificant to count against the wholesale defection of the militia. On the second occasion, as we shall see, all classes of the French proved loyal. Otherwise, beyond a doubt, they would have found themselves an American State. What would have become of their cherished language, religion and archaisms beneath the heel of the New England Puritan? As for the loyalists of Upper Canada, they would have been swallowed up in the vortex of that Republicanism which they so greatly loathed. Great offenders in the matter of fostering racial and social ill-feeling were the British officials sent out by the Colonial Office, and responsible to no one but the Department which had dispatched them. They and their wives seem to have made no effort to cultivate the best elements of the country, English or French, but held themselves aloof as a superior caste, in conjunction with the higher officers of the garrison and a very few leading French families. In fact, the Colonial Office of that day took far too much on itself in a country its officials knew nothing of, and was further encouraged by its nominees on the spot, very often newcomers equally ignorant, and by tradition complacent and self-satisfied.

Upper Canada, however, was then quite unaffected by these racial acerbities that really embittered life in Quebec and even in Montreal. The loyalists, who practically controlled the country, had, fortunately, no "French question" to grapple with, for there were no French to speak of in the province. As to the Colonial Office nominees, so far from being allowed to dictate or patronise, these importations were very soon put in their place, and either complained to the Home Government of the indifference shown to them, or took the line of least resistance and led lives of inglorious ease. Sir Francis Gore, who was Lieutenant-Governor for some years previous to the war of 1812, became the "tool of these self-constituted hereditary rulers" as a modern Canadian historian calls the little oligarchy of U.E. Loyalists who managed the province. There had in truth been little occasion for such political acerbities as had distracted the Lower Province. The widely-scattered population were too busy making a living to worry much about such things, though a few of the imported Americans had begun to make trouble. But the loyalist leaders, men generally of education and often of ability, and some of them by this time of comparative wealth, had such malcontents well in hand.

Toronto had as yet only makeshift public buildings, from which a Council of nine and their friends managed the affairs of the province and very often the Lieutenant-

Governor too! The revenue, chiefly derived from a share of the customs levied at Quebec, was not nearly enough as yet for the expenses of the Government. This gave the latter control of the situation, for though the elective assembly had nominal power over the money votes, it was hopeless to oppose a Government who had such power over the purse, as was represented by the ownership of all ungranted and unsold lands, and in the inevitable deficit on their budget had only to ask the Home Government for its liquidation!

Much the same political conditions existed in the Maritime Provinces, already developing somewhat similar oligarchies, which under the ever-menacing cloud of war was probably their safest course. That fraction of the public who cared anything for politics grumbled, but abstract theories of civic government were absurdly out of place with the fate of the country hanging in the balance. It is curious to note the manner in which many writers to-day discuss the politics of these small but historically pregnant communities, and declaim against the group of men who, generally better educated, more experienced and better endowed than the masses of their fellows, acquired power and held it with a somewhat high hand. They were in an exceptional position and they had sacrificed everything for the Crown. At a great expenditure of hardship and suffering, they had created this new colony. They had no wish to be followed into it by hordes of people from the country that had robbed them, and cast them out, and was at all times anathema to them. They can hardly be blamed when power came naturally into their hands, by virtue of their superior advantages and the colonial system of the British Government, for seeing in this great influx of American settlers a most dangerous republican element. Rightly or wrongly, Republicanism was a creed that the U.E. Loyalist element loathed. They had witnessed its workings during the post-bellum period in America, and that country, with its chaos of opinions, its debt repudiations and comparatively high taxation, its discontent breaking out here and there into riots, its Vermont intrigues and disintegrating schemes with Spaniards in the S. West, was a rather sorry advertisement of republican principles. They had witnessed, also, the loud acclaim in many States of the horrors of the French Revolution, a catyclysm which had for ever alienated the bulk of their French neighbours in Canada from their Mother Country. The detachment of the mass of French-Canadians from sympathy with their Mother Country is owing to their complete isolation since the Conquest in 1763, and still more to the antagonism felt by the Ultramontane Canadian Church towards the religious attitude of France. Lastly, the Canadian U.E. Loyalists saw their late persecutors obviously hankering after a quite immoral raid of conquest on the country they had themselves cut out with toil and suffering from the wild woods, converting it into a land of rich and fair promise. Can it be wondered at that the leaders of Upper Canada were chary of extending political rights to all and sundry, and used the machinery set up by the Crown and British Parliament, and subject to the exigencies of a young colony, to keep power in their hands? It does not matter that the American influx proved of little harm when the war cloud broke. There was every reason for men with such a past as the U.E. Loyalists to anticipate the contrary.

Successive Governors who came out found themselves pleasantly situated so long as they conformed in reason, as an easy-going man would certainly do, to the views of the socially agreeable clique that managed the country. Some officials sent out from England were severely criticised, and one at least was rejected, an unheard of piece of impudence for a colonial executive. The oligarchy were not all U.E. Loyalists, but had been reinforced by men of similar views, retired British officers and such-like. The small articulate element of the proletariat, the Americans more particularly, girded at them as "stuck-up aristocrats." For the present, at any rate, such voters as were interested did not feel their vote to be of the same importance as it had been in their native State. For the Governor and Council threw out with impunity any bill passed by the Assembly that they considered dangerous to the State. There are moments when autocrats and oligarchies are invaluable, and this was one of them, for no community of English blood had ever been in a more perilous situation than this one. That, having survived a successful war with honour and carried on for a generation afterwards under the familiar pseudonym of the Family Compact, it provoked an American-inspired revolution and led ultimately to Responsible Government, is not within our subject. It is quite certain that neither of the Canadas were ripe for Responsible Government at this critical moment.

During these years, before the war of 1812, which opened a new era for Canada, several groups of immigrants came over from the Mother Country into the Province. There was no urgent need then for such a movement, nor was anyone in favour of emigration from Great Britain during those long years of exhausting warfare. The fleet and the army and their auxiliary activities absorbed all the surplus manhood of the kingdom, over half a million men, out of a total population of fourteen millions. The balance was none too much for the task of producing the necessities of an island nation fighting for its life. But a great many Highlanders had flocked into Upper Canada. Those of the Johnsons from the Mohawk Valley, original loyalists, together with others—Grants, McLeans, Mackays, Hays and McDonnells—had settled at the eastern end of the province. There had come, too, a little later from Scotland, McGillies, Clanranalds, McDonalds, Macphersons of Badenoch and Camerons of Lochiel. It was not till 1804 that the large McDonnell movement, the whole regiment of Glengarry Fencibles with their families, arrived and settled alongside their compatriots in the county of Glengarry near Montreal. These last, and many others, were Roman Catholics. A few Catholic Irish had been introduced, while a good many recently disbanded soldiers were of that race and faith. Colonel Talbot, also an Irishman of the 24th Regiment, had broken ground on his own six thousand-acre grant near the western end of Lake Erie, to launch out a little later into one of the largest promoters of emigration, and pioneers of Canadian civilization of his or any day. Many narratives of these early movements are to be found on the back shelves of libraries—narratives in which men and women who helped to lay the foundation of now populous districts tell the tale of their early endeavours. No "travellers' tales" are these, but the records of work and hardship and hope, of humour and pathos, with peculiar fascination to some of us who may know the fields of those old strivings, as they appear to-day after a hundred and odd years.

Talbot was notoriously eccentric and was known as "Mad Dick Talbot." But mad or sane, there are said to be nearly a quarter of a million souls now living on the twenty-eight townships he acquired and opened for settlement. The anniversary of his birthday was celebrated as Founder's Day for years after the colonel himself had departed from this earthly scene, a touch of sentiment rather unusual in the somewhat hard atmosphere of Upper Canadian story. An equally picturesque and worthy figure of this period, though he left slight impress on Upper Canada, was the fifth Lord Selkirk, an able and warm-hearted young man of ample means and a fine *flair* for colonisation. Great clearances had been going on in Sutherlandshire under the economic demands of the erstwhile Highland chiefs turned landlords. Selkirk, who was not a Highland chief, took pity on the evicted tenants. He tried the experiment of taking eight hundred of the Duchess of Sutherland's outcasts to a grant of his own on Prince Edward Island, already partly colonised by the Nova Scotia loyalist group, The descendants of both now form the bulk of the 80,000 farming and fishing folk who quite thickly populate that prosperous little island.

It will not be amiss here to recall the curious grievance under which the island, a solid fragment of the old U.E. Loyalist country, with which this book is concerned, suffered for three-quarters of a century. It was in truth a scandal. Before 1783, the island had been granted to about a dozen proprietors at a quit-rent and was very sparsely occupied. At the main loyalist influx, these owners offered grants to the exiles on similar terms to those of the Government on the mainland provinces. The immigrants arrived, were allotted lands, and turned them into improved farms. They were then told that their titles were invalid, and they were evicted. Title-deeds were refused on every conceivable excuse, and when issued contained terms of ownership impossible for mere tracts of uncleared forest. The motive of these absentee proprietors of wild land was apparently to force the settlers to become tenants. The Governor himself, Colonel Fanning, owned a tract and was in the fraud, but on being threatened with exposure he recanted and issued his title-deeds promptly. Some of the proprietors, however, and their descendants after them, defied legislation of all kinds till within the memory of the present writer, when the "Prince Edward Island Land Question" was settled, and figured for the last time in the newspapers of England, where two or three generations of readers must have often had a languid curiosity as to what it was all about, and where on earth Prince Edward Island was! According to Professor Wallace, it transpired that nefarious juggling with the land records had enabled the proprietors from time to time to defeat justice in the local Courts. It need hardly be said that Lord Selkirk was not one of these egregious absentee proprietors. He purchased large tracts, too, on the Grand River, north of Lake Erie, and again at Chatham, in the western extremity of Upper Canada, offering to build a road right through the forests from one settlement to the other; but some hitch with the Government defeated his intentions. After this, he made that daring venture with his fresh colony on those remote prairies by the Red River in 1803. As a large Hudson's Bay stockholder, he brought about those dramatic and sanguinary episodes around Fort Garry, between the older company and its Montreal rival, the North-Westers, who struggled so hard to prevent Selkirk's band of farmers getting a footing there. In a sense, Lord Selkirk was the founder of the present province of Manitoba, though sixty years were to pass before the descendants of his isolated quasi-agricultural settlement on the Red River were to come within the purview of Canadian statesmen, and before the quiet efforts of the combined fur companies to belittle the farming possibilities of their vast domain were to be defeated by the Canadian Pacific Railway.

William Dickson, a councillor of Upper Canada, had

brought out a large group of farmers and labourers from his own county of Dumfriesshire, and founded the town and district of Galt, named after another and greater coloniser, the once famous Scotch novelist, now occupied by thousands of their descendants and others in the flourishing heart of the western province. Alongside of them, Pennsylvania Germans, voluntary fugitives from a State that in post-war dealings utterly belied its hitherto liberal tendencies, had founded the district which became Waterloo County, and to this day is in blood an almost homogeneous German district in the heart of a British country. A curious freak colony, too, was adventured by some French aristocrats, ruined by the Revolution. They applied for, and were granted, two townships just north-east of Toronto, which, it might interest the present occupants to know, were those of Pickering and Whitby. They were then, of course, primæval forest.

Count de Puisaye was leader of this curious company, and his French following of 150 souls were to form, not only a colony, but a militia regiment in the British-Canadian service. The scheme was devised on class lines, sound enough on the military side, but on the other fantastic in the extreme as applied to the backwoods. The party duly arrived at Quebec, two counts, two marquises, a viscomte, a dozen gentilhommes and a few ladies, with a rank and file in all amounting to forty, the remaining hundred having deserted at Plymouth! Windham, then British Minister, and Simcoe, who, as we know, had a weakness for class distinctions, were both rather taken aback with the scheme. De Puisaye wanted no association with French Canadians. They were inferior people, he considered, and moreover were not staunch enough in their loyalty. The Provincial Government, then under General Hunter, was puzzled, and no doubt amused, at the prospect of this exclusive group in the wild woods. After a brief glance at the forest primæval, however, the comparative civilization of the Niagara district was too much for the Count, and he bought a farm there. The leaders then quarrelled. A score of the others, together with the Viscomte du Chalus, settled on their grants, named after Windham, their well-wisher and supposed benefactor. But being without means, these poor, gently nurtured, ineffective pioneers came to penury, and Government had to assist them with rations. They soon, however, dispersed. De Puisaye died in poverty in England, and Colonel Quetton de St. George alone remained to perpetuate his family in British Canada.

Though of no importance, being merely a rather picturesque incident, this French venture was typical of a dozen schemes of group emigration founded on preconceived ideas, wholly alien to a new country and doomed to failure. There was, however, one great feature of these old colonial enterprises. The disappointed or disillusioned immigrant, when once planted, could not readily, as in later days, move on and follow some will-o'-the-wisp in futile search for an easier life. He had to remain where he was, long enough at least to survive the first feelings of disappointment that come more often to an Englishman than to a Scotsman or a German, and to acquire, so to speak, his "second wind." Thus he was enabled to become reconciled to the life and to "make good," as the modern phrase has it. Then, too, there were the children raised, if not born, in the new country. Compare the average of their future lot with those of the same class brought up in their native land! Yet even in those old days there was a vocal section of the British public who thought that the removal of a Highland crofter from his miserable patch and cabin caused pangs of nostalgia which more than counteracted the shift from poverty to comfort, not only of himself but of his children's children.

Strange, narrow people these! They regarded the ill-fed, ill-housed peasantry from their own comfortable and limited standpoint. They had never seen these folks and their progeny in their overseas surroundings. Very often, if it were only known, the shifting of such people from picturesque scenes in which to the spectator they form a pleasing ingredient is the real cause of offence, not the supposed hardship on the exiles themselves. When Highland peasants, as was often the case at this time, were driven into Glasgow slums at starvation weavers' wages, such sympathy was not misplaced. When the Catholic Macdonnells, for instance, were shifted, as already mentioned, from their mountains before the inexorable sheep, they were embodied in a regiment of Fencibles. Later on, they served in the Irish Rebellion of '98, and being subsequently disbanded, had no refuge but the cities, which held them in great misery of mind and body. At the instigation and under the leadership of their priest, afterwards Bishop Macdonnell, they came to Upper Canada, with their families a thousand strong, and settled, as already noted, in the county of Glengarry on the St. Lawrence, just west of Montreal, this long time a highly-developed rural area. The Macdonnells, retaining their old faith, still predominate among its occupants, and when I first knew Glengarry the old people still spoke Gaelic. In the ensuing war of 1812, these Glengarry Macdonnells like all the earlier Highland importations, proved of great military assistance.

The Church had, as yet, made small way in the Upper Province. The British of the Maritime Provinces, and of both town and country in Quebec, inspired from Halifax with its longer start, had the beginnings of a Hierarchy and an Episcopal Church, while the Presbyterians and other denominations had also organised among themselves. The Church of England was automatically the State Church of all the colonies, supported by the Church Missionary Societies at home. This often led to friction with the nonconformist bodies, but not serious enough nor permanent enough to claim any space here. Government had built a few churches in the Upper Province, while missioners from the other Protestant bodies travelled through the settlements till such time as material progress brought church building and its accompaniments in its train. The legality of marriages by other than the established clergy of England or Scotland was everywhere in those days unrecognised. But as the circumstances of Upper Canada had for years compelled an official recognition of the marriage knot as tied by local magistrates and even by Majors and Captains, it was hardly possible to revert seriously to the old restrictions on nonconformist ministers. In later times, with which we are not here concerned, there was a good deal of friction and resistance to such authority as the Church of England could legally claim, which was subsequently abandoned for all-round voluntaryism.

In the United States, the Church of England, virtually established everywhere but in New England, had been outrageously treated during and after the Revolution. The democratic element associated it, not unnaturally, with Toryism, as most loyalists were of that community. From eighty to a hundred churches were destroyed by mobs and their sacred vessels desecrated or melted down. The whole thing, it is generally conceded, was a disgrace to the Revolutionary cause. Even in Virginia, the higher classes, in a political sense, at any rate, staunch churchmen, though otherwise, according to a recent book on the subject, 'amiable deists and polite pagans,' submitted to these outrages by the common people of other creeds or no creed. They lacked the courage, or the energy, to interfere, though all classes had listened to Whitefield not long previously. For a whole generation the church of educated Virginia, such as it was, practically disappeared. The church of Washington, the Randolphs, the Madisons, the Lees, the Fairfaxes and other notable families, and probably of 150,000 humbler people who supported the Republic, had few buildings and no parsons, while half-educated Presbyterian Methodist and Baptist preachers from the back-counties in their log meeting-houses, ranted away on the happy destruction of the "church of Belial and the Scarlet Woman" (*sic*). It was an amazing interlude of some twenty years, and it is almost inconceivable that a gentry class who were so soon again to control the State should have sat down so tamely under it. But these iconoclasts, it must be remembered, were, according to the Adams and Jefferson phraseology, the 'most virtuous people on earth,' though Jefferson was himself an atheist. These little by-products of the Revolution are overlooked, probably not even realised, by most English writers on the period. They belong to the inner history of the various Colonies, which, apart from the unity of their common cause, were still divided from one another by the prejudices and traditions of a century and a half. As a last word to this digression, it may be mentioned that in South Carolina the Church of England went through the war unmolested and afterwards resumed its old position and influence without friction of any kind.

There was, of course, no such hostility to the Church in Canada, among what was probably a nonconformist majority, though certain financial calls on them to contribute to it were not often responded to. The only real troubles came with the allotment of lands to the Church, alternating with tracts destined for settlement. These blocks, held over for sale when of sufficient value, like those held by speculators, were a nuisance to actual settlers, retaining stretches of uncleared forest between occupied farms and adding greatly to their isolation. The " Church lands " question mildly agitated Upper Canada for two or three generations, till satisfactorily settled. Throughout this decade preceding the war, there was little to disturb the industrious, calm, and steady progress of Upper Canada. The constant fear of war and the doubts as to the American immigrants in their midst were the only disturbing factors in the minds of the small group of U.E. Loyalist leaders and their followers who controlled the province. A series of transient adventurers from outside came and went, who professed indignation at the placid way in which the populace allowed themselves to be controlled by a dominant group at York, as Toronto was still called. The settlers, however, were as yet much too busy and thinly scattered to worry about politics even had politics presented anything more serious than abstract questions to worry about.

Certain sharp-witted Irishmen coming into the country could not understand this devotion to clearing land, fencing and building, instead of a pleasant orgy of political agitation. Each of these gentlemen thought he could stir up the country and advertise himself profitably at the same time.

The first of these would-be rescuers of the Upper Canadians from thraldom was one Thorpe, an imported Circuit Judge. If there was some abstract justice in his conclusions, his ways were those of a demagogue and egotist, certainly not of a Judge. He got himself elected to the Lower House for the purpose of denouncing the irregularities of the Upper Chamber. They were too strong for him, however, and had him recalled as a nuisance. He had a friend and sympathiser, by name Weeks, another Irishman, who had graduated at New York as an election agent in the school of that father of corruption and intrigue, Aaron Burr, when the latter missed the Presidency through the influence of Hamilton, and shot him for it in a duel, as everyone knows. Weeks then transferred his political attentions to Upper Canada. In imitation, perhaps, of his late patron, he called out Mr. William Dickson, a member of the Council, on some slight provocation. Happily for the district of Galt, of which this gentleman, as we have seen, was the founder, the wrong man was not shot this time, while the other was killed on the spot. One Wilcockes, another minor office-holder from Ireland, was of the same faction. He started a newspaper called the *Freeman's Journal* in "the people's cause" and entered the Assembly, where his perorations so far exceeded legitimate bounds that the Government laid him by the heels in York jail. This made a martyr of him, and he was returned again by the American settlers of his district, and in the war of 1812 showed his true colours, turned traitor, and was killed. Wyatt, the Surveyor-General, was another of Castlereagh's Irish importations. Indeed, one might fancy that great man was using Canada as a dumping-ground for all his troublesome local firebrands. Wyatt's original offence, however, was of the kind that became so typical of his compatriot immigrants as to make New York to this day a byword among cities for political misgovernment. He dismissed his chief clerk, a Crown servant and U.E. Loyalist, for voting against his employer's friends. Wyatt was convicted and sent about his business, which took him back again to the "spiritual home" of his kind. Here he loudly proclaimed the people of Upper Canada to be ripe for rebellion, and thus added his contribution to the fatuous delusion which helped to plunge the Americans into their disastrous war.

Through all these pre-war years, constant efforts were made to win Canada back to that Republicanism which her makers had such good reason to detest. A third or a fourth of the English-speaking population were now from the United States, their political views an unknown quantity. As a matter of fact, most of them had none, and were content to remain as they were. Assuredly they had no intention of taking up arms in order to create in Canada the very conditions they had deliberately abandoned a few years previously. But the Government and Loyalist leaders could not know this. They are accused by latter-day democrats of taking a high hand. No doubt they did, and were surely justified in so doing. The eve of war, for Jefferson and his friends were bent on it, was no time for tolerating Republican and pro-American orators, or for quibbling about votes or abstract political questions, if, that is to say, the Empire was to retain her North American territory. At the moment, the prospects of this seemed dark indeed. Great Britain was engaged in a death-struggle with Napoleon, while in Lower Canada inter-racial relations were just then painfully strained. It was no time for Wilcockeses and Thorpes and Weekses and Wyatts, but for strong and loyal men, and in a good hour Isaac Brock had come to Canada, and subsequently in a still better hour to Upper Canada, as Lieutenant-Governor and Commander of the Forces.

CHAPTER VIII

THE WAR—1812

ISAAC BROCK came of a good old Guernsey family still prominent in the island. He had joined the 8th Regiment at fifteen years of age, and with it had seen much active service in Europe. At twenty-eight he was Lieutenant-Colonel of the 49th. In this capacity he had been ten years in Canada, and was now a Major-General, though not yet forty. He had served for a long time in the Lower Province under the Governor, General Craig, an honest, stout-hearted, old soldier, but in failing health and in truth not well suited to the complexities, racial and otherwise, of his position. He had recently been succeeded by the sociable and tactful General Prevost, who was far more conciliatory to the French than his predecessor. Sir James Craig, however, would have made a highly effective war Governor, while Prevost was to prove the very reverse. Prevost was the son of another of those faithful Swiss officers who were commissioned to the 60th Rifles. He was born in the regiment, while stationed at New York, before the Revolutionary War. He inherited wealth, together with charm of manner and person, from his mother, and spoke French like a native. He had served with distinction against the French West India Islands, won a baronetcy, and subsequently the Governorship of Nova Scotia, where, as now at Quebec, he had been extremely popular.

Brock had been Craig's right hand in such works of defence as were possible with their shortness of means. In Upper Canada, he had devoted himself to preparing the loyalists themselves for the storm that was undoubtedly soon to break upon them, and to keeping the discipline of the handful of British regulars which alone could be spared for the Province up to the highest mark. The

Militia, composed largely of the sons and grandsons of those who had fought the Americans thirty years before, with occasional veterans who had actually then served in the field, responded readily to Brock's magnetism. It is no mean tribute to his character that he had gained the affection as well as the confidence of the British Canadians generally. It was not merely because he fell on the day of victory that Brock has been so often compared to Wolfe, but also because he had many of the latter's qualities, especially his combination of studious habits with high practical efficiency. The few letters his biographers have printed rather suggest those of Wolfe, and I have read all the latter in the original. There is the same affectionate interest in his family and friends, the same keen sense of duty and patriotism. Of robust health and vigour, Brock was probably more popular with the ordinary civilian than had been the sensitive, highly strung hero of Quebec. Cut off for many years from active service, he had missed all opportunity of distinguishing himself in the field during the French wars. But in preparing the militia and regulars under his command in both the Canadas for the desperate business that lay before them, and himself leading them into it with dash and courage, he almost certainly saved British North America to the Empire.

Ever since the Peace, which was all in their favour, the Americans had been out of humour with England, abusing their Mother Country—as to most of them she then was—in season and out. Exactly why they did so Englishmen could not readily comprehend. The reverse would have been conceivable, but why should a nation that had issued victorious out of its struggle and got all it wanted persistently harbour these rancorous feelings towards the losers? That the English, who had then many other things to think of, did not worry much about this strange attitude may possibly have aggravated it. Received as gentlemen by gentlemen, as were the earlier envoys to the English Court, there is an absence of gracious acknowledgment. John Adams, like the rest of the family, a congenital hater of his Mother Country, was surprised and almost annoyed that George III had received him cordially. He seems to have been half prepared to treat the King as a public meeting and make a rousing speech on liberty and the virtues of his countrymen. He was invited everywhere and treated most hospitably. It made no difference! Every overture was suspected by this dour, captious Bostonian. Nothing English could be right. Compared to much of the Society in which he found himself, he was, figuratively speaking, a backwoodsman. He appears to have been almost annoyed because the standards of high society were not those of Boston Congregationalists. He seemed always to be buoyed up by the smug consciousness of superiority which characterises his letters to his wife.

Adams was but a type of those who should have known better, out of a larger American public without any such advantages. That some owed a great deal of money for goods received to English creditors, and evaded payment with excuses that their own historians of to-day account as flimsy,[1] may, perhaps, partly explain their attitude. Jefferson was, of course, obsessed by an anti-British craze. With him and many others it was a kind of cult they themselves could probably not have explained. French prepossessions and long residence in France should have cured him of this dogged provincialism. But in France he only learned to hate England the more, and his influence among the ignorant was very great. Yet he was a man of real culture, and what was still more rare, of keen artistic sense, as shown by his residence on a beautiful hill-top in Virginia, and more particularly by the University he designed and founded at its foot. For the rest, he was kind to his slaves, rather more than kind to some of them it was said, and a most enlightened and improving farmer.[2]

He was of plain though sound stock himself, but, allied with the Burwells and Randolphs, was socially a member of the governing class. Nevertheless, more than any other American of his day, he was responsible for the senseless abuse of England that distorted her every action and promoted the spirit which led to the war of 1812. There were, of course, many exceptions to this tiresome and in

[1] See Flick, Van Tyne and others.

[2] I knew both his estates, the larger and the lesser, in Albemarle and Bedford Counties respectively, and have read a most interesting series of unpublished letters mostly on agriculture which he wrote to a member of the Burwell family, still living in the eighteen-seventies and well known to me.

THOMAS JEFFERSON
From the original painting by CHAPPEL

truth rather ugly hatred among leading Americans. Alexander Hamilton, for example, though he was never in Europe, "divined it," as Talleyrand said of him. He never would have gone blundering into the European scene like some of these earlier diplomats. Jay, the negotiator of the Treaty of 1806, was another man of finer tact and perceptions, and the conciliatory nature of his Treaty drew an outburst of rage from all the baser sort in America. The French had for some years treated their former allies with contumely and insult. They had burnt one and a half million pounds' worth of their ships at one stroke, and had laughed at their remonstrances. Once or twice the worm did almost turn. But their indignation was quickly switched off to England, whose attitude towards them, according to all the laws of nations, was scrupulously correct. As we have tried to show, it was not the trifling taxes nor the theories of taxation that were the root cause of Revolution in America, but the Navigation Laws. It is also curious to note in this connection that when the Americans had deprived themselves by force of the Empire trade privileges they had so undervalued, and found that, like every other foreign nation, they were outside them, they made a grievance of the fact that they could not both eat their cake and have it. They had even the presumption to clamour for the old privileges of the Imperial bond they had themselves severed, and to add the plight in which they now found their trade, to the list of imaginary post-bellum grievances they cherished against Great Britain.

The English may have been, as Napoleon declared, a nation of shopkeepers, but overwhelming contemporary evidence shows that the passion for gain struck every visitor to America as that country's leading characteristic. Trade was the burden of every diplomatic overture to European countries. Ministers, particularly English ministers, were expected to give prompt attention to the discussion of those matters, regardless of the number and importance of greater questions which for the moment were urgent in other quarters. Complaints were frequent that British ministers were chary of the time demanded for discussing American affairs. Americans, generally speaking, knew nothing of Europe and cared less. Many of their diplomats were naturally crude and touchy, scenting patronage in every civility, and a snub in every interview. During all the years of friction over the Orders in Council and kindred measures to which Great Britain was forced, there seems to be little recognition among American officials that England is fighting for her life and also for the liberty of the world against its potential tyrant. With one after another, all that matters is American sea-borne trade, and that too for a nation of under six millions with half a continent to spread themselves over! No wonder European diplomats failed to understand them, and often gave them up as a bad job, except the French Republic, which treated the United States with incredible contumely. Napoleon, however, was all civility, intending to exploit them for all they were worth, as in fact he did to their ultimate undoing.

Jefferson himself, oddly enough, though he did so much to embroil the two countries, disapproved of all industries but agriculture. He had visions of a self-supporting Utopia, every man on his own farm, with the outer world forgotten and its vices kept from all contact with a simple, virtuous people. In leading up to the war of 1812, most American historians, echoed complacently by most British writers, fill pages with the ostensible causes of the dispute. These are three in number:—the Orders in Council against neutral trade with the enemy; the search for deserters on neutral ships, and, thirdly, the impressment of so-called American seamen. But the real purpose of the war was the conquest of Canada and the expulsion of the British from North America. A hundred instances of this avowed intention could be given, but the most convincing proof of it lies in the fact that the Maritime States of the North, whom all the professed grievances put forward as a cause of war chiefly concerned, were dead against an appeal to arms. They were assuredly no Anglophiles, but they hated Napoleon and all his works even more than they hated England. Moreover, the Canadians were, after all, their neighbours, and if not following the familiar precept of loving them as themselves they were in no mood to ravage and coerce them. No doubt, too, as a more travelled people, they understood better the sea-power of England. It was the South, broadly speaking, that was all the time clamouring for the conquest of Canada. For in the other questions at issue they had comparatively little interest and they had been always land-greedy, whether individually or in dreams of fresh territory. They were also obsessed by the notion that the British stirred up the Western Indians. Lastly, though totally unacquainted with France, they were strong Gallophiles and had complacently swallowed the insults heaped on them by the Directory and its envoys.

Jefferson's influence was, of course, much concerned with all this. When Adams, who was hardly a Gallophile, was elected as second President instead of Jefferson, France took it as a direct slight to herself. Jefferson, as third President, was in his element in the long quarrel with Great Britain, in which he was supported by the democratic party, the more provincial and ignorant of the two in world affairs. Despite his rage at British interference on the seas, he knew nothing of ships and trade, and in his heart thought that all Americans ought to stay at home, open out the country, raise crops, and live the simple life. Not a bad idea either, if practicable. Indeed he is credited with a wonderful theory that warships, if they must be built, should be so contrived that they could be hauled up on shore out of reach of the wicked English, among whom, he and his friends supposed, jealousy of the United States was the absorbing passion and their destruction the one aim. The truth of the matter was that the British were thinking all too little about the Americans. For though Jefferson was not a naval architect his compatriots were building beautiful ships, not of such an enduring kind as the British, but great sailers and of great size. What was more, they were making ships' guns of longer range than common. Hence their success in those duels between isolated ships early in the war, which left at least some naval honours to the American credit.

But British seamen were engaged to man those ships and fight these guns by the hundred. The higher wages offered were irresistible to the ill-paid but valiant Jack

Tars of those days. The right of search for deserters was a recognized rule of the sea with all nations. The Americans claimed to naturalize as a citizen by a stroke of the pen anybody useful who came along. Opinion was not in those days prepared to admit that a subject could abjure his country in twenty-four hours, and take refuge from his duty to it in the guise of a foreigner. It seemed a mere trick, and rather a low one. But when in legitimate search for deserters the British captain found his runaways on an American ship, posing as Americans, and being claimed as such, it can be imagined what a sea of troubles and difficulties ensued—the ships that fired on one another, the hot tempers, the formal apologies offered by one or other Government and formally accepted. All these incidents, sometimes dramatic enough in themselves, need not be laboured, though they helped to provide a pretext for the land attack on Canada. And again, when British ships were captured, persistent attempts were sometimes made to enlist the prisoners. Of 400 men on board the U.S. *Constitution,* which captured the *Guerriere,* half were British seamen and often "Captains of Guns." The captain of the *Constitution* used every art to inveigle the defeated crew to enlist in his service. The Commodore of the *United States,* after defeating H.M.S. *Macedonian,* declared to her captain that there was not a seaman on his ship who had not served from five to twelve years in a British man-of-war. In the famous duel between the *Chesapeake* and the *Shannon,* watched from the American coast by thousands of spectators, there were men, says James, the naval historian, on the former ship who had actually deserted from the British frigate.

Hildreth, the American historian, declares that, "so far from this being a war for the rights of American seamen, it was but a war to support the pretension of giving to British seamen by employment in American ships protection against the rightful claims of their own Sovereign." So much for the impressment of American citizens. Occasional mistakes were, of course, inevitable, particularly since all concerned spoke the same language though roughly differentiated in accent. The retaliation of the Americans for these measures was an embargo on

British trade, but this was found to act more detrimentally on their own people and abandoned. The Orders in Council, forbidding the carrying of enemy goods in neutral vessels, was duplicated by Napoleon, which made it difficult for America to fasten on that as a *casus belli*. Moreover, the British Government promised withdrawal on Napoleon's doing the same. This was a liberal offer, as Napoleon's edicts without naval power to enforce them were mere thunder, while the British orders were enforced. Pinkney, a more discreet envoy of the Jay type, had in 1806 framed a treaty with Castlereagh of a quite harmonious and satisfactory nature. But Jefferson, enraged at its friendly import, tore it up without even presenting it to the senate, a liberty hardly contemplated by those, himself included, who had framed the constitution! As war drew nearer, a hopeless pettifogger, named Russell, was unwisely, or perhaps designedly, chosen as *chargé d'affaires*. This envoy both misrepresented the opinions he was supposed to convey from British Ministers and substituted his own. "It was the misfortune of the American Government that some of its officials could not keep faith even with themselves," says the author of *The United States after the War of Independence*.[1] But all this may pass seeing that war had been determined on by the party in power.

While England was thus engaged in resisting the avowed attempt of Napoleon to destroy her, her difficulties were immensely increased by the ungenerous conduct of her offspring. "There was never any real neutrality on the part of the United States, from the time of Genet's escapade, down to Madison's declaration of war. If they did not send out ships of war they allowed their fellow citizens by hundreds to man the French privateers. Their moral support of France was so near to an open alliance that their own domestic affairs were deranged by the incriminations and recriminations repeatedly and unhesitatingly made by one-half of the nation against the other half. We have seen how the subjects of Great Britain were seduced from their allegiance in great numbers when not a sailor could be spared from the British Navy. We have noted the partial conduct of the Executive in frequently calling

[1] Edward Smith.

England to account for her shortcomings while condoning the acts of her enemy so far as to incur the oft-expressed contempt of that adversary. We have seen them enter into a sort of maritime war of their own, further adding to the difficulties of Great Britain, until they discovered that embargoes were unpopular and uncomfortable at home and non-intercourse only irritating. At length we have the spectacle of this presumptuous people, believing that the opportunity is at hand to acquire the long coveted possession of Canada, seizing the supposed time of Britain's extremity in which to execute their purpose. For this was the undoubted object of the declaration of war. The supporters, by their speeches in Congress, openly and frequently avowed it; the proof is complete in the reproaches hurled at them by their Federal opponents."

One famous Virginian at any rate spoke out. Probably thousands agreed with him but dared not oppose their rabid party leaders. "What is the question in dispute?" cried John Randolph, of Roanoke. "The carrying trade. What part of it? The fair, the honest and useful trade engaged in carrying our own productions in exchange? No, Sir! It is that carrying trade which covers enemy's property. It is not the honest carrying trade, but this mushroom, this fungus of war, a trade which as soon as the nations of Europe are at peace will no longer exist. It is for this that the spirit of avaricious traffic would plunge us into war. In case of Britain's destruction, France must inevitably succeed to the dominion of the ocean, and what then?" What indeed! That France as a conquering power, who already trifled with them as she chose, would ultimately do as she liked with them, does not seem to have occurred to these feverish Anglophobes. Fortunately, it did occur and in good time to the main trading States. They could not stop the war, though they violently opposed it even by threatening secession, but they did the next best thing. For they in great part withheld their support and left the slave States with the democratic half of New York, and Pennsylvania and New Jersey to pursue their immoral and inglorious attempt to capture Canada.

The leaders of the Democratic Party, "the war hawks,"

were mainly young men, to be sure, arrogant, inexperienced, provincial and with no knowledge of Europe. They thought Corunna had sealed the fate of England, and for reasons that seem amazing in men of pure British stock gloried in the delusion. Jefferson had done much to spread this nonsense among his followers. His hero, Napoleon, was now about to march his invincible army to Russia and complete the conquest of the continent, followed by that of England. That he would next turn his eyes westward does not seem to have occurred to these infatuated "backwoodsmen," to use that term in a world sense. Henry Clay, from Kentucky, declared in bombastic fashion, that the Kentucky backwoodsmen alone would wipe out Canada. "War is no terrible thing," he shouted in Congress; "there was no terror in it but its novelty." Clay had never seen war and was never likely to. Young Calhoun, of South Carolina, then barely thirty, who forty years later did so much to kindle the spirit that brought disaster on his own State and her sister States, was another firebrand in the "War Committee" of 1811-12.

Poor Mr. Madison, a follower and disciple of Jefferson, was a mild, cultured man, whose legal knowledge had been invaluable to his State and country. He lived on his modest estate in Orange County, Virginia, a delectable spot, with sufficient slaves to ensure the comfortable but simple life of his class. His wife, "Dolly Madison," was an accomplished housewife. Her mother had kept a boarding-house in Philadelphia frequented by Southern politicians attending Congress there. But she was also a lady of character, and the memoirs and letters relating to the Madison régime in the country draw a rather idyllic picture. With the Capitol but fifty miles to the north, Mount Vernon not too far off, and Jefferson at Monticello, but twenty miles to the south, there was much going and coming on horseback between the households over the rough, red and leafy Virginia roads. And the frequent hospitalities shown in later days by both households to distinguished travellers of the once hated race ("quite good fellows after all" as their hosts were surprised to find them) make pleasant reading. But Madison had all his life been accustomed to hear abuse of England, and the attitude had become confirmed. As, moreover, he was coming in for a second term as a "War President," this amiable, well-meaning man had no help for it, though he would have himself made peace within a month after the beginning of hostilities, when a most honourable chance was offered. But it was not peace his foolish friends wanted, but Canada. Jefferson had persuaded him that it was Great Britain who was "mad" in pursuing the only path that saved her from destruction. But this last meant nothing to that irreconcilable demagogue. In a short time Madison had learnt a good deal, and heartily wished himself back in Orange County, with his crops and his books, and all the domestic comforts ensured by the admirable Dolly. The irony of the whole business is that this was very generally known as "Madison's War." Just before the war he had actually suggested a compromise, when he got what the bellicose congressmen quite absurdly turned into a bad shock. This was the divulgence of a perfectly legitimate but confidential correspondence carried on between Craig while Governor of Canada, and a secret service agent he had commissioned to visit the States and ascertain the general feeling. The agent was an Irish adventurer named Henry, who, having had no legal education, was curtly refused a Judgeship by Gore, then Lieutenant-Governor of Upper Canada. Henry thereupon sold the private correspondence for a very large sum to Madison, who had it produced in Congress. Though it was merely the ordinary account of current opinion any government would expect and get from its secret service, Congress went wild with wrath at British "insolence." That was the stock epithet—though how applicable in this case one may well ask, and ask further why the fact of a President personally suborning for cash a blackguard and a traitor did not seem to detract from the dignity of the really respectable Madison.

The incident, however, wrought to a climax the fury of the "war-hawks," though in truth it was already boiling over. In spite of loud protests from several of the cooler-headed and more vulnerable States, war was declared on June 18th, 1812. Two days later, England, as yet ignorant of this, revoked her "Orders in Council" according to promise that on Napoleon's doing so she would follow suit. The news was over a month in reaching the seat of war, but when announced, the lust for Canada was, as we shall see, so overpowering as quite to neutralise the removal of the chief offence in the indictment against Great Britain. For there was no shadow of a doubt with the war party that Canada would fall an easy prey. Napoleon, they supposed, was busy completing the conquest of Europe by that of Russia. As a matter of fact, he entered Russia the very day war was declared at Washington. Jefferson had persuaded the Southerners that the War Lord of Europe was a democrat with a passion for the sovereignty of the people. Most Northerners, however, understood him better, and regarded him with nothing but hatred and dread.

We have no space for all the gems of eloquence that hailed the approach and declaration of war. "We are triumphantly asked," exclaimed a Southern orator, "if we expect to intimidate Great Britain. We do not expect to intimidate her, we expect to meet her armies in the field and to vanquish them. The power of England must be extinguished in America, she must no longer be permitted to corrupt the principles and disturb the peace and tranquillity of our citizens." Adams, too, was going about Europe airing his congenital dislike of Great Britain and spoiling for war. He was shocked beyond measure when Madame de Staël treated him to a long oration on the great qualities of England. His Bostonian outlook could not understand an enemy and French citizen taking this attitude. Even the suave and careful Percival revealed to this carping, peevish man "a violence and bitterness of passion against the United States." All these people spoke continually of the rancour and jealousy against them felt by Britain, a pure delusion and obsession. An ill-natured, ingrained suspicion seemed to flavour almost every dealing with England in these years, and it is no wonder that many British statesmen, with the best will in the world, gave up the Americans as impracticable. Jefferson said that an army would not be required to conquer Canada, only officers, whom both races, smarting under the tyranny of British rule, would rally to as one man. Clay thought the war would be "a promenade," and that the British must be driven from the continent.

The delusion that British Canada was ripe for rebellion was general with the war party and their dupes. When war was declared several of the New England legislatures and town meetings passed resolutions denouncing it. Even Maryland, as the fateful stroke fell, remembered the planters on her eastern shore, and her seaport city of Baltimore, perhaps with some premonition of what subsequently befell them, and commended the attitude of those States to the north who had opposed war. But the mob broke the windows of the local Federal press and maltreated every advocate of peace. A day of general fasting was appointed for invoking the blessing of the Almighty on the forthcoming crusade against Canada, an observance which must have edified Jefferson who did not believe in the Almighty, and Henry Clay, who called the mixing up of politics and religion "cant," and Russell, the late ill-chosen envoy to London, who used to "laugh aloud" when Adams' despatches of the "moral and virtuous people" type were received at Washington.

An appropriation had been made by Congress for the raising of 35,000 regular troops and 50,000 volunteers, while 100,000 militia were to be provided by the various States. Fortunately for Great Britain, most of New England's militia declined to muster. Though this was not done for love of their Mother Country, the speeches made showed a genuine reluctance to attack Canada as many believed wantonly, while, furthermore, the most really democratic community in America was actuated by that dread of Napoleon and all he stood for, to which we have alluded. Thousands, too, of their own people had settled in Canada, and the fact of their contentment must have filtered through all the valleys of New England, together with the idea that a rebellious Canada was a fiction. Some public men had the hardihood to declare that Canadians were either Frenchmen or Anglo-Americans of their own stock, and they did not see why they should be butchered and robbed because English captains on the high seas made themselves disagreeable. Moreover, they knew more of their neighbours, and did not expect the invasion to be quite the promenade imagined by the party in the Slave States and the deluded portions of Pennsylvania and New York in which loot was openly proclaimed as an incentive to "joining up." The militia from these States were most bitterly disappointed, as we shall see, when they found the loot had to be fought for. They declared that they had been betrayed, or at least basely deluded. Many thousands of them were massed at various times at various points within sight of the promised land. But I can recall scarcely any occasion on which they were effective, save behind ramparts or as skirmishing supporters of regular troops.

The plan of campaign against Canada was cast upon three lines, very much as in the case of the two former wars. It was quite a good plan, though in truth there was not much choice. To the east, the straight northward-thrusting route up the Hudson and Lakes George and Champlain to the St. Lawrence, near Montreal, was to be followed. But for the rest, Niagara was now to be the centre of the attack, the third point of invasion being shifted farther west to Detroit, a large post and station on the American side of the narrow waters between Lakes Erie and Huron, the western boundary, then as now, of Upper Canada. Then, however, unlike to-day, this last was a thinly populated frontier region, the fringe of advancing settlement over the rich peninsula of Upper Canada. The village of Sandwich faced Detroit across the St. Clair or Detroit River. On the Michigan side, American settlement had also been creeping up though still scanty. Detroit had an older importance than merely the chief seat of this new region, as a centre both of the old French and later British and American fur traders. It was here that the first blow at Canada was to be struck, for Upper Canada was to be the chief scene of invasion. That province conquered and occupied, a trivial business, the rest would be equally easy. A Dr. Eustis was War Minister, and was apparently one of those rather obscure politicians that a corrupt political atmosphere throws up. For Washington seems to have already grown rather murky in that particular, despite the fact that Madison and Jefferson personally were free at least of that sort of taint.

Till the very last, the British Government, then under Percival, had failed to realise the gravity of the situation. In any case they could have done little. They had been warned again and again of the danger by their officials in Canada, but their resources were now strained to breaking-point. There was no hope whatever of relieving Canada with an adequate armed force. The country would have to rely on itself and its small garrisons in fighting a nation upon its borders of over seven millions, already growing rich, and along an open frontier some 800 miles in length.

Prevost had so greatly conciliated the French Canadians, that early in the year, the legislature of the Lower Province had passed a militia bill enrolling 2,000 unmarried men, and furthermore had granted nearly the whole year's revenue for their support. The sedentary militia, too, showing a very different spirit from that of 1775, were now mustered and drilled. A regiment of Voltigeurs, also, was raised and placed under Major de Salaberry, a *seigneur* holding a commission in the 60th Regiment. There were present too the 49th and 100th Regiments with one battalion of the 8th, a few artillery and the provincial corps, the Canadian and the Glengarry Fencibles. Some of these corps, however, were only three or four hundred strong. Finally, £250,000 was raised by army bills, payable in five years. So much for the defences of Lower Canada.

In the Upper Province, upon which the brunt of war was to fall, things looked even worse. Brock had spared no effort to prepare for the inevitable contest. He had only with him the 41st Regiment, a thousand strong, and 250 of the 10th and Newfoundland regiments, respectively, with a handful of artillery. It needs no saying that the loyalists' militia had responded eagerly to his endeavours. Brock seems to have been as much beloved by the civil as the military element in the Province. Luckily, he was both Civil Governor and military Commander, though under final orders from Prevost which in his case were nominal. Though the ardour of the men could have swollen the ranks of the militia indefinitely, there were, unfortunately, only arms and equipment for under 2,000 in the country. There was no money to buy more, even had time and opportunity admitted. There was no war chest, and the United States was now closed as a market. Lower Canada had not enough of anything for herself, while the Upper Province was at that elementary stage of its history, represented by length without breadth, its people consisting of working farmers in a thin line 400 miles long, containing a large, uncertain element, and everywhere confronting an enemy country. Almost the only money crop was wheat, a modest bulk of which found its way into the Lower Province and thence, after leaving some toll there for non-productive bodies, garrisons, monasteries and the like, went across to England. There were few doctors and few drugs, most of the population having long been wont to gather, as we have seen, their remedies from their garden patches and the woods. Lastly, though one might extend the deficiency in supplies indefinitely, almost every man fit for service was engaged in making a livelihood for himself and his family by the labour of his hands under the exacting demands of agriculture. The food of the country itself, and that of its active defenders, depended on its people. There was no outside source of supply that it could tap.

Such was the country upon which, with a pæan of anticipatory triumph, and with the particular blessing of Jefferson, Madison's Government flung all the forces and all the talents it could muster. Such were the materials, or the lack of them, out of which Brock had to organize his defences. Upper Canada stood in the breach. It was to receive the first thrusts of the spearhead which was to clear the way to any easy conquest of Quebec and the Maritime Provinces. If arms were short, the loyalists gave freely of their wagons and horses and their own services for the vitally necessary transport over roads that were still mere tracks cut through the forest and corduroyed over the swamps. For lack of gunners, young farmers mounted the guns on their waggon wheels, drove them, and often served them in person as combatants. Brock's handful of regulars, however, were in the highest state of discipline, his militia burning with ardour and well officered. He had in addition a body of about 700 Indians under the great Shewanee chief, Tecumseh, who, of the three outstanding leaders of his race on the bloody pages of its history, was the most admired by all the white men who knew him.

Almost alone, he personally enjoyed an untarnished reputation for mercy in victory. He and his people, it should be remembered, had been driven from their homes, and their villages burnt by American troops, and that they should aid in defence of Canada, which had provided a refuge and a new home for so many of their race seems merely an act of self-preservation. Whatever their crimes in resisting extermination, there was, as Washington himself declared, little to choose in cruelty between the Indians and their opponents, except that the latter were supposed to be Christians and the former were not. No one nowadays, with the evidence of the ages before him, differs from Washington, who spoke at first hand. But as a political cry, the Indian alliance still served the Americans, despite the fact that both sides used the Red Man without hesitation, as opportunity offered. Tecumseh and his friends on this occasion had no choice. They did good service and committed no outrages, unless on the scalps of their opponents, a mutual compliment paid traditionally by both sides on the frontier. Very often they took no prisoners, but then the white men served them the same. This did not, however, prevent the old complaint against Indian allies figuring in the Napoleonic proclamations put forth by the invading General.

The Western campaign at Detroit was put in charge of General Hull, a veteran of the old war. It is impossible not to feel sorry for the poor old soldier. The physician at the War Office had reserved the full direction of this campaign to himself, as he had an eye on the next Presidency and success as a strategist on this occasion would be a distinct asset. He had obviously not studied the Germain-Burgoyne affair. As a medical man, and professional politician of the new type, he could hardly be expected to do so. Hull doubted his scheme, and may even have winced a little when he addressed the U.E. Loyalists in an oration written by Eustis. Hull was Governor of Michigan, and had a force of 2,500 men at Detroit, a fortified place with a small civil population. On July 12th, he crossed the river to Sandwich on the Canadian side, and then launched the doctor's engaging and remarkable address. "After thirty years of peace and prosperity," it ran, "the United States have been driven to arms, the injuries and aggressions, the insults and indignities of Great Britain having once more left them no alternative but manly resistance or unconditional submission. The army under my command has invaded your country, and the standard of the Union now waves on the territory of Canada. To the peaceable, unoffending inhabitants it brings neither dangers nor difficulties. I come to find enemies, not to make them, I come as protector." Separated by the ocean and the wilderness, the Canadians, so he declared, could have no possible interest in Great Britain, while they had felt her tyranny and seen her injustice. He then offered them the invaluable blessings, at present unknown to them, of civil, political and religious liberty. He begged them to remain at home and pursue their avocations, and as children of the same family, not to raise their hands against their brethren, for the army of friends he brought with him must be treated by them with a cordial welcome. They would then be emancipated from tyranny and oppression and restored to the dignity of freemen. "Had I any doubt of eventual success, I might ask your assistance; but I have none. I have a force which will look down all opposition, and that force but the vanguard of a much greater one. If, contrary to your own interests, you should take part in the approaching contest you will be considered and treated as enemies, the horrors and calamities of war will stalk before you."

Hull, speaking the words of Eustis, went on to denounce "the barbarous policy of letting loose the savages to murder American women and children." (Here the former were actually out for the protection of the latter.) He threatened that the first stroke of the tomahawk (on his own invading soldiers) would be the sign for a war without quarter and of extermination (on the U.E. Loyalist families !) an action that in the wildest moments of rage between white people in North America had never been suggested. "The United States," he concluded, "offers you peace, liberty and security. Your choice lies between these and war, slavery and destruction." Poor old Hull. As a reputedly experienced soldier, mistrustful, too, of the situation in which he had been placed, it must have irked him not a little to publish this effusion of his civic chief at Washington.

With two armies threatening nearer home, no British force had been able, as yet, to reach this Ultima Thule of Canada. But by way of comment on the olive branch Hull had just held out, his colonels raided freely up the river, which Simcoe had so patriotically named the Thames, and though it was but thinly settled, had secured a good deal of loot in the way of grain and cattle, the harvest being in progress. Brock, whose hands for the moment were full enough with both civil and military matters at Headquarters, had pushed a small force of three hundred militia, a hundred men of the 41st (Welsh), under Colonel St. George, and as many Indians under the famous chief, Tecumseh, to harass the invaders on the Canadian shore. These were followed by Colonel Procter and another handful of the 41st. They succeeded in convincing Hull that his marauding Ohio and Michigan militia were not much good as soldiers, and that Sandwich, though hastily fortified, was no longer tenable. Hull now recrossed the river to Detroit, having been in Canada about a fortnight. He had done some pillaging, lost a few men and killed one Indian, whose slayer wrote to his wife, that he had torn the scalp off with his teeth. Pretty fellows, these Westerners, whose morals were endangered, according to Jeffersonian theories, by the neighbourhood of British troops of the line. In fact, Hull was getting anxious. Things were not working out according to plan. Sandwich, when evacuated, had been occupied by the British, and guns mounted within range of Detroit. His communications and line of supplies ran southward down the waterways to the western corner of Lake Erie. Hull had loaded a schooner with stores and supplies necessary to his campaign, and he now heard that it had been captured by a British warship. There was a company of ladies, too, on board, officers' wives coming up to see the fun. They were doubtless thankful later on to Lieutenant Rolette for capturing them and sending them politely home.

Then there was a large supply of beef cattle, and other necessaries down towards the lake in charge of some militia. But the armed convoy sent for them was ambushed and routed by Tecumseh's Indians. Hull was now seriously concerned as to his supplies, and rather disillusioned as to his militiamen, who, he had assured the Canadians, would "look down all opposition." Still, he had a thousand regulars at Detroit, and he now sent Colonel Miller with six hundred of them, including cavalry and guns, down the American bank of the river to bring the convoys up. Half-way down, they found Captain Muir of the 41st, with 75 men of his regiment, as many militia, and some 200 Indians under Tecumseh, thrown across their path. A brisk fight ensued, which eventually resulted in the retirement of the Americans with a loss of over seventy killed and wounded. The boats brought down for the latter from Detroit were captured with their loads by the vigilant French-Canadian, Lieutenant Rolette. This may seem a chronicle of "small beer," but it caused the evacuation of Canadian territory and Hull's complete withdrawal of his troops to Detroit, to short commons and mutual recriminations.

And now Brock himself arrived from the centre of the danger zone, with 240 militia and about 40 regulars, travelling up Lake Erie by boats to Amherstburg, the farthest West Canadian post, at the mouth of the Detroit river. Characteristically, he at once sent a flag of truce to Hull with a demand for his immediate surrender. This was met by an indignant refusal. Brock then opened his little battery at Sandwich of five guns against the fort with some effect, the fort replying with none whatever. In the night, Brock sent a force of 600 Indians, under Tecumseh, and some British officers across the river to take ambush till morning. At daylight, he himself crossed with a force of 350 regulars and 400 militia, under a most effective fire from the Sandwich battery, and then, with his entire force, British and Indian, advanced against the fortress to carry it by storm. When about to deliver his attack, Brock was amazed to see a white flag run up, and still more so when an aide-de-camp from Hull came out proposing negotiations for surrender. Within Detroit was still the whole of Hull's force, save some three hundred or so absent in connection with the held-up convoys. There were also a good many non-combatants besides women and children. The affair was settled within an hour. Hull and his entire force of 2,500 men, including the absent detachment sent down the river, became prisoners of war, while thirty cannon, a supply of arms and stores, besides a captured brig, proved a welcome acquisition to Brock's scanty war arsenal.

This epoch-making event, ever memorable in the annals of Canada, took place on August 16th. The Indians, under Tecumseh's vigilant leadership, had on this occasion belied their general reputation, and upheld their chief in behaving well to their prisoners. Brock sent the Ohio and Michigan militia back to their homes, while Hull and his regulars, cavalry, infantry and artillery, were sent on as prisoners to Quebec. Eighteen months later, Hull was court-martialled and sentenced to be shot. Madison endorsed the verdict, but repealed the sentence. The horse upon whose back Madison's War Minister had hoped to ride into the Presidential chair had indeed broken down. How much of the catastrophe was due to the rider himself we may not know, but the spasm of rage which shook the country on learning that the first army of invasion with its general were all prisoners in Canada was not discriminating. The catastrophe was made worse by the jeers of the opposition and the dissenting States. There was no explaining it away. Twenty-five hundred American soldiers who had entered Canada with an assurance of easy conquest had not only been driven out, but captured wholesale on their own soil by seven hundred and fifty Canadians, more than half militia, with six hundred Indians. The humiliation on one side and the triumph on the other were out of all proportion to the numbers engaged, but it heartened and inspired the Canadians, British and French, still standing at arms, and steadied the doubtful element of post-loyalist Americans, so thickly settled throughout the country.

Brock lost no time in getting back to repel an invasion more formidable than Hull's, the attack now threatened by the "Army of the centre" on the Niagara river. Brock left Procter at Detroit with a small force to protect the frontier by carrying the war into the territory of Michigan. Procter's activities and adventures through the autumn and bitter winter of that frozen region must be left for brief mention later, and we must follow Brock back to a victory more glorious to him and his men and even more shattering to the exuberance of the invaders than the capture of Detroit.

But first a word on a new development of the political situation. For peace and war once again hung in the balance. Once more the American Government was given the opportunity to show that it was Canada they wanted and not the settlement of ocean amenities, though the latter, the world was told, and even yet believes, was the *casus belli*. As before stated, the Orders in Council were revoked by Great Britain almost concurrently with the American declaration of war, and of course in ignorance of that event. As the said Orders had been the chief cause of offence, the British Government naturally assumed that the way to peace was now open. Instructions were accordingly sent out to Governor Prevost and the Admiral commanding to propose at once a suspension of operations with a view to discussing the new situation. Prevost, without loss of time, sent his Adjutant-General to Dearborn, the American Commander-in-Chief, then at Albany with one of the three armies of invasion. The result was an armistice dating from August 6th. Prevost wished to include Hull's division, but Dearborn was powerless in this matter, as poor Hull's enterprise was, unfortunately for him, Dr. Eustis' own little affair, so it went on to disaster. Otherwise, with a month's delay, this might not have happened.

But this is merely by the way, for the grand result of the armistice was the blank rejection of peace by the American Government. The Orders in Council, which had been the head and front of their grievances, were now, it would seem, of small moment. Great Britain must abjure for ever the right of recovering her deserters, whom American captains had been seducing by hundreds with the offer of high pay and labelling with an alien citizenship in an offhand fashion hitherto unrecognised in the world. Madison had now a chance to follow his real inclinations, but he was too weak and the "war hawks" had their way. It was Canada they wanted, not peace, and the short armistice closed with their renewed attempts at its conquest on August 29th. As it was, the truce had been most unfortunate for the Canadians, for it had given the enemy an opportunity to bring up more troops and supplies to the frontier, and further enabled them to use the water transport of Lake Ontario, which was at present controlled by British ships. Among other advantages, too, it had allowed them to bring a fleet of merchant ships, blockaded by the British at Ogdensburg, to Sackett's Harbour, nearly opposite Kingston, where they were converted into ships of war. The control of the two lakes was a vital matter to both combatants throughout the war, as these waters divided the two countries. The far greater facilities and resources for shipbuilding on the American side made the maritime question a most difficult one for the British from the start, though they succeeded by vigilance and some hard fighting in minimising the effect of this unfortunate and futile armistice.

The two American forces now massed on, or near, the frontier for the impending invasion were on the Niagara River and at Albany respectively. The former was the most immediately threatening, though Dearborn, Commander-in-chief, holding the eastern command with its base at Albany, and its line of approach down the Lakes George and Champlain route, gave little trouble this season, despite his large force. Still he kept Lower Canada powerless to assist the other Province. For the moment interest chiefly centred on the Niagara frontier. Here the connecting river between Lakes Erie and Ontario runs a course of some twenty-five miles, broken rather beyond midway by the great Falls. Below the cataract for some distance are the furious rapids in their deep limestone trough familiar to thousands of travellers.

Below these, the river is navigable to Lake Ontario, and averages about half a mile in width. Above the Falls, it encircles in two channels the large area of Grand Island, then narrows again to the outflow from Lake Erie. Here, on the American side, is the city of Buffalo, even in those days a growing town. On the same side was Fort Rock, protecting Buffalo, and confronting it on the Canadian shore was Fort Erie. Just above Niagara Falls on the American shore, was Fort Schosser. Half-way between the Falls and Lake Ontario, below the stir of the rapids, the Canadian village of Queenston, to become so memorable, faced that of Lewiston on the American shore across a short half-mile of water. Below and within a mile of the lake, Fort George looked aslant to the American Fort Niagara, lying on the further side but still nearer the outflow of the river. Between this and Fort George was the pleasant little town of Newark, containing about 700 souls, and the original capital, it will be remembered, of Upper Canada.

The American force on this front consisted of 6,000 men, including 3,500 regulars. They were commanded by General Van Rensselaer. He was not a soldier by profession but represented much family and territorial influence. He had been opposed to the war, and was apparently appointed to this high command to convert him; a strange method! But Madison's government were politicians or nothing, and they gave brigades to political lawyers or country gentlemen, and regiments to regular officers. In this case, however, Van Rensselaer's cousin, a colonel in the army, was sent to look after him, but with singular fatuity, a Brigadier of regulars, Smyth, was appointed his second in command, and very naturally took the keenest pleasure in thwarting him. The troops were distributed at various points, the regulars at the two extremities, Fort Niagara and Buffalo, the militia in the centre at Lewiston, under Van Rensselaer himself. Smyth was in command at Buffalo, over twenty miles away from his chief, a situation he made the most of, though the conduct of Van Rensselaer, as a matter of fact, called for no criticism. The militia, mostly New Yorkers, had all the ardour of inexperience with the prospect of loot now within easy sight of them, as they still stood upon their own soil. They clamoured loudly to be led across at once, and chafed bitterly at the delay of ordinary military procedure.

Brock in the meantime was making such disposal as he could of his meagre forces. He had actually, for the moment, only 1,200 men in all, regulars and militia, at his disposal. Was there ever in modern history such a stake at issue under such odds? When one has said that Brock's regulars of the 41st and 49th were very first-class troops, though they constantly got drunk and were occasionally even mutinous, a paradox always possible with the old British army, and furthermore that the Canadian militia were ready to die to a man for their cause, it seems to mitigate little the discrepancy in warlike resources. There is no occasion to say more of what Brock himself counted for, though one might add that thanks to him the British regulars and Canadian militia were on the very best of terms—no mean achievement. Brock's second in command was Major-General Sheaffe, like many officers of his generation, of Colonial American birth, and Colonel of the 49th. Of the leading U.E. Loyalists, young Beverley Robinson, afterwards Chief Justice of the Province, had been with Brock at Detroit and was with him again here. Merritt, an old Queen's Ranger, of the Revolutionary war, whose lineal representative led Canadians in the Boer War, was here, in command of the Niagara Dragoons, as well as his son. Colonel Macdonnell, another notable loyalist of Glengarry, and Attorney-General of the Province, led the York militia to die at its head. Powell, son of the Chief Justice, commanded a local battery of artillery. Dickson, already mentioned as the founder of Galt, was a militia captain, besides many others whose sons and grandsons have worthily maintained their traditions through the succeeding century of Anglo-Canadian history.

CHAPTER IX

THE WAR—1812-13

OBSERVATIONS made by an officer sent on a mission by Brock to Van Rensselaer, led the Canadians to expect that the Americans would attack from their central camp at Lewiston. The American General had all his militia with him, and half his regulars at easy call, along a newly-made road to the Lake Ontario mouth of the river. Queenston lay opposite him, over about 400 yards of water, still moving briskly, but navigable. The militia were in such a hurry to get across into Canada that the general's first attempt miscarried, all the oars having been mysteriously mislaid. Though there were no casualties, the fiasco revealed the projected point of attack, and when, two days later, it was actually made, all was ready on the Canadian side for its reception.

The village of Queenston was to be the landing-place. Above it rose the then wooded ridge, 300 feet high, destined to give its name to a battle with consequences more vital to Canada than that of the Plains of Abraham. Three hundred regulars and militia were stationed at Queenston. Half-way up the "Heights" a single-gun battery was posted. The rest of Brock's scanty force was distributed at points along the seven miles of shore towards Fort George, near the river's mouth, and here for the moment was Brock himself, with about half his force. An hour before day, on October 13th, about 300 regulars and as many militia, pushed off in boats from the American shore, and headed for Queenston. Van Rensselaer's plan was to seize the village and make it a first base of operations against the rest of the province. Smyth, twenty-five miles away at Fort Rock (Buffalo), with his regulars, was to cross there at leisure and join him. But Smyth, as subordinated to a militia officer, objected altogether to the Queenston crossing, and was for making the first attack from his own station against Fort Erie, and probably felt personal satisfaction in the failure of his chief. For Van Rensselaer's approaching boats, under his soldier cousin and a Colonel Christie, were first espied by the three small batteries, which from different points commanded their approach. Considerable execution was done at once, and several men were killed. Some of the boats were washed lower down by the current, while several were stranded and their occupants captured.

Beverley Robinson, already mentioned as a militia officer present, has left a spirited account of the battle, which was published locally in the York paper a few days later. I have seen a faded copy of this print, now in the possession of one of the Brock family. "Grape and musket shot," says the writer, "poured upon the Americans as they approached the shore, a single discharge from a brass six-pounder destroying fifteen in a boat. Three of the *bateaux* landed below Mr. Hamilton's garden in Queenston, and were met by a party of militia and regulars, who slaughtered almost the whole of them, taking the rest prisoners. Several other boats were so shattered and disabled that the men in them threw down their arms and came on shore, merely to deliver themselves up as prisoners of war. As we advanced with our company we met troops of Americans on their way to Fort George under guard, and the road was lined with miserable wretches suffering under wounds of all descriptions, and crawling to our houses for protection and comfort. The spectacle struck us, who were not inured to such scenes, with horror, but we hurried on to the mountain, impressed with the idea that the enemy's attempt was already frustrated and the business of the day nearly completed."

But the young officer soon found that the struggle was only beginning. For some two hundred regulars had effected a landing and formed on the shore, with their backs to the high river bank. They were here attacked by some small detachments, but held their own till more boat-loads joined them. Brock himself now arrived on a reeking horse from Fort George, having left such troops as he could spare to follow at best pace, and rousing various small posts *en route*. He at once pushed on up to the small battery on the hill slope, and ordered down a detachment of the 49th stationed there and firing on the enemy as they crossed to the support of their friends on the river bank. Van Rensselaer, now seeing the hill-top to be nearly clear, determined to seize it. Some of his officers from Fort Niagara, familiar with the river, knew of a steep path up that same side, which, though it had not escaped Brock's eye, had been reported to him as inaccessible. Captain Wool, with some four hundred men, undertook the venture, and so successfully that they surprised and captured the battery on the slope just below, though its defenders got away. Brock, quickly grasping the situation, hastily collected about a hundred men, and charging up the hill recovered the battery, though at the expense of his life, for he fell dead with a ball through the breast.

Upon this, his little party again fell back, when Colonel Macdonnell, coming up with his two companies of militia, which increased the force to two hundred men, took the stricken general's place and again reached and carried the battery, though he himself was killed and Captain Williams wounded in the act. Outnumbered and without leaders, the men fell back once more down the hill to a battery at Vrooman's Point behind the village to await reinforcements.

There was now a long cessation from fighting. The Americans established themselves by degrees upon the Heights, to the number, as was afterwards proved, of about twelve hundred. General Van Rensselaer himself, too, came over and took command. Several boat loads of killed and wounded men had in the meantime been sent back to Lewiston. A British artillery officer, Holcroft, had succeeded in planting a gun in the village, and in sinking more than one of the American boats arriving with fresh soldiers. But prospects now looked bad for the British. The death of Brock had cast a profound gloom over the little army. An eye-witness tells us how a dragoon, without either helmet or sword, on a be-spattered, foaming horse, brought the news to Fort Erie, where, according to orders, a steady cannonade was being kept up against Smyth's answering batteries on the American shore. "Brock was dead, and the enemy in possession of Queenston Heights. Some wept, some swore, all worked the heavy guns with feverish energy as if they were field pieces, while triumphant cheers rang out along the opposite shore as the news which arrived there at the same time travelled from post to post." Away at the other end of the fighting line, too, the disaster only infused the gunners of Fort George with sufficient energy to silence the opposing batteries, which had been pouring red-hot shot on to the shingle roofs of Newark.

About three o'clock General Sheaffe, now in command, arrived from Fort George, having left a detachment there under Major Evans to keep Fort Niagara in check. He brought with him every available man, three hundred and eighty of the 41st and three hundred militia, with a hundred and forty Indians under their Chief, Norton, a naturalised Scotsman, who had already been skirmishing about the Heights, while two hundred more militia were hurrying up from Chippewa, a post near the Falls. Van Rensselaer, from the Heights, could make out Sheaffe's approach, and at the same time, noticing with anxiety that his own militia across the river, who were under orders to join, were suspiciously slow about it, he recrossed the water himself to hasten their movements. To his disgust, he found that there was nothing left of the warlike exuberance which had actually over-hurried him in his plan of attack. It seemed that the noise of battle and the returning boats crowded with dead and wounded men, had robbed these rustics of every spark of their martial fire. They had unanimously come to the conclusion that their terms of enlistment did not provide for service outside the borders of their own State, and they were quite resolved to stand by the Constitution!

Raw militia in many countries, on many occasions, have flinched as consistently as they have at other times, like the U.E. Loyalists beyond the river, performed doughty deeds. But seldom have they prefaced a panic by such vociferous ardour as had these hapless militiamen of New

SIR ISAAC BROCK

From a painting by an unknown artist

York on this particular occasion. So their disappointed leader, a brave and worthy gentleman, who, as stated, had disapproved of the war, found himself vainly urging his men to face a foe they had been clamouring for so long to meet, or, it might be fairer to say, to enter a country they had so long been clamouring to loot. It was fortunate for Van Rensselaer himself that he was detained at Lewiston, disagreeable as was the cause for it. Brigadier Wadsworth was now in command of the thousand and odd Americans who held the summit of the hill, which was nearly perpendicular on the water front, but accessible, though steep, on the other sides.

Sheaffe, leaving the force already at the village to hold it and guard the river bank, marched the rest of his men, some eight to nine hundred, inclusive of about 50 Indians, round to the back of the hill on the landward side, and prepared them for its assault. The men were comparatively fresh, and all highly disciplined, or burning with an ardour as effective, and a longing to avenge the death of their beloved chief. The Americans, on the other hand, were none too fresh. They had been on their feet since three in the morning and it was now nearly four o'clock. They were rather crowded, too, and had their back to the precipice and were open to attack on three sides. The British came up the hill at a great pace, unchecked by the rather irregular fire of the enemy. After a loud cheer and a single volley, they went in with the bayonet, It was soon over save for a brief but stubborn resistance here and there. Some of the Americans flung themselves over the precipice, some escaped down the narrow path which they had climbed in the morning. Quite a number seemed to have leaped into the river and perished. The confusion made further resistance hopeless, and Wadsworth sent an offer of unconditional surrender for his whole force. His envoy was Winfield Scott, thirty-five years later the hero of the Mexican War, Commander-in-Chief, and the object to this day of invocation in a familiar slang phrase. Over nine hundred surrendered, ninety were killed on the hill, numbers were drowned and many escaped. The American prisoners were sent on to join the earlier contingent from Detroit, in Lower Canada.

Of the British, Brock and McDonnell were the only officers killed, while seventy of the rank and file, and a dozen Indians were killed or wounded.

Such was the battle of Queenston Heights, of effect incalculable to Canada's destiny. Brock[1] was buried in a bastion of Fort George, and three more years of strife were to rage over his grave. He was irreplaceable, but his example and his memory inspired the defenders of Canada, who were to be led by many a good and daring officer, but by none with the peculiar magnetism of their lost general. Many years later, his remains were removed to Queenston Heights and a monument raised above them. This was blown up by an Irish-American miscreant in 1846, but subsequently a great concourse gathered on the spot, including all his old soldiers who could get there, and subscribed £10,000 for the noble and now familiar column, which on its lofty perch recalls his fame and the ever memorable conflict in which he fell.

The rage of the war party in America at this second disaster may be imagined. No general could be used this time for a scapegoat, as Van Rensselaer had committed no blunder, unless in expecting his militia to fight. It was on these last unfortunates that the weight of public invective chiefly fell, for the country had forgotten and probably never knew what Washington thought of irregular troops as reliable auxiliaries. Smyth, however, now free of amateur control by Van Rensselaer's retirement, was not ill-pleased at the fiasco, since he had favoured another spot for crossing the river. "Hull and Van Rensselaer," he declared, with dubious taste, to the men of New York, "were merely popular persons destitute alike of theory and experience in the art of war. In a few days the troops under my command will plant the American standard in Canada. They will conquer or die. Will you stand with your arms folded and look at this interesting struggle? The present is for renown. If you do, you will regret it and say, The friends of my country fell and I was not there." But later on Smyth ceases from invoking his fellow-countrymen and falls to depreciating the value

[1] Isaac Brock was gazetted a Knight a few days before he fell, but his promotion was of course not known in Canada till he was cold in his grave.

and prowess of the enemy. "Companions in arms! the time is at hand when you will cross the stream at Niagara to conquer Canada and enter a country that is to be one of the United States. You are superior in numbers to the enemy. Your personal strength and activity are greater. Your weapons are longer. The regular soldiers of the enemy are generally old men whose best years have been spent in the sickly climates of the West Indies. They will not be able to stand before you! you who charge with the bayonet." Why the rustics who mustered at Buffalo for the invasion of Canada should have been superior in physique to the U.E. Loyalist farmers of Upper Canada must have puzzled even those worthies themselves, while his men generally must have been exceptionally simple to believe themselves to be experts with the bayonet as compared with seasoned British infantry. If they had expected to handle weak, old men, they would have been surprised indeed when they got up against the "Green Tigers," as the 49th were called in America, though the militia, to be sure, were spared that unpleasant experience.

Above the Falls during this month of November, Smyth had 4,500 men, one-third of them regulars. Below, the remnant of Van Rensselaer's force, who had not had enough of it and gone home, remained to look across at the recent scene of conflict, now largely denuded of troops, to oppose the attack of Smyth on the Upper river. These last were extended over the sixteen miles between Lake Erie and the rapids just above the Falls. We have no space here for particularising the distribution of these small opposing forces, with an issue to decide so infinitely greater than was implied by their scanty numbers. It will be enough that on the 28th, at three in the morning, Smyth launched his grand attack. It was well conceived but entirely defeated. There was a great deal of confused fighting in the dark hours between such parties of his vanguard as succeeded in landing and about a third of the British force, the rest being occupied in serving the guns, or in guarding other threatened points, which the darkness and their small numbers and long line of defence made necessary. Many of the boats were sunk by artillery fire, but what fighting there was, was sharp, and when the attack was at length abandoned, eighty British and about twice that number of the enemy had fallen.

Next day, Smyth held a council of war in which opinions were divided. But he decided on another attempt that night, and issued a further heartening proclamation to his army with some frank hints at recent misdemeanours. "The General will be on hand," it ran. "Neither rain, snow nor frost will prevent the embarkation. The cavalry will scour the fields from Black Rock and suffer no idle spectators (a rap at the militia at Lewiston). While embarking, the band will play martial airs. 'Yankee Doodle' will be the signal to get under way. The landing will be effected in spite of cannon, for the whole army has seen that cannon are little to be dreaded." This was rather hard on the army, who on two occasions had seen so many boat-loads of poor fellows mutilated and sent to the bottom by artillery. And finally "Hearts of War! To-morrow will be a day memorable in the annals of the United States." But alas for this eloquent General! The "to-morrow" of his expectations never came. Disagreement among his staff caused a delay of two days. On December 1st, however, fifteen hundred regulars were successfully embarked when the Pennsylvania militia supporting them, dissenting from their General's view on the harmlessness of cannon fire, and mistrusting their own prowess with the bayonet, suddenly stood on their rights and refused to leave American soil. The defection spread, and after another council of war, the attempt was abandoned and the militia sent home, while the regulars retired into winter quarters, and General Smyth was given "indefinite leave of absence." So much for the "army of the centre" and its invasion of Upper Canada in the year 1812.

All efforts of the army to the eastward, under the Commander-in-Chief, Dearborn, had been equally futile. But on this field the attack had never been pressed home. Montreal, its object, was as vulnerable as it was important. Its old walls, useless enough, had recently been removed. Quite early in September, Dearborn had a force of 8,000 men, one-half of them regulars, at the foot of Lake Champlain on the Canadian frontier, and within forty miles of the city. There it remained, doing little or nothing till November, when it was reinforced up to 10,000. A few raids, answered by counter raids, summed up the year's activities in this field. The frontier here abandons the St. Lawrence near its Lake Ontario outlet, leaving a large slice of the Province of Quebec south of it and abutting on the New England States. Lower Canada was at any rate in a better situation for defence than the Upper Province. The French peasantry of the Richelieu country had refused to oppose, nay, had in great part welcomed, and in some cases even joined, the American invaders of 1775-6. On this occasion their sympathies were in reverse. A chain of posts had been drawn along this frontier by Prevost. The French-Canadians had responded readily to all calls made on them. Several companies of the sedentary militia organized themselves as garrison troops for Montreal and Quebec, thus releasing the British regulars and some companies of their embodied militia for active service along the frontier. There was a brigade of British regulars on this front near Montreal, consisting of the 109th, 103rd and part of the 8th regiments. The 1st Royal Scots, too, had just arrived. Some of these regiments, however, were nothing like up to strength.

The vital importance of "sea power" as regards the Great Lakes had not been overlooked. Kingston on the one side and Sackett's harbour on the other, of the narrowing eastern extremity of Lake Ontario, were for the moment the chief centres of naval activity. Brock had wished to attack Sackett's harbour and destroy the warships within it, but Prevost, henceforward almost as much the evil genius of this war as Howe had been of the former and greater one, had prevented it. He had misplaced ideas of non-provocative action, and that, too, against a most provocative and aggressive foe. He was also for conciliation where reciprocity was flouted, and for truces and armistices which merely gave the enemy more time for drawing on his great resources, whereas his own side had few to draw upon. Though a soldier with some good West Indian service to his credit, as well as much of the loyalty of the French-Canadians at this crisis, it would have been well indeed if he had now been replaced by some chief less complaisant to his foes and less obstinate with his friends. Fortunately, the country came through, despite him, and he, poor honest man, died under his impending court-martial, still half wondering why the soldiers anathematised him and why this trial!

Real distress now appeared in Upper Canada. Such a number of farmers and their sons had abandoned their homes in defence of the country as to lay a severe strain on a Province wholly dependent on agriculture of the "family farm" type. Provisions and clothing were both very short, and this too at a moment when the Mother Country, fighting for her life, and, as it seemed, with her last shilling, had little leisure to think of Canada. Clothing, above all, with winter now freezing up the land, was a most urgent matter, though the women in a thousand scattered homesteads, from Montreal to the remotest clearings on Lake Huron, worked their spinning-wheels night and day. A loyal and patriotic society was formed for providing these and other necessaries for the men in the field and alleviating the distress caused by their absence from home. Chief Justice Scott was President and the Treasurer was Dr. Strachan, then Rector of York, a famous schoolmaster, bishop and politician of early Canadian annals. Then again, there were the widows and orphans of the killed to be looked after. It is easy to realise how pitifully poor and ill-supplied was a young undeveloped Province like this with its 80,000 souls, for supporting a war against the United States! The Duke of Kent, who had formerly been quartered in Canada, collected £5,000 himself, and a further collection through the various Provinces produced £17,000. Such figures read to-day as utterly insignificant, and that these poor little sums were concerned with the fate of a nation-to-be seems incredible.

Lower Canada could not seriously help. It was all she could do to supply and defend herself. Her Legislature met before Christmas and Prevost congratulated them on the loyalty of the country and its successful resistance to the enemy, alluding with feeling to Brock's gallant death and the two glorious victories. The House voted a liberal sum from their slender resources towards the prosecution of the war. The Legislature of Upper Canada was also summoned to York by Sheaffe, now Lieutenant-Governor, and passed without opposition various measures of technical necessity to the defence of the country. In connection with the chances of war, particularly as regards Lower Canada, the lukewarmness of the New England States generally, already alluded to, must always be borne in mind. Their border regions became a field of war for the U.S. armies, but their people, to a great extent, excepting their seamen, took small part in the fighting, and carried on an inland trade with Canada as in normal times.

Though not actually part of the defence of Upper Canada in those years, 1812-13, still, as a war of aggression to that end, the campaign carried on in Michigan by the troops commanded by Colonel Procter, which had remained in the captured Detroit, must be briefly described. Action was, however, to some extent forced on Procter, for exasperation at Hull's defeat ran particularly high in Ohio and Kentucky, recently promoted to the dignity of States. Kentucky put 5,000 men under arms, and Generals Winchester and Harrison, the 'hero of Tippecanoe,' a big Indian fight, had no fewer than 7,000 men threatening a northward move on Detroit. This rapidly-increased force was due to one of Prevost's superfluous truces which had never even been agreed to by Dearborn, the American Commander-in-Chief. It had prevented Procter from hindering this concentration of enemy troops according to Brock's last instructions, an omission which drove away many of his Indians in disgust. The snow-bound winter of Michigan did not prevent the westward march of the Americans, so keen were they to avenge Detroit and then again to invade Canada. Procter's outposts now reached as far southward as Frenchtown, a fort at the western corner of Lake Erie, from which the American forces gathering at Sandusky, just to the south of it, drove out his small garrison after a smart defence. The object of the enemy was to push up the Detroit river from Lake Erie, that of Procter to prevent or delay them.

General Winchester was now at Frenchtown near the mouth of the river with a thousand men. Procter, without delay, set out to attack him from Amherstburg, on the opposite Canadian shore, with five hundred regulars and militia and rather more Indians under the famous Tecumseh. It was now the middle of January, and the whole river mouth, from shore to shore, was frozen tight. "Across this," says Major Richardson, who was with them, and wrote a history of the war, "we marched for four miles, a compact force, a small, resolute and martial company. The rumble of guns upon the icy track, the war-cries of the Indians, the glint of the bright wintry sun upon the burnished arms, left a lasting memory upon my mind."

In the dark of a bitter January morning, too cold, apparently, for even scouts to be posted, Procter found Frenchtown unprepared, though partially warned by the accidental discharge of a musket. After some sharp frontal fighting by the British troops, Tecumseh, with his Indians, moving swiftly round, took the place in rear and flank and completed the victory with considerable slaughter. Four hundred Americans took refuge in a block-house. General Winchester, being outside it without available troops, surrendered at discretion with 500 men, including those in the blockhouse. A hundred fugitives escaped to tell the tale to General Harrison some 20 miles to the rear. Four hundred of the enemy lay dead upon the snow, for the Indians, exasperated by the destruction of their villages, made no prisoners, and Tecumseh, always the restraining hand, was absent from this battle on other duty. Nor were they proof against scalps. One of those lifted at Frenchtown happened to be from the head of a brother-in-law of Henry Clay, a very leader among the war-hawk politicians. It may be imagined that such a scalp was worth more to the war press than those of a whole company without political affinities.

Procter lost on this occasion about a third of his meagre British force. He had more prisoners, too, than white troops to guard them, though he managed to get the unwounded away. The victory at least checked Harrison's advance on Canada and sent him, though tardily, into winter quarters. For this achievement Procter was made a Brigadier. He had not the men to follow up his victory, so retired with his prisoners to Amherstburg. Nothing of moment occurred on this front till the winter had broken. Harrison had built a strong fort on the Maumee river, and with over 3,000 men, either present or in sight, and larger forces in reserve, was preparing for a grand invasion of Canada by way of Detroit and Hull's projected route. Procter, now back at Sandwich, made a daring attempt to capture this same Fort Meigs on the Maumee. It was early May and many of his militiamen had gone home to sow their much-needed grain. He had been reinforced by some more men of the 41st, that much-enduring regiment which had fought in every engagement and endured every hardship in this arduous campaign. In killed, wounded and sick it had suffered heavily, and was yet to suffer still worse things. Tecumseh, however, was now back with over a thousand Indians whom he had collected from the despoiled and vengeful tribes to the southward. On the last day of April, Procter arrived before Fort Meigs with 400 of the 41st, some three-pounders, and 600 militia. The Indians, having travelled over land, joined him here. Some sharp fighting took place around the fort, resulting in the capture of 500 prisoners by the British; but they had not enough men or heavy guns to take the place itself. Harrison, who was afterwards President, could address his troops with a vigorous eloquence equal to that of any of his contemporaries in the field. He told those with whom he was invading, and incidentally looting, Canada that they were out to defend the freedom of their country and fighting Canadians 'who were driven reluctantly to the field by the bayonets of mercenaries.'

Soon afterwards, Procter made an attack on Fort Stephenson, where Harrison lay with a strong force, but failed to take it. Land fighting on this front was now at a deadlock. Procter, with his shrinking force, was no longer strong enough to take the initiative, while Harrison could not cross the river into Canada so long as it was commanded by British ships from Lake Erie. It was now necessary for the Americans to destroy the British fleet and get command of the lake. The summer had worn itself away with much marching and counter-marching over long distances in Michigan territory, and much futile bloodshed, and it was the 18th of September when the two fleets sailed out into the lake for the inevitable but unequal fight. For Captain Barclay, the British commander, who had lost an arm at Trafalgar, though he had much the weaker squadron, had no choice but to fight. Moreover, he was almost at his last crust for provisions. To man his fleet, he had 55 seamen and 102 Canadian sailors, who were mere boatmen, a deficiency which compelled him to ship 250 officers and men of the much-enduring 41st Regiment. The American commander, Perry, on the other hand, mustered 532 men in all, 329 of whom were seamen, 158 marines and 45 volunteers. There were two vessels of 300 tons on either side; the rest were much smaller craft.

The engagement began at noon and was most stubbornly contested for several hours. The flagships *Lawrence* and *Detroit*, carrying Perry and Barclay respectively, fought desperately together for half that time, and were terribly shattered, the former striking her flag after Perry had boarded another vessel. The guns of some of Barclay's six ships were almost useless at a range within the enemy's easy distance. His own ship, owing to the failure of a supply from the east, had been filled with old guns from the Fort of Amherstburg. Barclay himself was badly wounded, and after a resistance conducted with great skill and courage, and a loss of 140 in killed and wounded, his dismantled ships managed to escape from the two or three battered vessels that alone floated of the enemy's squadron. Thus the victory was complete, though for some time it hung in the balance, and the loss in men was about equal. It came as a god-send to the Washington Government, who were thankful for some modicum of comfort. Even Madison for once emulated his eloquent generals and pronounced it "a victory never surpassed in lustre if in magnitude." Yet Trafalgar was still fresh in men's minds!

Lake Erie was now in American hands, and the western part of the Province lay apparently at their mercy. Procter had no choice but to retreat through the peninsula of Upper Canada to his friends on the Niagara frontier, the main seat of war. His white force was now reduced to seven hundred men, harvest having imperatively claimed most of his militia, though a thousand Indians, under Tecumseh, remained with him. The retreating force sailed up the Straits into Lake St. Clair, and to the mouth of the Thames, and thence began their disastrous march up that river, with accompanying boats loaded with an amount of baggage pronounced superfluous by the court-martial which ultimately sat on Procter. Hitherto, that officer had been uniformly a bold and resourceful leader. His morale seemed now to break down, and he could do nothing right. He was hampered, too, by the presence of his wife and daughter, a superfluous burden, surely, in such campaigning as this! The veteran remnant of his troops, mainly of the 41st, were half of them in sore plight, worn out by two seasons' campaigning along unhealthy waterways, often on frozen plains and on half-rations, for the Indians had to be well fed as a first condition of service, and they were now his main support. Harrison started in pursuit with 3,500 men, including a swarm of Kentucky horsemen, under their old Indian fighting Governor, Shelby.

It is a melancholy and brief tale this retreat and pursuit. It is assuredly not one of the great retreats of history! No one in these days has ever heard of it. In those it was but a mere incident in a war the Imperial import of which people at home absorbed in their own tremendous anxieties, hardly even then understood. The incident, however, was tragic enough. A good officer, who for a year had held the open gateway of Western Canada by fighting the enemy on their own soil, with a handful of men, under every imaginable difficulty, had now given way before the approach of overwhelming forces. His duty and that of the gallant remnant of the men who had served with him, was now to retreat as rapidly as possible, to outpace his pursuers and get his men, and such of his supplies as would not hinder his movements, safely back to Headquarters on the Niagara front, about 100 miles distant. But Procter had broken down under the strain, and in retreat proved dilatory and inefficient. He encumbered his march with superfluous material. He refused, and perhaps rightly, to stand and fight, as Tecumseh at various favourable spots implored him to do, nor yet would he hurry, which was his first duty. In a week he had not covered more than forty miles, leaving stores and guns and invalided men to be captured by the enemy right upon his heels. Near the Mission Station of Moravian Town, he was at last compelled to stand or surrender. Of the sickly remnant of the 41st under 500 were able to take their place in the line, flanked by Tecumseh with about the same number of Indians, the rest having left in disgust.

Harrison's swarms of mounted men, backed by over two thousand infantry, after receiving a couple of volleys from the attenuated British force, simply rode them down to easy surrender. Sick, ill-fed and unused to retreat, the heart had been knocked out of them, and, worse still, their commander had deserted them. He was stationed in the rear and on the surrender of his men escaped on horseback. A sorry end to the career of a brave man. Tecumseh and his men fought with their usual, but here unavailing, bravery. The great chief himself fell at their head, his body being carried off by his men. Some Kentuckians falling on another mistaken for it, having first imitated the barbarous custom of some Indian squaws, then made razor strops of the skin, a singularly misdirected act of savagery, as Tecumseh himself had an untarnished reputation for clemency.[1] Harrison took 600 prisoners, including 150 in hospital and their attendants. He again showed himself subject to the prevailing weakness of his type by reporting that his men had achieved this crushing victory by "superior valour." Statistics make comment needless. Prevost was much worse in the other direction, for he publicly censured and with contumely this poor remnant of the gallant 41st. Later judgment emphatically denied the justice of this criticism, uttered by a man, who two years later, was to hurry back in retreat 6,000 enraged Peninsular

[1] See Life of Tecumseh (E. S. Raymond).

veterans from before a force so weak as to have no expectation itself of successful resistance!

Procter, court-martialled a year later at Montreal, was found guilty, from the beginning of his retreat, on every count except personal misconduct, his former services and bravery being fully admitted. A public reprimand, with suspension from pay and duty for six months, was the sentence. Harrison was now victorious all along the line. He carried his army back, however, to Detroit, burning the Moravian Mission for some reason and looting freely all the way such limited possessions as had yet arisen in those wild woods. He now sent his militia to their homes while he himself with a thousand regulars proceeded by water to reinforce his friends on the Niagara frontier.

But these doings in the West have carried us all through the open season of 1813, in which much had been done in the nearer fields of both politics and war. For one thing, to the joy of one portion of the American nation and to the dismay of the other, the news of Napoleon's failure in Russia had been received. There had been spirited debates in Congress. Josiah Quincey had denounced the invasion of Canada as "a cruel, wanton and wicked attack, in which neither plunder nor glory were to be gained upon an unoffending people, bound to the Americans by ties of blood and good neighbourhood. An attack undertaken for the punishment, over Canadian shoulders, of another people three thousand miles away, by young politicians fluttering and cackling on the floor of that House, half-hatched, the shell still on their heads and their pin feathers not yet shed; politicians to whom pity, reason, justice, were nothing, revenge everything." To this and like expressions from other New Englanders, Williams of South Carolina replied: "The St. Lawrence must be crossed by a well-appointed army of twenty thousand men, supported by a reserve of ten thousand. At the same moment we move on Canada, a corps of ten thousand more must threaten Halifax from the Province of Maine. The honour and character of the nation require that the British power on our borders should be annihilated in this campaign."

The regular army had been increased to 55,000 men, mainly destined for the invasion of Canada, supported by numerous militia. In the two Canadas this summer, there were about 7,000 regular troops, including the five Colonial corps, the 104th (New Brunswick), the 103rd (Newfoundland), the Glengarries, the Voltigeurs (French) and the Canadian Fencibles (mixed). In addition to these, were the whole or parts of the 1st, 8th, 41st, 49th, 100th, and a few dragoons. Later in the year, the 13th and the two de Watteville regiments (Germans) arrived. There came too, this year, Admiral Sir James Yeo, a young sailor of enterprise, with some other naval officers, and about 400 seamen for the Lake service. The virtual destruction of both fleets in the recent engagement on Lake Erie had at any rate left the British free of it for the moment. Thanks, however, to Prevost's folly in the previous year, the Americans had now the upper hand on the more important waters of Lake Ontario.

In the spring, before the ice had melted, General Dearborn was at Sackett's harbour, opposite Kingston, with five thousand regulars and two thousand militia. At Buffalo, watching that Niagara frontier, he had another three thousand regular troops. His orders from Washington, which had now got rid of that luckless strategist Dr. Eustis, were to cross the ice, attack Kingston, and thence move down the north shore of Lake Ontario and capture the little capital of York. This scheme fell through. Instead of it, a Major Forsyth crossed the St. Lawrence from Ogdensburg, and harried the undefended village of Brockville, looting it of goods and stock and fifty of its inhabitants. Colonel Prescott, who was in command of the troops extended from Kingston down the St. Lawrence, sent a vigorous protest to Dearborn against this style of warfare, but without satisfaction. Prevost, arriving at this moment, Colonel Macdonnell, of the Glengarries, requested leave to retaliate on the fortified Ogdensburg. The ever-deprecating Prevost, however, refused permission till the Colonel frightened him by hinting at the insecurity of his road to Kingston. Prevost then consented, but to a "demonstration" only.

Macdonnell, having his own views as to this, took five

hundred men, picked from various regiments, and crossed the frozen river, over a mile wide, under a heavy fire from the fort. Unchecked by this, his men landing the guns and dragging them through the deep snow up the hill, attacked the town, driving away the enemy posted in the windows with cannon fire, and leaving the rest to the bayonet. The adjacent fort, containing Forsyth, was next attacked, its batteries rushed or reduced to silence, and the garrison driven out pell-mell to seek shelter with the routed townsmen in the distant woods. Forsyth had been promoted for his raid on the town of Brockville. What blame, if any, attached to him for his failure at Ogdensburg so hurriedly we do not hear. But Macdonnell's was a great achievement, effected in broad daylight under heavy fire against a fortified town. His loss was sixty men. Among other brave deeds, Captain Jenkin, of the New Brunswick loyalist family, continued to lead his company of Glengarries after both his arms were shattered by grape, till he fell from loss of blood. A large supply of arms and stores was captured, the barracks were burned, as well as four warships fast in the ice. Ogdensburg gave no more trouble as a base of attack for the rest of the war.

The American fleet, now dominating Lake Ontario, was organized and led by Chauncey, a skilful but not over-enterprising Admiral, and consisted of thirteen ships carrying 84 guns and thirteen hundred seamen. So in late April, when the waters were ice-free, it was at General Dearborn's disposal. He had abandoned the attack on Kingston, and had decided to sail with a sufficient force across Lake Ontario and capture York. This was a small place as yet, and of slight importance, save as the Provincial capital and the centre of administration, but if held in force it would cut the communications between Eastern and Western Canada. Neither Prevost nor Sheaffe, who, since the Queenston Heights affair, had proved a poor successor to Brock, had done anything for its defence, though Sheaffe was there now with a trifling force. To shorten the story, lest amid the intricacies of this protracted struggle it becomes too lengthy and involved, it will be enough here that the Americans landed under the guns of their ships in the almost land-locked harbour along which a city of half a million souls now stretches.

The little garrison gave the Americans several hours' fighting in the surrounding woods before they surrendered the town. It comprised 400 of the local militia, and a hundred regulars, while 180 of the 8th regiment arrived accidentally *en route* for Niagara. Sheaffe got away with most of the regulars, while the militia were sent home on parole. The American, General Pike, commanding some 2,000 men, was killed but the one-sided skirmishing was dwarfed by the terrific explosion of a magazine containing 500 barrels of powder and quantities of shot, which killed 52 and disabled 180 of the Americans. By the terms of surrender, all property was to be respected. But the Parliament buildings, recently erected, were deliberately burned, together with their records and the public library, while several houses were damaged and looted. The American Admiral was shocked at this work of the army and even made some futile efforts to mitigate it. But the army sailed away to the Niagara front, making no use whatever of the capture, and leaving the little capital relieved of its captors and bereft of its defenders to contemplate the havoc within its gates, and two years later no doubt to remain quite unmoved when the capitol at Washington suffered a like fate as a just, if indiscreet, reprisal.

JAMES MADISON, ESQ.
President of the United States
From a painting by T. Gimbrede. *Engraved by* W. R. Jones

CHAPTER X

THE WAR—1813-14

WHY Dearborn did not fortify and garrison York, thereby cutting the land connection between Eastern and Western Canada, as his possession of Lake Ontario had already cut it by sea, does not appear. Probably, the War Office, still confident of overwhelming Upper Canada by numbers this season, did not think it worth while. By the end of May, Dearborn's force on the Niagara frontier, still regarded by the old plan as the chief point of attack, consisted of 6,000 men. Harrison's Western army, as we have seen, was to recapture Detroit, push on through Western Canada, brushing Procter aside, and join the Niagara forces in bearing down all opposition in front of it. With the peninsula of Upper Canada thus cleared of the British, the united army would then sweep down eastward unopposed, and joining hands with the force now threatening Montreal, would capture that city and advance on Quebec.

There is a much-quoted saying that Canada was unconquered till Quebec was won, and to that end sea power was necessary. Quebec city might, no doubt, have been held after 1812 by British sea-power, but a Gibraltar planted on American soil, and that, too, among a local population not of British stock, is surely unthinkable. Even if such a thing were physically possible, at what a cost of chronic ill-feeling, and how futilely, without territory of consequence, would such a post be held! If it had been a question of retaining a fragment of a lost British North America for maritime or strategic purposes, Halifax on the Atlantic was, at least, more conceivable in that capacity. But the American war party foresaw no such fly in the ointment of their triumph. The British Navy was in demand all over the globe, and there were hundreds of American warships of sorts already afloat.

Fort George, described in the Queenston affair as defending the British left, near the junction of river and lake, with the town of Newark lying inconveniently between its batteries and the river mouth, was the first object of this fresh American attack. Along the Niagara front, General Vincent, now in command, had eighteen hundred regulars and, owing to the exactions of the spring sowing, but six hundred militia. Of these a thousand regulars, drawn from the 49th, 8th, Glengarries and Newfoundlanders, with four hundred militia and a few gunners were all that could be spared for defence of the fort. On May 28th, four thousand Americans landed under the guns of Chauncey's fleet and of their own at Fort Niagara. A small party with a gun checked the landing for a moment, till they were mostly killed, and the Americans came on in columns, commanded by Winfield Scott and three brigadiers, two of them political lawyers. Six hundred British regulars and militia contested the advance outside the fort most stubbornly till, raked by musketry and by grape-shot from the fleet, they fell back with a loss of a third of their number, supported by a column led by Colonel Harvey, whose name stands out conspicuously throughout this war. But against such odds the fort was untenable, so after three hours' resistance and spiking the guns, Vincent brought his force away and retired to Burlington Heights, a ridge some 30 miles back, on which the city of Hamilton now stands.

In the meantime, he had sent word to Ormsby and Bisshopp, commanding at Chippewa, near the Falls and at Fort Erie, to join him, since the Niagara frontier was no longer defensible with the forces at his command. The Americans followed Vincent rather cautiously, lest Procter, retreating in good time before Harrison's approach, should suddenly join him; but poor Procter, as we know, was at this moment still holding up Harrison among the remote waterways of Michigan. Not far south of Vincent's fresh headquarters at Burlington, and near the site of the present railroad station of Stoney Creek, between Hamilton and Niagara, the American Brigadiers, Chandler and Windler, with 3,000 men in pursuit of Vincent, had pitched their camp for the night. The vigilant and zealous

Harvey, having reconnoitred it, found it, as he had more or less expected, of a force under the command of lawyers, rather carelessly disposed. It was seven miles distant, and a night attack was decided upon.

An exceptionally dark night favoured the enterprise, and by two in the morning Vincent and Harvey, with seven hundred men of the 8th and 49th regiments, reached the American camp unperceived. Attack was possible on one side only, but even this was negligently guarded. The outposts were bayoneted without a sound, and but for the foolish shouts and cheers of some British soldiers, the startled enemy would have had no more than time to leap to their arms before seven hundred of General Smythe's "decrepit old men from the tropics" would have been among them with the bayonet. As it was, the Americans had several minutes' notice, and time to form their line and man their guns. But the confusion in the darkness was complete. In the end, however, a party of British, with great gallantry, rushed the guns and bayoneted the gunners, while the rest of the force, after much confused fighting, was ultimately driven from the camp, leaving it with all its stores and guns in the hands of the British, who also took a hundred prisoners, including the two generals. Vincent drew off his men before daylight could reveal their paucity of numbers, with the loss, however, of two hundred rank and file.

The effect of this shattering blow was prodigious. The Americans retreated on the following day with precipitation, leaving their dead unburied, their wounded uncared for, and all their stores. At Forty-mile Creek, *en route* for Niagara, they were met by supports from Fort George under General Lewis, who now took command of the army, still some three thousand strong. But all intention of retracing their steps was now abandoned at the approach of a British fleet under Sir James Yeo, bringing reinforcements and supplies for Vincent, and firing grape-shot into the American ranks. Another panic now seized the Americans, and another hasty retreat took them hotfoot to Fort George, leaving behind them a further hundred disabled men, a big supply of flour, and their tents all standing. The rest of their effects were hurriedly shipped in twenty *bateaux*, all of which were captured by Yeo. Chauncey, for some reason, had slacked in his naval activities and allowed Yeo to cruise freely along the American shore, and seize magazines and supply ships bound for Niagara. Back again at Fort George with a loss, all told, of a thousand men, the expedition had failed dismally.

It was now July. Instead of sweeping victoriously through the country from Detroit with Procter on the run before them, Harrison and his forces were still in remote Michigan, greatly worried by Procter with his Indians, his militia and his faithful 41st. The Americans on this Niagara front were now once again across the water on their own shore, save on a little patch around Fort George which they still held. Vincent, too, had received fresh supplies and another regiment, the 104th (New Brunswick loyalists), embodied in the British army, which in the past winter had marched 200 miles through trackless snow and ice-bound forests between Fredericton and Quebec. Another general, de Rottenberg, an Anglo-Swiss, like Prevost, had been made Lieutenant-Governor of Upper Canada, and took some brief share in the fighting with Vincent, and there was much desultory but bitter warfare throughout the summer and autumn. The Americans had been forced back across the upper river by the energy of a strong force of Canadian-Indians, under the son of the famous Joseph Brant, combined with some well-led local militia. But the enemy had now themselves enlisted the services of three or four hundred Seneca Indians, whose villages in New York State had escaped destruction.

With all their protests, the Americans were themselves using savages for the invasion of an unoffending country. Most of the British Indians, on the other hand, belonged to that country, and like the British themselves, were fighting for their own homes. In short, both sides used the Indians when they could. The Red Man chiefly favoured the British because they treated him fairly and the Americans did not. This is the simple truth of the matter. It is admitted that Canada has from the first kept faith consistently with her Indians, while every well-informed American is conscious that their Indian policy in the past has many dark pages. But the Senecas of the late Five, or, to be precise, Six Nations Confederacy, were now persuaded that President Madison, not King George, against whom they really had a technical, though unavoidable, grievance, was now their father. But he, poor gentleman, as may be imagined, was now getting very unhappy. The victories his planter friends had foretold with such unmeasured confidence had not come off, but instead of them only disastrous failure. The New England States were jeering at him, when they were not cursing him, for his obnoxious embargoes and restrictions on their commerce, already half-crippled by a war most of them detested. It was almost ludicrous. Here was half a nation of landsmen calling Heaven to witness the violent outrages of Great Britain on American ships and seamen, when the other half, or, let us say a third part, who owned most of the said ships and seamen, thought the war a deplorable blunder, and—particularly since the Orders in Council had been revoked at the very opening of it—a folly and a crime. As the very birthplace, too, of liberty and freedom in the extremist American sense, this alliance with the tyrant of the world seemed to them monstrous. A minority thought otherwise, of course, just as in the Middle and Southern States there were many saner people who disagreed absolutely with the war craze. And there were a great many more now who did not like it than there had been a year before! The produce of the plantations was beginning to pile up in the warehouses and there was every prospect of it remaining there and rotting.

A sentimental offset to these practical disadvantages and disappointments to be sure, was afforded by four or five single-ship naval victories, when the large frigates and long-range guns that the Americans had been clever enough to build with a view to the war, overmatched as many British frigates of the same nominal rating. But the result had no more effect on the war than so many international boat-races, and by the end of the year the American coasts found themselves effectually blockaded. The only people at all enjoying themselves were the privateers of various nations, and the British Maritime Provinces, where the U.E. Loyalists of Nova Scotia and New Brunswick were making money rapidly. This, too, was actually the beginning of that split between the Northern and Southern States, that half a century later almost disrupted the Republic, and in resisting which the North had to deny those very rights of freedom of action inserted by their grandfathers in the Constitution.

Many American writers of to-day consider that it was through all those troublous times, immediately following the Revolution, that the loss of the collective wisdom, experience and balance of the expatriated loyalists was most felt.[1] If they had been treated with sanity, there is no doubt that the temper of the nation would have been better balanced, and the inter-State quarrels less fractious, while in all probability the futile war of 1812, with its fresh legacy of hatred, would never have been fought. Yet if the loyalists had been wisely treated, there would have been no such Canada as we know to-day! They did not suffer in vain.

The British Government, on realising the temper and feeling of the New England States, gave instructions to their officers on active service to discriminate so far as possible when causing loss or damage, between those who wished to be their enemies and those who did not. Surely a normal and prudent measure! This, however, was not Madison's opinion, for he and his colleagues were thrown into a frenzy of indignation. They did not see, or apparently did not see, the obviousness of such a procedure to any sensible statesman. They only detected a diabolical design of the ever-malignant British to undermine the harmony so painfully achieved by a kindred nation of whom they were jealous. "Great Britain," Madison announced to Congress "introduces into her modes of warfare a system equally distinguished by the deformity of its features and the depravity of its character." Such was the verdict of the War Cabinet on the discrimination of Great Britain between active and passive enemies. It will be remembered that just before the war Madison had given a big sum of money to a rascally Secret Service

[1] See Fiske, Van Tyne and others.

agent of a Canadian Governor for his papers. These consisted of quite harmless confidential letters respecting the current state of opinion in the United States, information concerning which was vitally necessary to the Governor of a country living under the threat of war. If this commonplace incident threw Madison and his friends in Congress into an uncontrollable uproar, one may well ask what was the clamour about, and were all these people quite mad? New England trading-ships were treated leniently, whereas the blockade from New York southwards was rigid. The Washington Government passed non-export regulations, mostly futile. Was it likely that States who denounced the war were prepared to sacrifice what remained of their trade for a pack of Southern planters and landmen, because they had chosen to raid Canada and embrace the arch-fiend Napoleon? Something like this was their point of view. It was all very deplorable, of course, that this recently formed Republic, the model for the world, which the world, the British world at any rate, had been watching with much real interest and little of the jealousy attributed to it by its hyper-sensitive protagonists, should talk disruption. It was altogether sad that at the very first serious test it should thus threaten to fall in half.

To return to the land war, which along the Niagara frontier consisted of raids and counter-raids across the river. The most notable incident, and one moreover with an undying romance attached to it, was in connection with a post at Beaver Dam on the Canadian side. A young Lieutenant Fitzgibbon, with a selected detachment from the New Brunswick regiment, and Grant's Indians, had been making such damaging raids over the border that Colonel Boerstler, with 570 regulars, was sent by Dearborn on an attempt to destroy it. Starting from Queenston, just then in American occupation, some officers were there overheard discussing the enterprise by one Laura Secord, the wife of a local landowner and officer then serving in the militia. This gallant young woman lost no time. Starting before daybreak and avoiding the sentries by circuitous forest trails, she eventually, after twenty miles of rough travelling, stumbled upon an armed Indian camp, whose peremptory challenge was alarming enough. She explained her mission, and the Indians took her to Fitzgibbon, who, thus warned of the attack, made full preparations for it in the form of an ambush. The result, after some fighting, was the capture of Boerstler's entire command, including some guns. Laura Secord remains the heroine of early Canadian history. She lived to a good old age and her tomb, surmounted by her bust, may be seen in the graveyard at Lundy's Lane, a fitting spot as the scene of the fiercest battle of the whole war.

Wilkinson was now appointed Commander-in-Chief *vice* Dearborn. He had served under both Arnold and Gates in the Revolutionary War. He was also a friend of Aaron Burr, and had been under suspicion of being concerned in that subtle politician's intrigues in the south-west, for which he stood trial. The intentions of the Washington Government were now bent on a combined attack in force on Montreal, the heart of the Canadas. Late in this summer, therefore, Wilkinson began to concentrate his forces at Sackett's Harbour for a descent of the river. In consequence of this, public attention was now largely withdrawn from the Niagara front, and some of the troops engaged there were shifted eastward. There had been some disagreement at Washington as to whether it was better to conquer and occupy Western Canada before attacking Montreal. Wilkinson pronounced against this, and was for leaving a sufficient force only on that frontier to hold the British troops occupying the Peninsula and keep them amused with raids. He did not take into account what might happen to the American frontier!

For soon after the Beaver Dam affair, a force of 250 British crossed the river to Blackrock, stormed the batteries, scattered the garrison, carried off or destroyed eight guns, and burnt the barracks and other houses, besides a ship in the harbour. Unfortunately, their leader, Colonel Bisshopp, a young loyalist who had done fine work throughout the war, was killed. And now the Canadian traitors, the disaffected, an always suspected though vaguely known element, came out into the open. They even formed a corps under Wilcockes, who had been turned out of the Legislature and the country, it may be remembered, some time previously. The American General in Command, naturally enough, welcomed their assistance and highly commended their efforts. They seem, however, to have been chiefly active in the looting of loyalist families when some temporary advantage gained by the Americans had made it safe. They hung about Harrison's pursuit of Procter and got large pickings in his trail. Isolated groups of militiamen home from the war on farm duty, joined for defence against these miscreants. They caught a score of them red-handed on one occasion and shot them offhand.

When Perry's victory on Lake Erie followed by Procter's collapse before the advancing Harrison was known, the latter general was expected in force on the Niagara front, so Vincent withdrew his troops again to Burlington Heights, the best defensive position against an American movement eastward. But Prevost took alarm and ordered an evacuation of the whole West of the Province, and a retirement to Kingston. Vincent and his officers, however, decided to ignore the order and stayed where they were. Their decision was fortunate. For Harrison and most of his force, after crushing Procter, went on to join Wilkinson's grand attack on Montreal. We must now follow him there and leave the Niagara frontier as no longer for a time the pivotal spot of the war, and return later to tell what happened there during the rest of 1813. Suffice it to say here that when the threat of Harrison's invasion from the West passed away, Vincent returned to the river front, and the former situation of the opposing forces all along that line was more or less restored. As above mentioned, men from both the British and American forces had been withdrawn for the great attack on Montreal. But this did not prevent the interludes of bloody fighting and raiding that continued to distinguish this border-line for the rest of the year.

Little of moment had occurred in the eastern area of war since Macdonnell's successful attack on Ogdensburg, described in a former chapter. A much larger display of force had been made by the Americans than at the Niagara front, but it achieved almost nothing. On May 28th, the day on which Vincent had been forced out of Fort James, Admiral Sir George Yeo, with his fleet carrying seven hundred and fifty regulars, advanced against Sackett's Harbour, the American naval headquarters opposite Kingston, its British equivalent. The garrison consisted of nine hundred regulars and five hundred Albany militia. Unfortunately, Prevost himself was in chief command. For the troops were actually in the boats ready for a surprise attack, and full of confidence, when he whistled them on board again, nobody to this day knows why. After this timely warning to the garrison, he decided to make a fresh start the next morning. But now there was not a breath of air, and the ships could not get near enough to cover the landing from the boats, or even to use their guns. Still Prevost pressed the attack under these untoward conditions and without artillery, as he had rejected his opportunity the morning before with every condition in his favour. A landing was effected, however, on Horse Island, connected by a causeway with the mainland, where the Albany militia were posted. These ran, almost at the first shot, but the British and American regulars had a fight so stubborn that the enemy set fire to their ships in the harbour, and even to their barracks preparatory to an evacuation. At this moment the fatuous Prevost ordered a retreat! Major Drummond, of distinguished service through this war, guaranteed him success if he might have but a few moments more. But Prevost, as obstinate as ever in his scuttle policy, and timid in all forward action, silenced the protests of his officers, and reshipping his force sailed away with a loss in killed and wounded of 250 officers and men. Yet a few months later he was publicly accusing of cowardice the exhausted, half-starved remnant of a gallant hard-fighting regiment for surrendering at Moravian town to more than five times their number of fresh, well-fed troops! This was the most important of several equally inconclusive incidents of that summer along this central section of the frontier.

But now preparations were going forward for a conclusive and final attack, this time directly on the Lower

Province, the conquest of which must eliminate Upper Canada from any further resistance. By October, General Wilkinson was at Sackett's Harbour with about 8,000 regular troops, preparing for a descent of the St. Lawrence to Montreal. He was delayed for nearly a month, according to his own account, by bad weather. He was to be met before approaching Montreal, at the junction of the Chateauguay river and the St. Lawrence by a second army, mustered at Plattsburg on Lake Champlain and thence descending to the St. Lawrence by the old war route. This force consisted of 4,000 regulars, ten guns with artillery, some cavalry and 1,500 militiamen. It was under the command of General Wade Hampton, a South Carolinian, who, after uniting with Wilkinson, was to resign to him the chief command. By the end of September, he had moved forward to a point known as Four Corners, where the Chateauguay river entered Canadian territory between 30 and 40 miles from Montreal. There he lingered, waiting for notification of Wilkinson's long-delayed start.

The two armies broke camp the same day, Wade Hampton beginning his march down the Chateauguay Valley. A dilatory, ineffective general, he moved slowly for four days through a forest country towards an open region which would be greatly in his favour. Astride his path in an interlude of woodland stood De Salaberry, the French-Canadian officer, immortalised by this day's achievement, with his 300 Voltigeurs, while Colonel Ferguson, with 80 Fencibles and 200 Indians, was beside him. This little force was merely intended to harass and check Wade Hampton's advance. Some miles behind it was a corps of 600 French militia, well drilled and disciplined by Colonel Macdonnell, of the Glengarries. De Salaberry opened this extraordinary engagement to which even Hull's surrender at Detroit offers scarcely a parallel. He extended his few hundred men with 50 Indians in line, partially protected by an abbatis across Hampton's path, their left on the river which covered Hampton's right. Just across the river, Macdonnell, with his 600 militiamen, was marching up. General Izard, another South Carolinian, commanded the American advance, which was moving down the left bank of the river towards the open country. This was on October 25th. On the preceding day, a force of 3,500 men, under Colonel Purdy, had been sent down the right bank of the river through the woods to cross a certain ford in the rear of such enemy force as might be opposed to them. But Purdy and his men had lost their way, or had been purposely misdirected, and spent all night in the forest, and were still wandering vaguely about the next day when they hit off the ford of their intended destination.

Here, however, they were met by a volley from a band of militia. Pushing past them, they ran into a part of Macdonnell's militia stationed on the same bank, and soon afterwards encountered a heavy fire from the Canadians on the further bank. This threw the Americans into confusion. They dispersed in the woods, got lost again, and began firing indiscriminately on each other. Ultimately, exhausted with their long day and night of woodland wanderings and entirely demoralised, they did not get back to Headquarters till the next day, when the battle, such as it had been, was over. But the dramatic part of the fight was along a barricade of tree-trunks thrown up in the rear by De Salaberry's men, to which they retired after the first exchange of fire. Both Voltigeur's and Macdonnell's regiment, together with about 200 Indians, seem now to have been in touch with each other, though the accounts are confusing. De Salaberry caused all his buglers to blow, while all his Indians raised the war whoop, and the Canadians yelled with such effect that Izard thought he had a whole army in front of him, and after waiting in vain for Purdy to join him faced about and marched his men back to Headquarters. Wade Hampton was so upset that he lost his head. With such a force, he could, of course, have walked over that in front of him. Instead of this, he faced about and carried his whole army back to Plattsburg, whence he had started a week before.

The whole affair was little more than a series of skirmishes, with the loss of but a hundred men to the Americans and about twenty to the Canadians. But the result was in effect momentous. It broke up this most formidable advance on Montreal, which could not have maintained a siege by about 14,000 regular troops and artillery, and stopped dead the advance of Wilkinson. That general was furious when the news of Wade Hampton's fiasco was received and wrote to him in unmeasured terms. Wade Hampton's excuses seem to have been feeble. It was said that he drank. It is difficult otherwise to account for his amazing conduct. His indignant officers were said in after years to shrink from any admission that they had been at Chateauguay. The country was subjected to yet another burst of indignation. But unlike poor Hull who, much less culpable, was sentenced to be shot, Wade Hampton was not even court-martialled. His performance remained a mystery, subject only to the before-mentioned solution more than hinted at by some American writers. Though in effect but a mere skirmish, the incident known as the "Battle of Chateauguay" stands out deservedly in Canadian history, for it almost certainly saved Montreal, and, further, it was achieved solely by French-Canadian troops. De Salaberry, leader of the vanguard, for his extraordinary coolness in the action and resource in imposing himself on Hampton as leader of a large force, has achieved immortality, though his senior, Colonel Macdonnell, equally deserving, no doubt, was the actual recipient of official gratitude. Some American writers brush away Chateauguay as a battle and describe it as a mere check which gave Wade Hampton a poor excuse to thwart Wilkinson whom he hated, and back out of an expedition he disapproved of because not inaugurated by himself. Probably sectional jealousy and politics had some share in this astonishing fiasco, but French-Canadians do not look at it from that point of view and regard Chateauguay as a kind of Thermopylæ.

But in these late October days, Wilkinson was slowly descending the St. Lawrence from Ogdensburg towards Montreal, about 100 miles distant, quite ignorant of Hampton's defection. He had nearly 9,000 men, a force sufficient in itself, one would have thought, to overwhelm Montreal, garrisoned as it was chiefly by French sedentary militia, well intentioned enough but without serious discipline. Wilkinson had some good officers, too, for the politicians were being gradually shed and efficient regimental leaders were coming to the front. The British were dogging Wilkinson's steps. They could do no more, for Colonel Morrison, in command, had only the 49th and 89th regiments, both much under strength, a few artillery and 300 militia from Glengarry and Dundas, in all under a thousand men. Several slight skirmishes were engaged in, till on November 11th the more serious action of Chrystler's Farm was fought on the Canadian bank of the river, just above the Long Sault rapids, which Wilkinson was in the very act of descending. It was a much tougher fight than Chateauguay, and in a manner shared with that the honour of saving Montreal. For it decided Wilkinson that without Wade Hampton he could not, or at any rate would not, advance on Montreal, and it was on the morning after the battle that he heard of Hampton's defection. The vanguard of his army had just descended the rapids, and another brigade were to follow, when Morrison, aided by Harvey of Stoney Creek fame, forced it to a rearguard action.

Morrison drew up his force in line between the St. Lawrence on his right and woods upon his left, leaving the open farm land, which gave the battle its name as a clear field of action. Against this, Wilkinson, according to his own account, threw two and a half brigades, numbering eighteen hundred men, soon followed by a further six hundred under General Boyd. Persistent attempts to turn Morrison's left by the woods were made in vain. Then a strong attack supported by cavalry was launched on his river flank without result. By most skilful handling, one flank of the British was hurried over to the support of the other when threatened by disparity of numbers. Their guns, too, were preserved, and they even succeeded in capturing one of the enemy's. Finally, the Americans were repulsed all along the line with a loss of over 400 men in killed, wounded and prisoners. That of the British was 180. Wilkinson was not himself present at the battle, being ill at the time. Like Hampton, he has been accused of intemperance.

The action did nothing more, of course, than shake Wilkinson's nerves into a state ill-fitted for the shock they were to receive next morning. Unlike Hampton, however, he called a Council of War, which decided that the march on Montreal, fifty miles down the river, must be abandoned. Why 8,500 pretty good troops, well-found and equipped, should have been unequal to the attempt on an unfortified, ill-defended city, because a thousand or so of the enemy were hanging on their rear, has never been satisfactorily explained. Whatever the true reason, all thoughts of Montreal were abandoned, and Wilkinson, with wrath in his heart, and as much gall on the point of his pen, put his army into winter quarters, some in the immediate neighbourhood and the rest at Lake Champlain. Wilkinson's wrath, however, was certainly not less than that of the public when they got this second shock so quickly on that administered by Wade Hampton.

But American troops were fast improving, and good officers developing *vice* politicians retired. There was no hope yet, moreover, of substantial relief to the British from the Mother Country, and despite the stubborn resistance so successfully made, the future was still dark enough. On sea, however, the Americans were feeling the pinch. Their early frigate victories had possessed only spectacular value, and now the British battle squadrons were achieving a virtual blockade of the whole American seaboard, with particular attention to the southern half of it. So the crops of Virginia, Maryland and the Carolinas were rotting away in their warehouses, and their coasts subjected to frequent naval raids, which made these chief instigators of the invasion of Canada call Heaven to witness the savagery of the British. But these things do not immediately concern us here. The omen most cheering to Canada at that moment was the almost solid opposition of the New England States to a war professedly waged on behalf of their own sea-borne trade.

The close of the year 1813 saw more hard fighting along the Niagara frontier. The Americans, under McClure, name of sinister memory, were in possession, it will be remembered, of Fort George, and a fresh riot of raiding and looting now followed on the Canadian side. For since so many British troops had been withdrawn for service eastward, Vincent, still in command, had marched his dwindling force back to Burlington Heights. In November he received reinforcements and reassumed the offensive, and with Murray, his second-in-command, an officer of daring and enterprise, not only pushed the Americans back into Fort George but pressed them so closely that McClure evacuated the fort, recrossed the river to the American side, and occupied the old Fort Niagara. By this move some fifty or more civilians, whom McClure had carried off from the farms and imprisoned in the fort were released. McClure had taken the opportunity to loot much of the vacated country, which would have been legitimate enough had not the invaders posed as the friends and deliverers of Canada. But this truculent Scotch-Irish militia Colonel had carried off many civilians and their families and imprisoned them in Fort Niagara. Before rather hurriedly evacuating Fort George, which had been vastly improved by the Americans' occupation, McClure committed a deed which cost his own people dear and made his name to be remembered with execration and loathing in Canada.

The pleasant little town of Newark, the original capital of the Province, it will be remembered, stood close to Fort George, and contained, with churches and public buildings, some 150 houses. Before vacating the Fort and Canadian soil, and with but half an hour's notice, McClure set fire to the town, and four hundred inhabitants, at that moment largely women and children, were turned out into the rigours of a Canadian winter night, and all their possessions destroyed. There was not the slightest military excuse for this cruel deed. It was a purely wanton action. His own Government reprimanded but did not remove him, and he remained to receive condign chastisement from the friends of his victims. For Sir Gordon Drummond, just now arrived as Governor and Commander of the forces in Upper Canada, automatically relieving Vincent of the latter post. Drummond was one of the many fine soldiers whom, despite her world-wide engagements, the Mother Country, by good judgment or good luck, managed to spare for Canada in this her hour of need. From Vincent, Drummond also took over Colonel Murray, a worthy lieutenant for the intended campaign and well able to put the new chief *en rapport* with the situation on that front.

The result of this combination may be stated in brief. Murray, having taken all the available troops across the river, carried the old American stronghold, Fort Niagara, by storm with a loss of 400 men to the defenders. Lewiston and Fort Schlosser, on the American side, were next captured, and an aggressive campaign was instituted. In less than a month's time this onslaught laid waste the entire American frontier from Fort Niagara, held by the British till the Peace, to Lake Erie, including the town of Buffalo, now reduced to ashes. Thus ended the second year of the war in Upper Canada, leaving the Province cleared of the enemy, and the principal enemy post in British hands. McClure, with 2,500 men, was in charge of this now devastated frontier. He had been pushed into Buffalo, from which he was now burned out. He only appears again as a writer of despatches in which he has the hardihood to complain of the brutality of the British in wasting the country. But McClure disappears from the scene, and under the stress of war better officers pressed to the front, by degrees displacing the many incapable commanders appointed through political interest.

The dearth of provisions and supplies of all sorts in the Upper Province was a constant difficulty with those responsible for its defence. The chief means of transport from the East, the source of all such things, was by Lake Ontario, though a rough road had been made from Montreal to York. Even then it was a question whether it was controlled at the moment by the fleet of Chauncey or of Yeo. The militia, who were practically all producers of foodstuffs, could not farm and fight at the same time, and their fighting services were indispensable to the small force of regulars in the Province. They were divided into two grades, the Active and the Sedentary. The former served more or less permanently, the latter were called out in emergencies. A great deal of havoc had been wrought among their homesteads. Bands of adventurers, nominally attached to the American service, pounced here and there on undefended districts, burning and looting, and carrying their booty across the border. Renegade Canadians of the recent immigrations joined these "free companies" and vented their spite and indulged their greed on the property of loyalist farmers absent at the front. In some cases these marauders were accompanied by Indians from those tribes across the border already mentioned as taking service with the Americans. Prevost, with all his deficiencies as a war Governor, was most active and diligent in all these matters of organisation and supply. Strange as it sounds, a large proportion of the foodstuff, grain and cattle, for the armies came up from Vermont, which carried on a roaring trade with Canada throughout the war. For that reason the Vermont people must have become quite reconciled to it, more particularly as they had neither sought nor perpetrated any of its horrors. It was a long road, however, for supplies to travel, even when that road was open, from Montreal to the seat of war in Western Canada.

The shape of that Province, as of Ontario to-day, may be briefly indicated, the shape, that is to say of its developed and occupied area. Roughly, it forms a strip only grown broader in the past century, running from Montreal and the junction of the Ottawa and the St. Lawrence, westward, skirting the great river and the great lake till at the latter's western extremity it expands fan shape into a region sometimes called for convenience the peninsular of Ontario. This is a little misleading, as its shape is roughly an axe head. To be more precise, it rather curiously resembles Wales in outline on a map, and like Wales, is washed on three sides, north, south and west by wide waters, those of Lakes Erie and Huron. To complete the simile, it is about the same size, or not very much larger. There all physical comparison ends, for its surface is the reverse of that of the Principality, being gently undulating like Suffolk or Norfolk, with but few ridges sufficiently high to invalidate the comparison. It is better watered, too, and with clearer and swifter streams than East Anglia, and is the finest agricultural region in the Province and in all the old Provinces. First settled from Niagara, it will be remembered, by Butler's Rangers, later immigration from other parts, from the American side and even from the Mother Country, had penetrated through most of it with scattered settlements of promise that time has more than justified in such names as Brantford, Woodstock, London, Galt, Burford, Stratford, Goderich and many others. Greatest of all is the flourishing city of Hamilton, covering the site of the old fortifications on Burlington Heights, the defence and key of the peninsula in its more precarious moments, and never captured by the American invaders.

Toronto stands just on the eastern edge of what, for descriptive purposes I, like many others, have thus styled the "Peninsula," now more generally defined as Western Ontario. The strip of territory extending thence for 300 miles along the water line to Montreal and Lower Canada, which in 1812 comprised the eastern half of Upper Canada, though widened and developed and punctuated by little waterside towns, and closely settled this long time with well-equipped farms, is still but a strip. A strip, that is to say (40 to 50 miles in width) compared to its vast northward-stretching forest hinterland, long ago rejected for good reason by the serious pioneers of agriculture, though of abiding interest to the miner, the lumberman, the holiday camper and the sportsman. In 1812, the northern fringe of this long belt had not been nearly reached, and most of it from Toronto (York) to Montreal, was still practically a water frontage.

CHAPTER XI

THE LAST PHASE OF THE WAR—1814

THE Legislature of Lower Canada, mainly of French composition, met at the opening of the year. The army bills issued in 1812 and payable in London had proved a success, but there was still a great lack of money for war purposes, so the credit was further extended to a million and a half sterling, all paid off in the following year. The French-Canadian attitude to the war was sound enough, but from the situation of the Province, there had been no need to call out more than a fraction of the militia, especially as they were valuable at home. The City of Quebec, more particularly, was far removed from all scenes of war, and the politicians, reverting to what they held to be civic grievances, matters often of old date, were again giving trouble in the Lower House. Fresh from a despotic past, and as yet quite inexperienced, these people, in their new rôle of vote-elected legislators, got out of hand and contracted a notion that their House was entitled to an absolute control of their Province, a catastrophe which, fortunately at that immature period, the Government, having the actual power over the purse, could readily avert.

The French-Canadians lacked, of course, the hereditary self-governing instinct of their British neighbours on both sides of the border, and had not yet grasped the difference between Representative Government, the natural inheritance of a British colony once really set going, and Responsible Government, which was wisely reserved till that colony was large enough to produce a choice of men capable of assuming the graver responsibilities towards their own country and the Empire. None of the Canadian provinces were yet ripe for this, least of all French Canada, whose immature politicians, in twenty years, had hardly yet learned that they were sent to the legislature to do anything but air their own grievances and talk. Governor Craig had more than once unceremoniously sent them home to study the uses and limitations of a Legislature at their leisure, and they hated his memory, as heartily as the defenders of their country must have wished the old soldier back again at Quebec. But Prevost had "a way with him" in handling the French, and kept them from doing the mischief they might have done at this critical moment, a merit that must always be weighed against his military shortcomings.

The Legislature of Upper Canada was summoned in February by Sir Gordon Drummond. War was much too near these men, who had been burned out of their very Parliament House, and some even out of their own houses, for wordy broils or civic trifles. Most of their talk concerned the defence of the country, and ways and means so far as they could forward them, for carrying on the war.

Early in this year, before the ice had melted, Wilkinson set about an attempt to retrieve his failure of the previous year. Leaving Brown, the ablest of the new American generals, at Sackett's Harbour, with 2,000 men, he had gathered the remaining 4,000 under his immediate command at the old camp of Plattsburg on Lake Champlain. With these he made, in March, the forward movement against the frontier of Lower Canada that was to retrieve his reputation. The details of his failure need not long detain us, but just across the border, on a small tributary of the Richelieu, the Lacolle, which crossed his march, he encountered a much smaller force of British and Canadians under Major Hancock. Here a stone-mill and some adjoining houses had been fortified and formed the chief point of contention. After a fight lasting several hours, in which the 13th Regiment particularly distinguished itself, Wilkinson failed to force the position, and retired again to Plattsburg, and this time to a very lenient court-martial. It is significant that Wilkinson's chief line of defence at his trial lay in the desperate bravery of his opponents, as related by his witnesses, among others an artillery captain stating that one company "made a charge on our guns receiving their fire and that of two whole brigades of infantry at the same time."

This was the last attempt of the Americans on Lower Canada and Montreal. Wellington's Peninsular veterans, now released from Spain, were already embarking for this scene of action, to put an end to the long strain and to all American hopes of conquering Canada. The next fighting on this front was six months later, when the Americans were on the defensive on their own soil, with small hope of stopping the British advance, till Prevost, in the last of his many fatuous actions, called it off, as we shall see. Away up at Sackett's Harbour, near the Lake Ontario outflow, two hundred miles westward of these scenes in the Montreal area, Chauncey had been busy building ships all the winter. His opponent, Yeo, across the water, at Kingston, who had finished the year with some advantage over him, had been equally active with his more restricted resources.

In March, General Brown was ordered away westward to the Niagara frontier, which was now once again to become the chief theatre of the war. This gave the British an opportunity of attacking Sackett's Harbour and its shipping on the ice. But Prevost's tenderness towards all enemy ports once more thwarted his more enterprising subordinates, in this case Drummond and Yeo. When the lake was ice-free, however, they persuaded the reluctant Governor into a combined naval and military attack on Oswego, that famous old fortress of French war memory. It was now a large depot of military stores and garrisoned by no more than 400 American regulars. Fortunately, Prevost did not this time accompany them, for at the very moment of attack a sudden gale sprang up and blew the flotilla out to sea again, and such an opportunity to spare Oswego would have been altogether too much for him. But Drummond and Yeo returned next day, though the delay had given time to the defenders to call in all the neighbouring militia. They were not much good, however, as they ran away the moment they came into action. Under a heavy fire, between ships and fort, Drummond's men, about one thousand in number, drove out the garrison, dismantled the fortress, burned its auxiliary buildings, and captured several ships in the harbour and a large supply of stores, always of priceless value to the ill-furnished Canadians. Following this, in early May, Yeo took his fleet to Sackett's Harbour, where Chauncey, busy with his preparations for the summer campaign, was unable to come out and had to submit to a blockade, which entailed much difficulty in getting his naval requirements into the yards.

But the chief interest of the war was now once more shifted to the Niagara frontier, where some of the heaviest fighting yet experienced was to take place. General Brown, succeeding Wilkinson, was in command here with five thousand men, and headquarters at Buffalo. He had proved himself a keen and clever soldier, and by constant drill and exercises had wrought a vast improvement in his army. His orders now were to take Fort Erie opposite him, and then to push through the country to Burlington Heights, always the key position of the British. After capturing those works, he was to sever the connection between Forts George and Niagara and the Eastern districts. Chauncey was expected by this time to be out with his new ships, and dominating the lake. But whether moved by jealousy, of which he was accused, or hampered by Yeo's persistent attentions, Chauncey failed to join his friends. General Riall, for the moment representing Drummond in command of the British in the peninsula, had in all about 4,000 men, including 1,000 at York and 400 at Burlington Heights. The remainder were distributed along the Niagara river between the two lakes, with headquarters at Fort George. Brown led off with the easy capture of Fort Erie, lightly garrisoned. Riall's main post of defence, however, was the Chippewa river, which falls into the Niagara just above the Cataract, and lay across the enemy's line of march towards Burlington Heights, and the British posts down the river.

Here Riall prepared to contest the American advance. He had actually with him rather more than 2,000 men, consisting of a battalion of the 8th just arrived, about five hundred strong, from the East, and as many from the Royal Scots and the 100th respectively, with a squadron of Light Dragoons, a few artillery men with three light guns and six hundred militia and Indians. With doubtful wisdom, Riall crossed the Chippewa and advanced to a smaller and parallel stream, a mile or so beyond, named Street's Creek. Here the American force, about four thousand five hundred strong, met him, their right flank resting on the Niagara river, their left on the woods bordering the intervening fields, so frequent a situation in the limited battlefields of this war. Riall attacked first, according to the British custom; Generals Winfield Scott and Ripley led the two brigades of American regulars, and were supported by a third of militia and Indians. The militia along the woods did not give much trouble, but the regulars were now of a different mettle from those the British hitherto had never hesitated to attack with much inferior numbers. This time, though throwing themselves on the enemy with their usual courage, the British failed to break the lines, and being themselves played on with nine field pieces, they were gradually pushed back to and across the stream of the Chippewa, a position they successfully defended till the close of a day which terminated in the loss in killed and wounded of a fourth of Riall's small army. The American loss was less, and not without reason they claimed a victory. For with hardly any artillery, with the Chippewa indefensible higher up its course, and with his force so greatly reduced, Riall had no choice but to retire, which he did unmolested to Fort George. Here he was joined by 800 Glengarries and some more militia, with whom, after leaving his wounded at the Fort, he marched towards Burlington Heights, then held by the 103rd New Brunswickers and part of the 104th Newfoundlanders.

The field was now open for the looting and ravaging propensities of the New York militia, who had saved their skins by a rapid retreat at the battle of Chippewa. All this region being now temporarily clear of the British, the New Yorkers, in company with the renegade Canadians, followed their usual course, among other exploits burning the village of St. Davids, near Queenston, for which General Brown, always correct in these matters, though not always able to control his rapacious irregulars, immediately cashiered their commander, Colonel Stone. "My God," wrote an American officer of regulars, who was killed immediately afterwards at the head of his regiment at Lundy's Lane, "what a *service!* I have never witnessed such a scene. If their commanding officer had not been disgraced and sent out of the army I should have handed in my commission." Brown pressed on to Fort George, but swerved aside with the intention of following Riall, who, now reinforced, was but a dozen miles off on the road to Burlington Heights. There was no sign of Chauncey's fleet, expected to co-operate in these movements, and while manœuvring and considering whether to attack the fort before following Riall, Brown suddenly heard that the latter was behind him, near Queenston. He at once fell back up the river to the old ground on the Chippewa, where he had successfully fought three weeks previously. Riall's vanguard followed him up, and halted for the rest of his force, about a mile short of the Falls on the morning of the 25th July.

A stretch of plateau ground was here traversed by the byway which was to immortalise its insignificant name of "Lundy's Lane." The converging movements of troops towards this point had begun before daybreak. The Americans advanced from up the river, the British from the posts below. At midday, only Riall with about 1,000 men, and Scott confronting him with rather fewer, to be shortly much increased, were in contact. Drummond, in chief command, had crossed the lake from York to Fort George in the previous night, and was either leading or pushing up all the available troops towards the Falls and to Riall's support. The latter was, at the moment, retreating before superior forces, when, at about five o'clock, Drummond came up with 1,600 men, took command, faced about, and received the American attack 4,000 strong, well delivered and well led. The British guns were planted on a ridge crowning the field, and around this the battle raged long and furiously. It was not, however, till after seven o'clock that Brown had launched his whole force against the British, who in their turn still lacked the third and final instalment of their total in Colonel Hercules Scott's regiment, which of all the British forces had to make the longest march.[1] While the heaviest

[1] About twenty miles.

fighting took place along the ridge that carried their batteries, the British felt their inferiority in numbers most on their left flank, where, upon the edge of the cliffs, lashed by the whirlpools of Niagara, the American right wing was pushing the eighth regiment back, and threatening Drummond's rear. They pulled up and reformed in time, however, and encouraged by the arrival, at nine o'clock, of Hercules Scott's foot-weary men, succeeded in recovering their ground, though General Riall was wounded and made prisoner on this flank.

It was now pitch dark, and a fierce conflict raged, mainly at close quarters and by the light of its own gun-fire. The Americans before Hercules Scott's arrival had actually carried the ridge, captured though not withdrawn the guns, and pressed the British hard all along the line. After one or two repulses, Colonel Miller, with 700 picked troops had rushed the British batteries, but, as above noted, to no ultimate purpose. For Drummond, with his belated and weary reinforcements, had renewed the attack with vigour and recovered his position at almost all points. None of Wellington's troops had yet arrived in Upper Canada. Those engaged in this fateful battle consisted of the ubiquitous New Brunswick and New-foundland regiments, the Glengarries and companies of the 1st Royal Scots, the 8th, the 89th and the 41st, a few dragoons and gunners and a strong and effective force of militia. The heat of the July day had been overpowering, and the night was still and airless. Half the British had been tramping in the sun all day clad in the dreadful trappings of that period. Flung without halting into the very thick of the fight, these indomitable troops, regulars and militia, shook off their deadly weariness and went into action, an enthusiastic sergeant declared, "as if they were just out of bed." The Americans had come fresh into the battle, but are described as by this time absolutely parched with thirst.

Soon after midnight, and more than three hours' fierce but indecisive fighting, both sides had fought themselves literally to a standstill. General Ripley, now in command *vice* Brown, wounded, called off his troops, who went limping in any sort of order back to Chippewa. The

British dropped exhausted where they stood on the battlefield. Such was the battle of Lundy's Lane, the last serious offensive effort of the Americans in this war.

The British lost one-third of their number, the Americans one-fourth of their somewhat larger force. General Brown and Winfield Scott were both badly wounded. Drummond himself was severely wounded, but kept the field. So too was Morison, of Chrystler's Farm repute. Riall was both wounded and taken prisoner. The 89th lost more than half its numbers. The Royal Scots, in the two battles of Chippewa and Lundy's Lane, lost four hundred of all ranks. The militia lost about half those engaged, including their Colonel, Robinson, badly wounded. Both sides claimed a victory. As the battle had resulted in the final failure of the Americans to break through into Upper Canada, and in their return very much battered, to Fort Erie, we may safely leave the decision so far as it matters, to the reader's judgment. That the British slept their sleep of exhaustion upon the disputed field of battle amid the dead, while the enemy abandoned it as well as the guns they had captured earlier, would surely score a further point in military reckoning, if again that mattered.

General Ripley, next in command to Brown and Winfield Scott, had orders from the former to return to the attack next morning, but the exhausted condition of his men made any such attempt out of the question. They had done their best, indeed their best effort of the war, and they could do no more. Seldom too have British infantry on the top, as in this case, of arduous marching under a burning sun, shown their great qualities more conspicuously than through this black and stifling night within reach of the very spray of Niagara Falls. The Loyalist militia, too, not merely the incorporated but the sedentary companies, who returned after the battle to their just ripening harvest fields, fought with equal staunchness, rallying when hard pressed with the coolness of regulars around the regimental standards planted along that fiercely contested ridge. Within sight of the lofty shaft on Queenston Heights commemorating a noble soldier, and the repulse of the first invasion, there rises near the edge of the mighty cataract a humbler obelisk, in memory of the last and fiercest attempt, and of the stubborn infantry, British and Canadian, who fell in opposing it.

The Americans had fallen back across the Chippewa, and now, throwing much of his stores into the Niagara river, Ripley retired again into Fort Erie. But it was too late for this improvement in the American soldiers to avail them anything. Those 16,000 veterans, just landed at Quebec had put the result of the war beyond doubt, just as their absence from England in the following year caused Waterloo to be the narrow shave it was, a fact generally overlooked in all but the most authoritative accounts of the battle. Waterloo's risk, in short, was Canada's salvation. On the face of it, a world-famous crisis is here opposed to a remote struggle for a thinly populated colony, which within living memory had been balanced in exchange value against a small West Indian island. But how different the matter appears when looked at in the right perspective! Would victory at Waterloo have reinstated Napoleon, already broken in health? Even had it done so, would this have been to England as the loss of her North American provinces? Surely not, whatever the turn of European affairs for the moment.

But if suspense was over, and the crisis in Canada past, peace was not yet, though the bellicose States were by now as sick of their war as all the rest of the world concerned with it. This, however, did not stop hostilities on the Niagara front. Drummond determined to attempt the capture of Fort Erie, the sole spot left of American occupation on Canadian territory. It had now become a fortress of great size and strength, and the army in and around it had been reinforced by General Izard from the East, and numbered in all about 8,000 men under the command of General Gaines. He was a new man at the front, probably a politician. At any rate, he was a despatch writer of the old Smyth, McClure and Co. type. The attack on Fort Erie, delivered on August the 15th, proved a ghastly and expensive failure. Possibly Drummond should have recognised that the enterprise was not now worth its probable expenditure of life. Assuredly, it was not worth what it actually cost.

A night attack, delivered at three points, it was met at each by a withering fire, for there was no surprise. On the left, the de Wattville regiment that had recently come west and was composed of foreigners, hitherto steady, now stampeded carrying with them the 8th. Deprived of their flints so that bayonets only could be used, and with scaling ladders too short, they were severely tried. The left of the works, which were half a mile in length, was attacked by Hercules Scott with his Colonial Regulars. They were met with a most destructive fire of musketry and grape, which killed Scott and knocked over a third of his men. In the centre, Drummond, with a small force composed of the 104th New Brunswickers and the rallied survivors of Scott's battalion, achieved one of the most heroic feats of the war, though disastrous in its results. After three or four desperate attempts on the *abatis*, in the face of a hail of fire, they won a position in a bastion and held it against every effort of the enemy. General Gaines, writing to his Government of the approach of the British on this night, describes them as "enveloped in darkness as black as their designs and principles." Why the occupant of a fortress in an enemy country should write thus viciously of the owners who were naturally trying to turn him out, even the writer himself might find some difficulty in explaining.

But at this moment, Gaines was informed by an officer that there was a big store of powder under the bastion, which he could fire in a moment if the word was given. Gaines gave the word, and with a terrific explosion the whole masonry of the bastion with three or four hundred of its brave defenders was blown into the air. It was characteristic of this particular general's mentality that in reporting to Washington he should write that the bastion "was carried at the point of the bayonet with dreadful slaughter." This fearful explosion put an end to everything, and the attempt on Fort Erie cost in all over 800 men killed and wounded. Two of Wellington's regiments were now sent west to Drummond. But Izard, though still in command of a big force, shrank from pressing on through Canada, as Chauncey had again lost control of Lake Ontario to Yeo. A few raids were made on the sparsely settled Canadian shores of Lake Erie, and seven hundred Kentucky horsemen, under Colonel McArthur, swept once more across the much-harried farms of the peninsula from Detroit as far as Burford on the Grand River, which, being in flood, held them up. As the main American army at Fort Erie was making no forward movement, the Kentuckians turned about and rode homewards after less than a month of ravaging and looting in the country. Early in November, the Americans abandoned Fort Erie, and crossed back to their own side of the river, and the war in Upper Canada, as it so turned out, came to an end, with no hostile foot within that area and the British left in possession of the American Fort Niagara.

It only now remains to tell how the war was finished off in Lower Canada. Often and severely threatened, this Province had been scarcely even singed. The Americans made no attempt on Montreal during this summer. With 16,000 of Wellington's troops on guard, it was out of the question. Only about a thousand of these had been sent, and that late in the season, to the Niagara front, but their presence in the country had automatically released other troops for that service. The Americans in the east were now on guard upon their own frontier in the neighbourhood of Plattsburg and Lake Champlain. But the British had, of course, no designs of conquest upon American territory unless for rectification of the boundary line here and there, or indirectly perhaps for use in the Treaty of Peace that was obviously not far off. So Prevost can hardly be much blamed for keeping these peninsula troops inactive. But the Home Government did not think so, and wrote him rather shortly that they had not sent him out the cream of the army to do garrison duty, but expected him to make use of them. It was a most natural though, as it turned out, a rather unlucky reproof.

Prevost accordingly set out, unfortunately in command himself, for the invasion of the State of New York, with 11,000 of what were then perhaps the best troops in the world. It was early autumn, the finest season of the year in Canada. The way to Plattsburg and the north-western shores of Lake Champlain lay through a partly settled country, easy to travel. For these men, inured to all weathers and all seasons, and every kind of hardship in Spain and Portugal, it must have seemed like a holiday trip, with no foe in their path but what could be brushed easily aside. For at Plattsburg there was only General Macomb with 1,500 regulars and a mob of militia. A good soldier, Macomb was throwing up breastworks across Prevost's route by the lake shore, hoping to give a temporary check to these terrible veterans and at least to save his face.

But there was a small American fleet at Plattsburg of a few armed ships, and a still smaller British squadron lower down in the out-flowing river. Yeo had sent a Captain Downie to command it and get it fit for sea. When Prevost arrived at Plattsburg, he found him only completing the one big ship, necessary to his, in any case, weak squadron. Prevost decided that he could not move against even the weak opposition ahead of him, without the destruction of the American squadron. So the troops marked time, and General Macomb worked on unmolested with his entrenchments, and Downie, with scarcely completed preparations, sailed out to encounter Macdonough the American commander, under every disadvantage of wind and approach. The fiercely-contested little sea-fight resulted in the death of Downie, and, partly due to that misfortune, in the defeat of his fleet after a severe engagement. Prevost, in the meantime, had begun a half-hearted attack on the American defences. But when he learned of Downie's defeat, he decided that he must abandon his enterprise. He seemed to be obsessed by the notion of "naval co-operation." It was in vain that officers of experience in a score of battles assured him that he could scatter the American defences in twenty minutes, and if necessary destroy Macdonough's crippled little squadron from the shore. But no arguments had ever yet convinced this obstinate wrong-headed man. Even had a farther advance into American territory along the lake shore been thought not worth while, a quite conceivable point of view, though not that of either the British Government or his own officers, the manner of Prevost's change of front was still deplorable. For having started an attack on the American lines, he simply turned tail, destroyed his stores and marched his troops, who had chased the French across the Pyrenees, back to Canada. Their wrath and that of their officers may be imagined. No one was more amazed, or more delighted, than Macomb. He had not intended even a serious opposition. He put in writing the admiration with which he had watched the approach of these veteran troops against his batteries. His militia, he says, had run at the first approach of the British, but when his artillery opened a heavy fire upon them they came on, in column, "even scorning to deploy as the balls fell among them."

There seems to have been a good deal of desertion as Prevost marched his army back again through the pleasant Richelieu country. Possibly, the men thought it was better to turn farmer than be led any longer by such a man as this! Such was the closing scene of the war in Lower Canada, while the curtain, as we have seen, was dropping on the last act in the Upper Province. When the report of his futile expedition reached England, Prevost was summoned home to stand his trial at a court-martial. He appears to have been quite pained and surprised at being held to blame. But the poor man did not live to be called to account, dying soon after his return to England. His family erected a monument to him in Winchester Cathedral, on which his virtues are duly recorded, but probably they were spared the knowledge of his failings. His retreat into Canada was of little practical consequence. It was the manner of it and the moment he selected to face about that was so galling to his troops, and at the same time gave cause to the enemy to claim a sort of victory over Wellington's veterans, in that they were called off, after making a first half-hearted attack on the American entrenchments. It was enough at this late date that Canada was safe. An invasion of U.S. territory was superfluous, and above all, so near New England, indiscreet. Prevost should have attacked and scattered Macomb's force regardless of the sea-fight, which a special naval court-martial found that Downie had been hurried into by Prevost before he was ready. The latter's influence in almost every enterprise he was personally concerned with throughout the war, which may be fairly said to have been won in spite of him, was unfortunate. Above all, he spoilt the finish, so far as Canada is concerned, of a struggle in which it is but the simple truth to say that nearly all concerned had covered themselves with honour.

This advance over the border was part of a policy of aggression that the British Government had decided on as a check to the destructive American raids in Upper Canada. With one trifling exception, the other blows were directed upon the coasts of the Southern States and as neither Canada nor Canadians were concerned with them, they may be dismissed in a few lines. In this autumn, General Ross was landed with 4,000 men, mostly brought direct from Wellington's army in France, at the head of the Chesapeake Bay. The fleet transporting and co-operating with them was commanded by Admiral Cochrane. Washington was the first and main objective. Small raids had been maintained upon the coast, even during the maritime preoccupations of the French war. But now that England's hands were free, something more forcible was to be executed in retaliation, as was definitely stated by Lord Liverpool's Government, for the outrages perpetrated by the Americans along the Canadian frontier, and as a warning against their repetition.

The landing and march on Washington gave little trouble. Some 7,000 militia collected for its defence at Bladensburg, east of the city, were scattered in an hour, and the entry was unopposed. The Capitol, with its affiliated buildings and two private houses which had fired on the entering troops, were burned. Otherwise, all private property was punctiliously respected. The British force then re-embarked and sailed on to Baltimore, landing a dozen miles from the city. An engagement with an intervening force of some five thousand Americans was finished in about half an hour by a frontal attack with the bayonet, though unfortunately Ross was killed by a shot from covert. He was held in such high regard, both as a soldier and a man, that Parliament voted him the monument in St. Paul's that records his worth. Obstacles to navigation having blocked Cochrane's lighter craft, Ross' successor, Pakenham, though within sight of Baltimore, did not think its occupation, which had not been a definite object of the campaign, worth while, and the troops were re-embarked. The Washington affair became, naturally enough, the subject of bitter invective. The outrages for which it was a retaliation were conveniently ignored. Madison, Jefferson and their friends declared " that ancient and modern history might be searched in vain for a parallel." But no blood was shed. Many people in England, till now much too preoccupied with their own pressing dangers at home to know even the names of Toronto, Newark, St. David's, or St. Catherine's, or other little towns callously destroyed by the American troops, echoed Jefferson's sentiments in less dramatic language.

The American Government protested that they had repudiated in the last three cases the action of their commanders, though what this amounted to when, as in McClure's case, they retained them in command, is not easy to see. But as for the fourth instance cited, that of the burning of York (Toronto) by General Pike, all mention of it was studiously avoided, yet this was the very point, and rightly, that the British Government had most in their minds. There was, of course, no answer to it. For it was idle to plead that the public buildings of Toronto were smaller than those of Washington, and the capitol that of a smaller country. Upper Canada had been created by the very people whom the Americans had driven into exile and penury, and it seemed a double outrage that they should be followed into the land of their refuge by their old persecutors, and their works wantonly destroyed. In any case, the relative size of the two capitals was neither here nor there, especially in view of the peculiar circumstances of the two contending peoples. The British Government considered the matter seriously in regard to its equity before giving the order for the burning of the capitol, and held the above views, which seem unanswerable. The sincerity of the Jeffersonian outcries, apart from the exaggerated language in which they were uttered, may be gauged by the fact, as stated above, that the burning of York was not alluded to when they stated their case. To this day, even English writers constantly denounce the burning of Washington as an inexcusable act, while knowing nothing of the context. But whatever the equity of the act, it was undoubtedly impolitic. To the world in general, though most of that world burned and hacked its way remorselessly about enemy countries, it appeared equally wanton and out of keeping with Britain's professions and usual practice. Above all, it was straining the forbearance of the New England States, who might not care what happened to Baltimore or New Orleans, but to whom the national capitol was another matter.

No untoward results, however, came from that quarter. Nor did a small expedition actually made into Maine, then an outlying territory of Massachusetts, upset the mutual understanding, if it may thus be called. A glance at the map will show that a large slice of the present State of Maine thrusts itself northward between Lower Quebec and New Brunswick almost to the St. Lawrence Gulf, cutting off Lower Canada from the Maritime Provinces. It proclaims itself a geographical anomaly without sense or reason, calling for rectification. Even in these days it is a sparsely settled country of small agricultural value, and in those was still unimportant and its very boundaries rather vague. It seemed a good opportunity to occupy this unnatural protuberance, hold it as British territory and settle the matter definitely at the coming peace. The militia of the district, Washington County, which had been unavoidably ordered out in face of what was actually an armed invasion, readily promised the British commander to remain quietly at home if he would leave them and their property unmolested. This was, of course, acceded to, and formal possession of this obtrusive tongue of country was taken. Unfortunately, the question of ownership, then a comparatively slight matter, was not properly settled at the Peace, and later as "the Maine boundary question" became for some time a dangerous source of friction between the two countries. Its ultimate settlement, as generally happened in these Anglo-American affairs, when left to diplomacy and a Commission, went in favour of the Americans, and in this case a glance at the map will sufficiently illustrate the fact.

The final event of the war was remoter from Canada

and its interests than even the Chesapeake expedition. And as the unsuccessful attack on New Orleans by Pakenham did not take place till the preliminaries of peace had actually been signed in Europe, there is still less occasion to do more than allude to it here. It will be enough to say that Andrew Jackson, the successful defender of the Southern city, provided his country both with its outstanding military figure for the war of 1812 as well as its next President. And it is a curious thing that this rough soldier and party man, contrary to all expectations, showed a far more friendly and rational attitude towards Great Britain than any of his more polished political friends and contemporaries, civil or military, or indeed any of his predecessors since Washington. The Treaty of Ghent was signed at that city in April, 1815. As early as 1813, the Emperor of Russia, prompted by the Americans, had interested himself in the matter. But as the American demands apparently showed no abatement, the British Government held aloof. By August, 1814, however, when the conquest of Canada was obviously hopeless, the Washington Government had shifted their ground. By the time the Commissioners had finished, the claims on which they had declared war were wholly abandoned, and the Treaty placed matters on the *status quo ante* footing in every particular of any consequence. The mutual restoration of outposts was quite trifling, the Maine wedge occupied by the British alone excepted. For the moment, that was given up, quite possibly, as suggested by the most authoritative historian of the war,[1] owing to the vigorous protests of Massachusetts, who then owned it, and had proved friendly throughout the contest. Nor were the Indians forgotten in this Treaty, as in the last, and, so far as paper could serve, they and their possessions were safeguarded against all American reprisals. Fishery rights were restored to the Americans, and, as a concession to Great Britain, no armed fleets were to be kept on the Great Lakes by either nation. In short, the war, productive of so much loss of life and treasure on land and sea, altered nothing. To Britain it had been an

[1] Sir Charles Lucas.

aggravating side-issue to the gigantic struggle to which she was committed in Europe. Nevertheless, this American war might have brought forth results of far more lasting importance to her, a fact, of course, less obvious in the heat of the struggle with Napoleon.

CHAPTER XII

PEACE AND ITS FRUITS

CANADA had not only emerged triumphantly from the war of which she had been the potential victim, but, in common with the other British provinces, had actually gained in material prosperity. It is true that the Western districts of Upper Canada had suffered much from war's ravages. But then it was a region still without towns worth mentioning, and in the first stage of agricultural development. In many parts the year's crop was destroyed, while houses and barns were burned; but nearly all such buildings were of the rather provisional kind, to be more solidly replaced in the years to come, when the expanding acreage of these amazingly rich grain lands should justify it. In short, the losses of this kind were soon made good by the hardy and energetic race that suffered them. The rest of the country, together with Lower Canada and the Maritime Provinces, reaped nothing but profit from the war. The furnishing and feeding of a large body of troops, the victualling and repairing of warships, the building and sailing of privateers and a brisk trade with the New England States, had given all the Provinces an actual leap forward, while their powerful but disconcerted foe was suffering all the annoyances, moral and physical, and many of the positive evils of an unsuccessful war. But still more, the sense of victory following the long and anxious strain which preceded the arrival of Wellington's troops, gave a feeling of pride and a new status to the Canadians, more especially to the U.E. Loyalists of the Upper Province, whose militia throughout the war had fought with the courage and discipline of the regulars with whom they had stood shoulder to shoulder. Their services had been handsomely and gratefully recognised in a special message from the King.

They had given their answer to the taunt that they were the slaves of British tyranny and had definitely settled the question of the " fourteenth State."

However much the two races in Canada might quarrel among themselves, the French parishes would never again give an ear to the American propagandists, such as had fooled their fathers in 1775-6. The whole country, in short, had given a decisive answer to the always smouldering talk of annexation. Among the later settlers in Upper Canada, persons of hitherto wavering or indifferent opinions, American prepossessions were no longer brooded over or discussed. The Peace which had fallen upon a war-weary Europe in 1814, and had been clinched by the Anglo-American Treaty in the following spring, proved, as will be remembered, to be premature as regards Europe. For soon came Napoleon's escape from Elba, followed by the " hundred days " and the final climax of Waterloo, the most epoch-making date of modern times, prior to that other one falling with such strange coincidence exactly a century later. Nor is it often recalled, as I have before pointed out, how intimately that forgotten and overlooked struggle for Canada was bound up with the fateful conflict of June 18th, and how nearly the needs of the former had lost us the victory of Waterloo. For a not greatly inferior force to that which filled the British squares at Waterloo was through sheer ill-luck then kicking its heels in Canadian garrisons having had little fighting, even while producing a moral effect quite incalculable.

But 1815, as a mere date, had a significance in the story of Canada, wholly apart from the fact that it fixed her place permanently by power of the sword among the British Commonwealth of nations. Canada ceased henceforward to be mainly a colony of Americans, created by Americans, living by choice under British rule, side by side with a conquered French Province in a rather uneasy fellowship under the same flag. In other words, the country had not yet been seriously regarded as an outlet for surplus Britons, though incidentally many groups from the Mother Country had adventured there. Great Britain had no people to spare through the long Napoleonic wars. Emigration was rigidly discouraged, nor indeed was there much pressure at home to stimulate it. Moreover, before the war of 1812, the attractions of the United States in its new Western territories seemed far greater than those of a country whose rigorous climate was the chief thing known about it, though most people were quite willing to regard it as a suitable refuge for Highlanders! But now, with the hosts of men turned adrift at the Peace, and the bad times consequent on the cessation of war, the question of emigration came to be taken seriously.

From this time onward, British North America became a recognised field for the surplus population of the Mother Country. Between the Peace and about 1840 the movement, compared with anything formerly known, assumed vast proportions. Apart from personal initiative, the Government, as well as private societies, promoted it on a generous scale. No less than 50,000 souls, an unprecedented figure in those days, were landed at Quebec in a single year, while the records show a fairly proportionate number from all three Kingdoms. There was then a large surplus of agricultural labourers in England, while the weavers of Scotland, as well as her farm labourers and small farmers, squeezed out by the rapid enlargement of holdings, swelled the volume. Ulster, as always, contributed a sturdy tribute, while Catholic Ireland, not yet the factor in transatlantic emigration it became later on, gave a considerable contribution, though the French Catholic Province, which probably possessed some attraction, never really assimilated its Irish co-religionists with its own church. The Maritime Provinces, too, got a larger proportion of all these settlers than was the case in later days.

Once again Canada became the refuge of soldiers. She might almost be called the very child of war. For many regiments were disbanded at the Peace, and thousands of soldiers who had fought in the long wars were cast upon the world. They were assisted in thousands to Canada and to grants of land there. All endeavours were made to plant men of the same regiments or from the same districts in contiguity. Hundreds of retired officers, too, went to Canada and took up or purchased land, turning for preference to Upper Canada, though all the Provinces came in for a share. For the most part, these gentlemen-immigrants, often attracted by the prospects of sport, an old, old story, found the conditions of clearing land and Canadian farming too severe, and shifted in time into one or other of the many little market towns that were springing up all over the country. Through most of the nineteenth century necessities were extraordinarily cheap and life even among the well-established classes remained upon very simple lines. The position of the U.E. Loyalists' circles which had hitherto controlled Upper Canada, became interesting in face of this large immigration, coupled with the rapid increase of the pre-war population, all engaged in a healthy occupation.

The note of the U.E. Loyalists throughout had naturally been antagonism to the United States and what it stood for, coupled with a close attachment to the British connection. Their attitude of suspicion towards the wave of immigration from the United States that followed on their heels has been already described. It was only partially justified, as we have seen, in the war. But it was they themselves who led and mainly filled the ranks of that invaluable militia which tipped the scale on the side of victory for the British arms, and with them must be numbered those Loyalist regiments raised in New Brunswick and Newfoundland and in the Glengarry district, embodied in the British army, and that took part in almost every fight. The loyalists had, of course, a start of all other elements in the Province and for obvious reasons had a larger share of capacity and education. They had thus obtained a strong lead in the direction of affairs which the war had strengthened and apparently justified, and they intended to keep it. They have been accused of arrogance and aristocratic pretensions by later Canadian writers. It is true that they had no great respect for the popular vote, but they had grown up in times of constant international peril when their country included a large element of doubtful patriotism and a further one so buried in remote woods and absorbed with their early struggles for existence as to be almost indifferent to all current events. Not that your true democrat considers it necessary for his voter to know much of the subject he is asked to decide. But the

U.E. Loyalist leaders were assuredly not true democrats. They have come down to posterity as invincible Tories and autocrats. But as these bigots not only created these provinces, wresting them from the wilderness with their own hands, but defended them successfully from democratic alien hordes anxious to annex them, their attitude is easily understood.

It is difficult for the orthodox democrat of later days who still really believes in the counting of heads and mob rule, as it is sometimes unkindly defined, to criticise doings of a body to whom they virtually owe their existence to-day as Canadians. Not that this prevents a great many severe things being said about these early patriots as politicians. The modern Whig, to use a convenient term, has a trick of justifying every agitating or rebellious reformer of one epoch by the fact that at a much later one the privileges he fought for were conceded. He seems to imagine that a colony considered ripe for complete self-government at one period had been of necessity sufficiently developed for it fifty or a hundred years earlier. Unquestionably, however, the Canadian oligarchy, fortified by their achievements and successes in the late war, carried matters with a tolerably high hand. A kind of aristocracy existed, originating to some extent in the antecedents of so many of these American loyalists, or rather in the qualities such antecedents had engendered and transmitted. They had brought these out of the woods at the first opportunity, and displayed them both in peace and war as natural leaders. Their ranks had been recruited from time to time by men of similar class and creed from the Mother Country. The military spirit and close association with the British army, moreover, had helped to foster a certain exclusiveness that surprised early visitors to Canada, who expected to find a democracy of emancipated backwoodsmen. The farmers, who formed the bulk of the population, whether of American or Old Country origin, outside the late fighting ranks at any rate, began to resent the idea of natural or inherited leadership. They were mostly, too, Dissenters or Presbyterians, while the governing class, like most of their American forebears, were Church of England, which, apart from the usual sectarian prejudices, was unpopular on account of the public lands allotted to it and its designs, or supposed designs, of fastening an established church permanently upon the country, as the Roman Church had been fastened upon French Canada. After the war this group of influential persons and families kept as strong, or a stronger, grip on the Executive of Upper Canada than even before. They came to be known as the "Family Compact," not literally as a clique of relations, but something so nearly approaching it as to suggest the convenient application of an historic precedent. They maintained their hereditary dislike of democracy and the growing democracy did not like them. Many, too, of the less important offices were tending to become hereditary as in England; many educated Englishmen, military or otherwise, who came into the country after 1815, found this element the most congenial, and together with the numerous British garrisons, helped to preserve the caste feeling in British Canada till within living memory. Since then, however, the Dominion has become rich and populous, and "caste" has long been replaced by different standards, not necessarily democratic in a social sense!

The stronghold of the class which evolved the Family Compact was in Toronto, and in the many pleasant little lakeshore and market towns that came to reproduce its life. Unlike the governing class in most of the old American colonies, that of Canada regarded land as having no social significance, whether possessed by a landlord or a large employer of labour. It was not adapted to either type, but only to the working freeholder, who from a poor man with one or two hundred acres of uncleared land, found himself in middle life or old age, after a life of toil and all its marks upon him, a yeoman with a well-appointed farm. Such, with negligible exceptions, was the country from end to end. The aristocracy, the gentry, if I may use the term, which they used very definitely themselves in those days, were officials, lawyers, bankers, merchants, clergymen, owners of town property, timber-lands or mills. They more or less represented the old U.E. Loyalist, if not necessarily of their actual blood. Though farming land meant nothing, either socially or often profitably, to those not living on and working it, the vast tracts of wild Crown lands meant a great deal, and just as in the old American colonies privileged persons with influence got patents for large tracts and founded families and fortunes, so those with power, or interest, at headquarters in Canada dealt with the Crown lands at Government disposal, to be sold later at a profit in a manner calculated to arouse the opposition of the growing democracy in a country where the franchise was fairly liberal. All the Government appointments, too, were virtually in the hands of the controlling faction.

Family Compact rule culminated in 1841, when the two Canadas, the French Province with its small British minority, and Upper Canada almost homogeneously British, were rather infelicitously united. The ineffectual and rather farcical rebellion of William Lyon Mackenzie, a Scotch-American importation into Toronto, and an agitator with American bias, called attention to the discontent in Upper Canada, while Papineau's more serious rebellion in Lower Canada, partly on race, partly on privilege grievances, synchronised with the other. Hence the Durham Commission and Union of the two Provinces. If it partially failed, it provided at any rate a common platform for the development of both French and British statesmen. And when Federation came in 1867, there were many able politicians from the two Canadas equal to the difficult task of reconciling the Maritime Provinces to merging themselves individually in the common union, and furthermore to draw up a Federal Constitution in some respects better than the famous American Charter upon which it was partly modelled.

The story of Nova Scotia and New Brunswick, from the settling down of the U.E. Loyalists onwards, lacks the dramatic nature of that of the Canadas. There were neither wars nor rebellions. Their peaceful story and steady advance in population and development is only coloured by the long political struggle for Responsible in place of Representative Government, which was conceded to the Canadas soon after their union. In these Eastern Provinces there was a somewhat similar oligarchy of family and privilege, arising from much the same sources and opposed by a rising democracy for much the same reasons. But then their progress towards Responsible Government, though marked by political acerbities, brought no serious friction, nor any outbreaks, as in the Canadas. Indeed, Nova Scotia was so thoroughly satisfied with herself in 1867, that it was with the utmost difficulty that she could be persuaded into Federation, an achievement ultimately brought about by Joseph Howe, the son of a U.E. Loyalist refugee, and one of the ablest statesmen British North America ever produced.[1]

The proportion of U.E. Loyalist blood to-day in the Maritime Provinces would be hard to guess at, but despite some shifting of population in the early days, it must be very large. Local historians and genealogists have discussed the matter in the pages of their own periodicals, but not one of them, unfortunately, has treated the matter in available book form. In no case, however, would that be likely to interest an English reader unfamiliar with the country. For such, it will be enough to say here that it is very seldom indeed that one encounters a "Blue-nose" of native parentage, who does not claim and with justifiable pride to be of U.E. Loyalist stock! If the claim may be occasionally a trifle obscure, that matters nothing, it only proves a proper pride in such worthy origin. The time-honoured sobriquet of "Blue-nose" applied to the people of the Maritime Provinces by their neighbours has no such reference to the cold climate that it might suggest. Nor, indeed, were the Canadas in any position to jeer at their Eastern fellow subjects on that account. But the term was a gibe, no doubt of New England origin, at their invincible toryism as symbolised by the colour in question. The bearer of it too will always tell you that his Provinces have supplied in the past far more than their proportion, as compared with the Canadas proper, of men distinguished in law, politics and the arts, and Canadian history, till recent times, will more or less justify the boast.

Halifax, again, whatever the commercial rivalry of St. John has done to it in recent times, has always been the social and representative capital of the Maritime

[1] But Howe, who in the 'forties had won responsible government for his Province, was now an old man. He shifted his views on Federation, and only at the urgent appeal of Sir John Macdonald appeased a violent and critical opposition that he had himself encouraged.

Provinces. And if you know it and also the rest of British North America, you will not require its natives to tell you that among its politer classes the "English accent," as all our transatlantic friends and relatives style it, has been preserved and even cherished to an extent elsewhere unknown short of British Columbia, where the reason is plain enough. Whether the English atmosphere and intonation of Halifax is due to its age-long association with English naval and military folk, and consequent intermarriages, or to the polished accents of distinguished U.E. Loyalist ancestors, is a moot question I will not attempt to answer. But whatever the genealogical conditions of the Maritime Provinces, the far more rapid growth in the wealth and population of the old Upper Canada, as Ontario, has to a greater extent dimmed the memories of its U.E. Loyalist origin, or at any rate partially submerged them under new wealth and new claims. The identity of the once prominent U.E. Loyalist families, like that of other stocks of that kind elsewhere, has tended to fade away before the rise and power of wealth. Ontario was within memory a purely agricultural country with a vast hinterland regarded as practically worthless and without a future. Now the money value of its manufactures is actually greater than that of its food products, though the land is fertile and well farmed, while the once forbidding, almost worthless hinterland, now counts in mineral products among the most favoured districts in the world. And as Ontario was the foremost factor in pioneering the great North Western Prairie States, the descendants of the loyalists will now be found scattered over the whole Dominion as far as the Pacific. But how many are aware of this descent is another matter. Genealogy, even their own, has not much place in busy lives absorbed in the problems of to-day. But in Ontario, names and their traditions have survived the recent social and material transformation of the country. At any rate, the sentiment is there among those, not too many perhaps, who have the temperament and can feel the past.

BIBLIOGRAPHICAL NOTE

BIBLIOGRAPHICAL NOTE

A BIBLIOGRAPHY of authorities and sources of information used in this work would be both impossible and superfluous. But for the benefit of such readers as may be inclined to some further acquaintance with this period of American history, I subjoin a list of a few books of direct bearing on the subject (not mentioned in the text). All these works are available at the more important libraries.

The two American works on the United Empire Loyalists are by Sabine (about 1845) and Professor Van Tyne (1902). The former lived near the New Brunswick frontier and devoted many years to gathering oral information from the original refugees or their sons, a valuable feature of his work being a brief biographical sketch of about 3,000 of these settlers.

Van Tyne's *Loyalists* is a full and most impartial account of the whole movement, in which the author does not spare his countrymen, and to which I gladly acknowledge many obligations. The same author has recently published a work on *The War of Independence*, which, from among the many American accounts of that struggle, may be specially mentioned here.[1]

A short book on the U.E. Loyalists has been recently published in Canada by Professor Wallace, of Toronto, and another on *The Family Compact* by the same author in the same series.

The most recent authoritative history of the United States is by Professor Morison, of Harvard, while Professor Eckenrode, of Virginia, not long ago handled *The Revolution in Virginia* in a very masterly manner. Flick's *Loyalism in New York* is a standard work, while Chief Justice Jones' contemporary account of that Colony in Revolution is invaluable. The subject has been reawakened by Willbur E. Abbott in *New York in the Revolution* (1931), while that unique backwoods magnate, Sir William Johnson, has just found two fresh biographers in A. Pound (Macmillan) and F. W. Seymour (Longmans).

In connection with the Loyalist settlements the biographies of Haldimand and Simcoe (" Makers of Canada " series) and my own *Life of Dorchester* (Oxford University Press) may be read; also that of Brock, in the above mentioned series. As to general histories of Canada, Kingsford's (10 vols.) is the most exhaustive. Many shorter ones will be found in the library lists, as well as histories of individual Provinces such as Nova Scotia and New Brunswick. American biography, apart from the bulkier lives of the more famous characters, may be read in the compact single volumes of the " American Statesman " series, edited by Coit Tyler, while Colonial History is dealt with in the Commonwealth series, edited by Lodge.

[1] Also John Fiske, the distinguished American writer on this period.

For the war of 1812, the books of Lucas (the fullest), Hannay and Richardson, all British, are the only works, for perhaps obvious reasons, dealing exclusively with the invasion of Canada. The last-named, though his book is otherwise inferior, served through the war himself.

I have here omitted works that I know to be unavailable to the ordinary reader. While the above brief list includes but a few of those bearing on the period and available, it is, I think, sufficient for the purpose.

Note.—Oxford University, though rather liberally endowed 20 years ago by Mr. Otto Beit for the study and popularisation of Colonial history, appears to have been almost silent on lecture platforms, while the few publications issuing from that source are rather in the nature of textbooks for students and examiners than encouraging to the general reader.

INDEX

INDEX